TRADITIONAL FOOD
IN NORTHUMBRIA

Traditional Food in Northumbria

PETER BREARS

Excellent Press
Ludlow

Traditional Food in Northumbria

by

Peter Brears

First published in 2013 by Excellent Press
9 Lower Raven Lane
Ludlow SY 8 1 BL

ISBN 978 1900318 45 7

Printed in Great Britain
by TJ International

CONTENTS

ACKNOWLEDGEMENTS

Firstly, I would like to thank Mr Duncan Davis of The Black Bull, Frosterley, for his suggestion that I should write this book on the food of the North-East. However, it would have been impossible to have written this book without the substantial help of two of my closest long-standing friends, John Gall and Rosemary Allan. My knowledge of the North-East is largely based on visits to them over the last forty years, seeing John construct most of the buildings and Rosemary furnish the interiors and build up the magnificent social history collections at the open-air museum at Beamish.

I am most grateful to Mr Richard Evans, Director of Beamish, and to his staff, for access to the records and collections housed there, and for granting permission to reproduce a number of the museum's historic photographs. Further thanks are due to Ms Anne Moore, Museums Officer for the Woodhorn Charitable Trust, for her help at the Morpeth Chantry Bagpipe Museum. The staff of Tyne & Wear museums were similarly helpful in arranging for me to reproduce their fine portrait of the redoubtable Euphemia Scott, the fishwife.

I also wish to thank Mr Ian Forbes for his information regarding the diet of the Weardale leadminers, and Mr George Muirhead regarding that of the fishing communities of the North-East coast.

My warmest thanks are due to Mrs Susan Houghton, for her invaluable help in bringing this book to completion, to my publisher, Mr David Burnett, for his care in putting it through the press, and Pete MacKenzie for the design and layout.

Peter Brears
Leeds 2012.

1. The North-Eastern counties of Northumberland and Durham

INTRODUCTION

This book tells the story of traditional home cooking in the counties of Northumberland and Durham during the most regionally distinctive period between around 1800 and 1920. Everyday life here at this time was enormously different from that of today. Most working men were employed in industries that demanded long hours of hard physical labour, discomfort and even danger. Their mothers, wives and daughters worked similarly hard in homes without labour-saving appliances, constantly battling against cold, dirt, hunger and potential poverty to keep their menfolk and children clean, happy and well-fed.

To them, the foods served in cafés, bistros and restaurants were totally unknown, ready-meals a thing of the future, and take-aways limited to fish-and-chips and hot pies. Even the purchase of ready-made bread was seen as a shameful admission of domestic incompetence. Instead, all their food was home-made using fresh, local and often home-grown produce, perhaps supplemented with some professionally preserved meats and fish.

Over the centuries the region's housewives developed hundreds of really practical, economical, efficient and satisfying ways of feeding their families. Recipes were passed on from one generation to another more by practical example than written instructions, being absorbed by children around the kitchen fire, as they grew up. Since then, and especially after the 1960s, this tradition virtually disappeared as most women took up work outside the home, incomes increased, and modern fashionable lifestyles were embraced. Foreign holidays, new Chinese, Italian, Greek and Asian restaurants and the celebrity chefs promoted through the media all offered new, purchasable taste sensations. Now all good, plain English home-made food was considered bad and boring. Even the honest hospitality provided for friends in the family home had to be abandoned to make way for imitations of commercial restaurant meals, preferably using only those ingredients without an English name, and served in restaurant style.

The whole tradition of English regional cookery could easily have been lost, had it not been for the people of the late Victorian and

Edwardian years who set down their experiences for the benefit of future generations. Some did this by studying local history, customs and dialects, some by composing popular songs and verses, and some by writing their memoirs. More usefully, many women donated their favourite and well-used family recipes to the communal fund-raising cookery books published by local churches, chapels, and hospitals. In addition, Northumberland and County Durham were extremely fortunate in having two major collectors of recipes and food habits. The first of these was Peggy Hutchinson, a local farmer's wife and one of the finest food journalists of the 1930s. Writing for local newspapers throughout the northern counties, and with a uniquely keen perception of the real importance of good local dishes, she collected hundreds of their recipes and published them in her books on Old English Cookery, Northcountry Cooking Secrets and Preserving Secrets. The second was Rosemary Allan, who as Senior Keeper at Beamish, the North of England Open Air Museum, carried out an extensive questionnaire survey of the region's traditional foods. This gathered together a unique group of recipes, menus and recollections mainly from informants born before the First World War, which otherwise would have been lost forever.

Compared to today, the home lives of working families of the past varied enormously according to their personal circumstances. Of these, the most important was occupation, each having its own distinctive environments, problems, rewards and foods. Here, the first chapters set the scene by describing the ways in which just a few of the many occupational communities in Northumberland and Durham lived and fed themselves, the pitmen, small farmers, farm workers, lead miners, fishing families, and the poor. Then follow studies of each different type of food, placing it within its social context and giving numerous recipes, most being provenanced to a specific person or place.

As a cookery book, this is quite different from most others, since its recipes are not those of a particular celebrity chef or food writer, but those of a whole vibrant regional community of housewives. Its dishes are all quite basic, although some demand real skill, and are intended more to substantially and comfortably satisfy the heart and stomach, rather than to flatter the eye. The contrived pretentiousness of Nouvelle Cuisine or of tower-building will not be found here, and there is nothing deformed 'with a twist'. Instead, all is good, honest, unadorned home cooking, the stuff which fuelled the people of one of Britain's major industrial and agricultural regions for centuries. Its specialities range from the everyday stotty-cake and pan haggerty to the celebratory singing hinny and yule cake, along with bride cake for weddings and death cake for funerals. Hopefully these and all the other recipes will be used rather than merely read, for they represent some of the best of regional foods, not only in Northumberland and County Durham, but in the whole of England.

Peter Brears

A NOTE ON THE RECIPES

Since many historical recipes were written as aides-mémoire by cooks who assumed that everyone knew what they were doing, they frequently omit such essential details as methods, oven temperatures and timings. For this reason they are presented here in their modernised, rather than manuscript forms. The original quantities and procedures are all followed as closely as possible, but are now expressed in standard Imperial and Metric measures. Spoon measures all represent their level, rather than heaped quantities, while medium-sized eggs are used throughout. Temperatures, meanwhile, are those of standard ovens, and should be reduced accordingly when using a fan assisted oven.

CHAPTER ONE

THE PITMEN

What is it that gives us cakes o' meal?
What is it that crams our wame se weel,
With lumps of beef and draughts of ale?
What is't but just the coal trade[1]

For over four hundred years the coal-mining industry provided the economic driving force which changed the hinterland of the Tyne, Wear and Tees into one of the world's most important manufacturing regions. Its output was of far more than local significance, since it heated homes and fuelled industry in England and the adjacent continent, as well as steamships traversing every ocean. The wealth it created for the landowning nobility and gentry, the merchants and industrialists, was truly vast, as seen in their castles and houses, the streetscapes of Newcastle, and its various cultural institutions. None of these could have been created had it not been for the pitmen, the individuals who expended their energy, health and lives in damp, dark, dirty and dangerous underground seams, hewing out the coal with their sharp picks. It then had to be dragged to the bottom of the shaft by the putters, raised up to the surface, selected and sorted on the screens, and tipped into the chaldron wagons which carried it down to the harbour-side coal-drops.

Pits were sunk wherever there was coal, often in areas where there were few people to operate them, or perhaps no settlement at all. The owners therefore had to provide basic accommodation for their new and expanding workforces. As a model, they appear to have followed the pattern of the older generations of farm labourers' cottages, giving each family a single-storey one- or two-room cottage, perhaps with another room above. Some were built back-to-back, as at Long Row, Haswell, with a kitchen and bedroom on the ground floor and a sleeping loft above, accessed by a steep ladder. Dr Thomas Wright of Newcastle visited a number of similar houses at Heaton in the 1820s describing how they were being used. In one;

Dinner is on the table. The frying pan unsullied by dish-clout for the last six months stands on the fire sending forth savoury fumes of a few fat slices of bacon. A dish of half-boiled potatoes is under the bars and a half dozen broken plates, dirty spoons and one-pronged forks strewn about the chairs and table, if the furniture be worthy of that title. A mess of cabbage leaves and hot water with some bread in it serves the bairns for broth and washing fingers in.

In many others, the scene was completely different, with;

> The clean mahogany bedstead, patchwork quilt and shining inlaid chest of drawers immediately fronting the door, an eight-day clock in one corner, and glass-fronted cupboard, stored with 'wedding china' and tastefully displayed in the opposite one; a *mahogany polished* table covered with a bit of green cloth and surmounted by a *betterme* [best] teaboard and looking glass each rivals the honour of reflections; chairs which you seem afraid should slip from under you – so glassy their surface; 'The wife' – a picture of neatness with half a score of brats around her and the gudeman at the chimney corner smoking his pipe after his ablutions on coming from work.[2]

A reporter from *The News Chronicle* was similarly impressed when he visited a pitman's house in 1849-50; his description is well worth quoting in full, since it presents such a complete picture of probably the best working-class homes of the period.

> We will now enter one of the ordinary class of houses. As a general rule, the furniture is decidedly good: some articles are even costly ... especially ... the bed and chest of drawers. The bedstead is very frequently of carved and turned mahogany, and the bed, clean, soft and comfortable, with white [hangings] and a quilted coverlid. The chest of draws ... frequently costs from £8 to £10. It commonly rises almost to the ceiling, only leaving room for a few old-fashioned china or stoneware ornaments placed upon the top. The chairs are sometimes deal, and sometimes mahogany. The mantelpiece is generally crowded with little ornaments of china and glass; the plates, cups and saucers are usually kept in cupboards; but highly polished brass candlesticks, placed on shelves, or hung upon nails, glitter from the walls. Birds and birdcages abound. The women are great agents in getting the houses so well

2. The miner's cottage at Francis Street, Hetton-le-Hole, as remembered by Mrs. Huntley, who grew up here during the First World War.

furnished as they are ... When a young couple get married, they generally go to a furniture broker in Newcastle or Sunderland, with perhaps £10 of ready money, obtaining a considerable part of their 'plenishings' upon credit, and paying for it in instalments ... The colliery folks have a great notion of clocks, ... a great proportion of the pitmen's timepieces are regular eight-day clocks with metallic dials. I have good reason to believe that most industrious pitmen can attain to a state of comparative domestic comfort. [3]

At this period the cottages might still have floors of beaten earth, but by the 1850s most were of hard-wearing stone flags, paving bricks or firebrick quarles. Their design was also improving with the ground floor having both the best bedroom and a well-equipped kitchen fitted with a sink and a cast-iron cooking range and with an attic bedroom above.

Within these homes, the rhythm of everyday life was ruled by the shift pattern worked at the pit. In the earlier years it was a regular eight-hour day shift, but when trade boomed there were double shifts, and eventually full twenty-four hour working was implemented. This placed an enormous burden on the housewife, especially if husband and sons were on different shifts. A vivid example of this is provided by the following timetable for one north-eastern pitman's wife in 1920;

3 a.m.	get eldest son's bait, to start work at 4 a.m.
4 a.m.	back to bed for an hour
5 a.m.	get another son's bait, to start work at 6 a.m.
6 a.m.	husband back from work, prepare his bath and breakfast
8 a.m.	get 3 children up, breakfasted, and off to school
10 a.m.	prepare bath and dinner for eldest son's return at 11-11.30 a.m. and
to 1 p.m.	make dinner for the children returning from school
1 p.m.	get 3 sons' bait, to start work at 2 p.m.
2 p.m.	bath and dinner for son returning from 6 a.m. shift
4 p.m.	tea for children returning from school
9 p.m.+	get husband's bait, to start work at 10 p.m.
10 p.m.–midnight, baths and dinners for 3 sons returning from 2 p.m. shift.	
12 midnight to bed, ready to start again at 3 a.m.[4]	

This relentless routine, having to meet one unavoidable deadline after another, day after day with hardly a break, was challenging enough, but represented only one part of the responsibilities of a pitman's wife. To keep the house and family clean and healthy, she usually adopted another, weekly timetable which started on Monday as washing-day. This meant a constant stoking of the wash-boiler, the boiling of 'whites', lading water into wash-tubs, possing, scrubbing collars, cuffs and stains, wringing out, rinsing in blue-stained water, mangling, and filling the ceiling racks, clothes horses and outdoor clothes lines

3. This communal oven at Mickley Square, Mickley was typical of those provided to serve the families living in the rows of cottages built by the colliery companies. Here Florrie and Bessie Howden are removing their tin-loaves.

with every item, hoping that most would be dry by the end of the day. Tuesday was devoted to housework, especially cleaning and ironing. Thursday was baking day, Friday cleaning and polishing ready for the weekend, Saturday polishing the brasses etc., and making ready for Sunday, when no domestic work was done, but the week's best dinner had to be cooked, and time spent in preparing everyone for Sunday schools and church services. Each family might vary this timetable to suit its own needs, changing the washing day to avoid that of others in the same yard, for example, or baking two or three times a week. This could be a necessity when so much bread was consumed, and buying in loaves from a shop was seen as slovenly dereliction of duty. Given these demands, it is surprising to find that miner's wives found time for interests of their own, but many participated in the communal lives of their local chapel or church, and also enjoyed knitting, rug-making and quilting at home, even though these were economical ways of producing household goods.

Within the home, the pitman's wife often acted as managing director and chief financial officer, receiving either a housekeeping allowance from her husband, or even his entire wages from which she returned sufficient for his own needs. With careful budgeting, she would then pay all the bills, buy all the necessities, and accumulate savings for special events or emergencies. Unlike most others, she had no rent to pay, since the house came free with the job, as did the coal needed for cooking and heating. Most of her vegetables would be home-grown, since the majority of miners maintained excellent gardens or allotments, and perhaps kept a pig as well, to provide pork, bacon and ham. In this the miner on shift-work had a great advantage over many other workers, since he had free daylight hours to devote to his allotment, its vegetables, flowers, and sparrows. This common garden pest was caught, cooked and eaten in many northern mining communities, giving rise to the riddle, 'How do they catch sparrows in Gateshead?'

> Hoo they larnt aal thor art an' thor cunnin',
> Just ask 'What's the best, horsehair or fine wire,
> Or catch ye mair waakin ' or runnin? ...
> Say 'Hoo de ye snare them, an' keep yor trade gaen',
> An' this they'll reply 'Well, the best way we can!'
> That's hoo they catch sparras at Gyetshead![5]

Since the pitmen were paid fortnightly, every other Friday, their wives had to budget for the whole of the two-week period. They usually went on a major shopping expedition on Saturday to buy in most of the groceries they would need to keep their families supplied until next pay-day. This involved a long walk into the nearest town, and an equally long walk back with heavily-laden baskets, 'all merry and happy and trudging home with their spoils, while the husband is 'half-seas-over' (drunk) wrestling with a pig with a string tied to its back leg.' Some colliery owners even provided long carts to carry the men and their lasses into town and back 'at a smart pace.'[6] These fortnightly payments were not without their difficulties. There was a risk of the cash wage disappearing at one of the gambling 'schools' held just after the pay had been received, the dire consequences of this being fully described in the song 'I wish Pay-Friday Would Come'. If too much was spent on the next day, the Pay-Saturday holiday, or the ensuing pay-week, times could be bad over the following Baff-week.[7]

The most difficult period for all mining families was when virtually all income ceased during periods spent on strike. Even if they were not evicted from their houses, as sometimes happened, strikes brought distress to the whole community. As James Gordon described during the strikes of 1844;

> The wife that to his manly breast
> In hopeful youth he clasp'd
> Must sink beneath the deadly blow,
> By stern starvation grasp'd.
> His children clinging to his knee
> Have begged of him for bread;
> And in the bitterness of soul
> Sobbing, he hangs his head ...

or;

> Our wives and bains ha nowt to eat
> This twenty weeks an' mair;
> We ha' ne' tyeble, nor ne' meat,
> A man, that's vara sair.[8]

This was as true in the nineteenth century as it was in the early twentieth, as Tommy Armstrong recorded;

> In our Durham County, I am sorry for to say,
> That hunger and starvation is increasing every day.
> For want of fuel and coals we know not what to do,
> But with your kind assistance we will stand the struggle
>   through ...
> Our work is taken from us now, they care not if we die;
> For they can eat the best of food, and drink the best when dry.
> The miner and his partner too, each morning have to roam
> To seek for bread to feed the little hungry ones at home.
> The flour barrel is empty now, their true and faithful friend,
> Which makes the thousands wish today the strike was at an end.[9]

The other cause of poor living was a sackless, lazy and incompetent wife, such as one miner complained of in 'The Pitman's Pay';

She buys me, tee, the warst o' meat
Bad bullock's liver, houghs and knees,
Tough, stinkin' tripe, an' awd cow's feet,
Shanks full o' mawks [maggots] and half-nowt cheese

The crowdy is wor daily dish
But vary different from MINNY'S,
For she gets a' her heart can wish,
In strang-lyced tea and singing hinnies ...

She peels the taties wiv her teeth,
And spreads the butter wiv her thoomb;
She blaws the kyel [broth] wi' stinkin' breeth
Where mawks and caterpillars soom!

Fortunately such wives were comparatively rare, and most mining families enjoyed plenty of good, plain food. This is clearly demonstrated by the accounts of a Northumbrian miner's family in the mid-nineteenth century. It should be stressed, however, that it is a family at its most prosperous, with four males in full employment. There would be much less generous catering before the boys started to work, when they left home, and if injury or death left dependant relatives.[10]

		£	s	d
Income for 2 weeks	Father [a hewer]	2	4	0
	1 boy, putter	1	16	8
	„ „ driver		13	9
	„ „ trapper		9	2
		5	3	7
Expenditure	Mutton 14lb		8	9
	Flour 70lb		13	0
	Maslin			
	[wheat & rye flour] 42lb		7	6
	Bacon 14lb		9	4
	Potatoes		2	3

	£	s	d
Oatmeal			6
Butter 2lb			
& milk 3d per day		6	0
Coffee 1¼lb		3	0
Tea ¼lb		1	6
Sugar 3lb		2	0
Candles			6¼
Soap		1	8
Pepper, salt,			
mustard etc.			6
	3	0	6¼
Shoes 9s per month		4	6
Clothes, stockings etc.		17	6
Sundries		2	6
Benefit club		1	3
	4	6	3¼

The main interest in this account lies in the types and quantities of food being consumed. They are eating 2lb/900g of meat a day in the form of mutton and bacon, and 8lb/3.6kg of flour, representing about 10lb/4.5kg of bread. This suggests that the miner is eating about 8oz/225g of meat and 2lb/900g of bread a day, plus his home-grown vegetables, amongst the highest consumption of any manual worker of the period. The reasons for this were twofold: firstly, he needed plenty of nourishing food to keep him fit and healthy when performing such a physically demanding job; secondly, he needed to enjoy the food while he could. In this industry, sudden death and crippling injury always threatened, and wear and tear on the body, exacerbated by occupational diseases, meant that the expectancy of long-term high earnings was very low, and of early death very high. As a totally reasonable and practical response to these conditions, coal miners have always lived life to the full while they still could, enjoying their good and plentiful food regardless of the expense, where others in safe, sedentary occupations would have saved as much as possible.

The food taken to work down the pit was known as bait; always something plain and easy to carry. As described in a story current about 1816, it could be 'a Great lump ov White Butter an' Breed in ma

4. This tinplate water bottle was found by the rescue men after the Seaham Colliery disaster of 1880, when 164 lives were lost. It was scratched with the following last message;

"Dear Margaret,

There was 40 of us altogether at 7a.m. Some was singing hymns, but my thoughts was on little Michael that him and I would meet in heaven at the same time. Oh Dear wife, God save you and the children, and pray for me ... Dear wife Farewell. My last thoughts are about you and the children. Be sure and learn the children to pray for me. Oh what an awful position we are in "

clogs', while in the 1840s it was just a hunk of bread and a tin bottle full of either water or cold tea.[11] In 1853 it could be 'huge hunks of bread and cheese, with a bone or so of meat, drinking at that time coffee or milk out of a tin canteen.'[12] In 1873 it might be bread and butter with tea or coffee, and around 1890 a piece of bread with a bottle full of cold water or tea.[13] Later it might be bread and jam with the water or tea.[14] These represent individual variations on the same theme, however, rather than any great change from one period to another.

The miner's main meal of the day, his dinner, had to be ready on his return from the pit, whatever his shifts. Back in the 1840s 'Pies, dumplings and puddings, with the best of beef and mutton etc. were their common fare'.[15] Rather like the Yorkshire Pudding of the West Riding miners, the boiled suet puddings or dumplings were eaten as a first course to take the edge off the appetite, the roast beef or mutton, potatoes and vegetables coming later.[16] This custom had largely disappeared by the early twentieth century as shown by these weekly menus from the mining communities of Durham and Northumberland;

Mrs O.B. Bannister, West Auckland, c. 1919.[17]

	BREAKFAST	DINNER	TEA	SUPPER
Sun.	bacon & egg	roast beef, Yorkshire pud.	fruit pies & cakes fruit & custard	cold meat etc.
Mon.	boiled egg	steak & kidney. pie etc	scrambled egg on toast	sandwiches, milk
Tues.	jam & bread	liver casserole etc.	scones, teacakes	biscuits & milk
Wed.	boiled egg	chops etc., rice pudding	kippers	bread & jam
Thurs.	jam & bread	hot pot, baked dumplings	rhubarb & custard	ham sandwiches
Fri.	poached egg	baked fish, parsley sauce, peas & potatoes	veg. soup	soup
Sat.	boiled egg	boiled bacon or ham, pease pudding	pies, cakes, cheesecakes, scones	fish & chips

Mrs Howey, Stakeford[18]

	BREAKFAST	DINNER	TEA	SUPPER
Sun.	boiled egg bread & jam	roast beef, Yorkshire pud., veg., milk pud.	bread & butter	toast & dripping or a bacon or cheese sandwich
Mon.	porridge bread & marg.	cold meat, panacalty, jam roly poly	bread & jam	„
Tues.	„	stewed liver, leek pud., potatoes, milk pud.	„	„
Wed.	„	Scotch broth, cornflour mould, jam	„	„
Thurs.	„	sea pie, stewed fruit & custard	„	„
Fri.	„	mutton stewed with black pud., & onions, bread pud.	„	„
Sat.	kipper or baked herring bread & marg.	tripe & chitterlings fried in onion batter	„	fish & chips

These menus fail to mention one dish which, above all others, was associated with pitmen's families - the singing hinny. Rich in butter and currants, this was seen as a luxurious and expensive indulgence. These 'rich kneaded cakes that sung with their exuding fat when baking on a girdle', were made for the pitmen when at home, after work.[19] One Victorian visitor to the region had even seen one of these huge girdle cakes 'set edgewise on a table, leaning against the wall, from which each little urchin would help himself by tearing off what he wanted with his dirty hands', while another spooned up sugar from a torn-open parcel of sugar on the table.[20] To the middle-class observer, these, along with other plentiful foods, were sure signs of the pitman's profligacy. He would have changed his mind, however, had he ever worked at the coalface, or stood among the families at the pithead as exhausted rescue men recovered the bodies of fathers, sons and workmates. Would he have denied some of the good things in life to those seen in this pitman's house, after a fire-damp explosion underground in the 1830s?

> On one bed lay the bodies of two men [grandfather, 60, and son, 40] burnt to a livid colour. On another bed in the same room were streaked three fine boys [grandchildren all under 15] all destroyed in the same instant by the same destructive blast. Outside, the garden was full of vegetables, the father's spade still there where he had worked that morning ...[21]

CHAPTER TWO

FARMING FAMILIES

The lives of individual farmers in the north-east varied enormously, depending on the size of their holding, its location, the fertility of its land and the demand for its produce. Those with the largest acreages of rich lowland arable and grazing were extremely prosperous, enjoying the social standing and standard of living of the gentry. Others worked hard to earn little more than their subsistence from the cold, sour Pennine uplands, often relying on a secondary income from lead mining etc. to make ends meet. The majority, however, and those described here, lay midway between these extremes.

The size and quality of the farmhouses was similarly variable. William Cobbett described those of Northumberland as being 'big enough and fine enough for a gentleman to live in'.[1] These were the fine model farms established on the vast new enclosures of the eighteenth century, as illustrated in Bailey & Cully's *'General View of the Agriculture of ... Northumberland'* of 1805.[2] Many of the home farms associated with major country house estates were of the same scale. Beamish Hall's home farm, now part of the museum, provides an excellent example. Other farmhouses were far older, still occupying the defensive tower houses and bastels built up to the time of the Tudors and early Stuarts, or the lesser halls and smaller houses of the sixteenth to eighteenth centuries. A further group of small farms was built in the late Georgian and early Victorian period, as the uplands were laboriously brought into cultivation to meet the demands of the expanding population and the lead mining industry. These very different kinds of farm had many different plan-forms and facilities, but their functional heart was always the kitchen.

This was a large room with a stone-flagged floor to take constant wear and scrubbing, and a large table which served partly for food preparation, and partly as a dining table for the entire household, only the grandest farmers retiring to a separate dining room. Usually most of one wall was occupied by a great fireplace. One at Greives Farm was drawn by S.H. Grimm in 1778. Shielded from the doorway by a hallan, or fixed screen, it had a wide, open fireplace, at the centre of

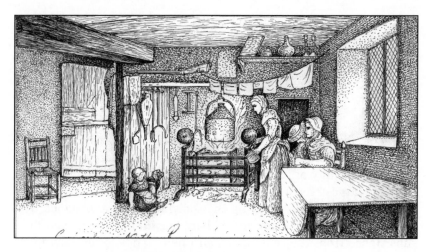

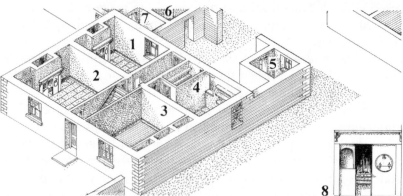

5. In the late eighteenth century most farms still used large open fireplaces, as drawn by S.H. Grimm at Grieves Farm, Northumberland in 1778 (top). In contrast, the model farms of the early nineteenth century often had two kitchens, each fitted with a Newcastle round oven and a side-boiler. Designed in 1824 by John Green of Newcastle for the Beaufort Estate, Hallington New Houses near Barrasford (bottom) featured;

1. back kitchen	5. coal house & shed
2. kitchen	6. ash-house
3. parlour	7. privy
4. dairy & larder	8. kitchen range with 20" oven & 12 gallon boiler

which stood a large coal-burning grate, ideal for both roasting and boiling. Up to this time many stone-built farm kitchens also had open fireplaces, but bridged by a single, massive masonry arch. Then the openings became narrower, with an almost square elevation with a pair of vertical jambs supporting a horizontal lintel, flanked by a pair of recesses.

Now the fireplace began to be filled up with separate units, one at Fell Close, Waskerley, having a central general purpose fire at its centre, with a small hot air oven and a boiler at its sides, and a domed brick 'beehive' oven in one of the recesses. Such arrangements were usually replaced by massive cast iron ranges in the Victorian period, the most convenient and practical cooking devices of their day. Given access to cold larders, dry store-cupboards called presses, a good supply of pots, pans and dishes, and a long-case clock to keep everything punctual, the farmer's wife and her maids had everything required to feed her family and its servants. It still needed considerable skill, experience and sheer energy to keep everything under control, being no place for the laziness jocularly attributed to Elsie Marley, the alewife of Picktree, Chester-le-Street, who was, in truth, renowned for her energy.

> *Do ye ken Elsie Marley, honey,*
> *The wife that sells the barley, honey,*
> *The wife that sells the barley ...*
> *Elsie Marley's grown so fine,*
> *She won't get up to feed the swine,*
> *But lays in bed till eight or nine,*
> *And surely she does take her time ...*

In general, these farming families enjoyed the good basic diet needed to keep them fit and well able to tackle their energetic outdoor lives. Since they were the prime producers of food, they bought in only essentials such as sugar, salt, dried fruits etc. which they could not grow, everything else coming from the farm. Margaret Stafford, one of six children at Brockley Hall, Alnwick, remembered that in the 1920s a 12 x 20 yard/11 x 18.3m garden was maintained by the farm men so as to produce all the potatoes, cabbages, sprouts, beans, peas, carrots, beetroots and cauliflowers for home use, as well as herbs such as sage, mint and parsley. They also kept two pigs for the farm; one could last a year when its respective joints were either dry- or wet-salted. The kitchen was always busy. Every morning soup had to be made for the first course at mid-day dinner, vegetable, scotch broth, pease, lentil or chicken being the usual varieties. The main course of meat, potatoes and vegetables followed, and then a substantial milk pudding, fruit pie, or a dish of stewed fruit, custard, trifle, jelly, or fruit fool. All the bread, whether white, brown or teacakes was also home-made, as were the fruit cakes, sandwich cakes, gingerbreads, rockbuns and buttermilk cakes ready for teatime every afternoon. A typical weekly menu at this farm was certainly substantial by any standards. Except for Sunday, every day started with a bowl of porridge. This was not made from rolled oats, but from coarse oatmeal, which gives a much better texture and, some think, taste.

Oatmeal Porridge

1½ tbs coarse oatmeal   ½pt/300ml water
& a large pinch of salt for each person.

When the water is at a rapid boil, stir it round with a wooden thyvel or porridge-stick, then sprinkle the meal into the pan gradually, so as to avoid forming lumps. This is not as easy as it sounds. Continue stirring until it begins to thicken, then cover, reduce the heat, and leave to simmer very gently for 30 minutes. Alternatively remove the pan from the heat and wrap in a few layers of thick towel, and leave for up to an hour to cook using its own heat. Finally stir in the salt.

	BREAKFAST	DINNER	TEA	SUPPER
	Always with porridge (except on Sundays) and coffee	Always with a soup and pudding, the meat accompanied with potatoes & vegetables and water to drink.	Served with tea	Served with milk, cocoa or chocolate
Sun.	boiled eggs	roast beef	afternoon tea	beef salad
Mon.	bacon & egg	cold beef	white & brown bread	ham & pease pud.
Tues.	bacon, egg & tomato	stew	white & brown bread	liver & onions
Wed.	kippers	rabbit pie	scones & teacakes	scrambled eggs
Thur.	bacon & egg	pork chops	grannie loaf	ham salad
Fri.	sausages	roast lamb	rock buns, cakes	fish
Sat.	bacon & egg	[lamb] mince	sandwiches	soup & sandwiches

The menu clearly shows evidence of good housekeeping, the Sunday roast providing Sunday tea, Monday dinner and probably Tuesday dinner too, in the form of a hash. Similarly Friday's roast lamb reappeared as mince for Saturday dinner and perhaps in Saturday afternoon's sandwiches. Saturday was always busy, since there might be shopping expeditions etc., and the house had to be cleaned and prepared for Sunday. It was for this reason that only easily-prepared mince, soup and sandwiches would be served.[3]

Mrs V.O. Archer was brought up as a farmer's daughter at Turnpenny, Alston, around 1912. Here, high up in the middle of the Pennines, there was plenty of good and substantial home-grown food, but necessarily a more economical use of roasts and bacon.[4]

	BREAKFAST	DINNER	TEAS	SUPPERS
		always served with potatoes & vegetables		
Sun.	porridge	roast mutton, onion pudding,	jam, with bread, scones or teacakes	fry-up
Mon.	„	cold mutton, suet dumplings & syrup	„	kippers
Tues.	„	shepherds pie, bread & butter pudding	„	broth
Wed.	„	bacon hotpot, spotted dick	„	leek pie
Thur.	„	egg & potato fritters, roly poly	„	macaroni cheese
Fri.	„	bacon, onion & potato pie, spotted dick	„	broth
Sat.	„	bacon & chips, fruit & custard	„	lentil soup

Here again the Sunday roast also provided the Monday and Tuesday dinners. One of the major differences from the previous menu, however, is the greater role played by boiled suet puddings, and dumplings. Today these are usually considered unhealthy, but they provided the very substantial, satisfying and energy-producing foods required by everyone working hard in this cold Pennine environment.

It would be a great mistake to believe that everyone living in the countryside fared as well as this, for many fell on hard times. This was certainly the experience of Miss E. Pearson who grew up at North Row,

Cambo, in the middle of the 1914-18 war, when her father was away on active service.[5]

BREAKFAST	DINNER	TEA
bread & butter	soup, rabbit, or mince & dumplings	Bread, butter & jam
toast on Sat. & Sun	milk pudding or fruit pie	

Here there was no roast, no bacon, no eggs, no cakes, no cooked suppers, and cooking time was cut to a minimum at mid-day. Only real skill and careful budgeting enabled such a single-parent family to maintain its independence and keep itself out of the workhouse.

CHAPTER THREE

THE FARM WORKERS

The labour employed on a farm depended largely on the needs of the land. In less fertile areas the few men needed to run the farm usually lodged in the farmhouse, receiving their keep and a wage in cash. Daytil men, casual labourers paid by the day and providing their own accommodation, were generally available, but the characteristic form of labour used on the large and fertile Northumbrian farms was that of 'bondage'.[1]

Unless a farm worker's employer had been 'speaking' to skilled 'hind' or to the farm labourer, inviting him to stay on for a further year, his contract ended on 12th May. Therefore, in early March, he went to one of the local hiring fairs, where he agreed to work for another farmer for the coming year, on the usual terms and conditions. Up to around 1840 these meant that he was to receive the use of a cottage and garden plot, transport for his coal, the keep of a cow with grass in summer and a ton of hay in winter, the use of a thousand yards of potato row for his own consumption, 7lb of wool and £4 in wages, paid half-yearly. In addition, the farmer provided six bolls of oats, four bolls of barley, two bolls of beans and half a boll of wheat. These were variable customary measures. Around Hexham, for example, a boll of barley or oats was five bushels, and peas, rye or wheat, four bushels, while at Alnwick it was six bushels of oats or barley, and two of wheat. In cash terms these represented:[2]

	£	s	d
36 bushels of oats	6	12	0
24 „ „ barley	5	12	0
12 „ „ peas	3	0	0
3 „ „ wheat1	5	0	
3 „ „ rye	1	15	0
36 „ „ potatoes	2	14	0
24lb of wool	1	0	0
Keep of cow	9	0	0
Rent of cottage & garden	3	0	0
Carrying of coals from pit	2	0	0
	£ 35	18	0

In return, he had to do all manner of farm work, rising at four-thirty in summer and an hour before dawn in winter to get the horses ready, and work through to six p.m., before feeding the horses and settling them down for the night. Some two-and-a-half hours were allowed for breakfast and dinner, but that still gave a working day of over 12 hours. In addition, his wife had to rear the farmer's chickens, spin linen for the farmer's wife, shear corn, clean out the byres, turn the manure heaps, and in later years spread guano in the fields and feed corn into the thrashing machine. In Northumberland the 'bond' was the worker's agreement to provide a female 'bondager' to undertake these tasks if unable to do so from his own family. Usually a 16–19 year-old, she was paid a wage and received her board and lodging from the hind, but in addition to her farm work, had to do his milking and housework.[3] This system began to break down from around 1840, when such women started to be employed by the farmer on day wages, with a cottage, carted coals and potatoes, but hind's wives still continued to work in the fields.[4]

Most farm staff lived in rows of single-room farm cottages built for their accommodation in the years following the eighteenth-century enclosures. The drawing, based on descriptions of the 1840s, shows their usual design and layout, with the partitioned porch, dairy and box-beds. Some had a firegrate mounted in the fireplace between two stone hobs, while others had a round oven for baking at one side, and a cast iron boiling pot at the other. Sometimes these were provided by the farmer, but some were owned by the worker, along with the window frames, these being removed every time he and his family 'flitted' from one farm to another.[5]

Inside the cottages, everything was arranged so as to be as comfortable and convenient as possible, but even so they were relatively crowded when occupied by a large family. As Mrs John Grey of Dilstone House described in the 1830s;

> There are a couple of neatly-painted or fir-wood *press-beds*; a dresser and shelves, on which are ranged a goodly display of well-hoarded delft, or of modern blue-and-white Staffordshire ware. There is also a *press* or cupboard, in which are kept the nicer articles of food, and below which are drawers for the clothes of the family. A clock, in a handsome oak case, ticks, not behind the door, but in some conspicuous situation, and, in many families, is added a *mahogany* half-chest of drawers for the female

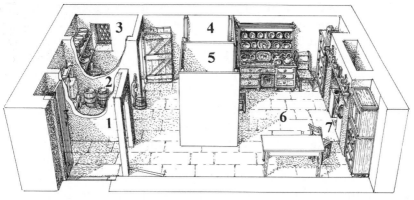

6. Most farm cottages were built to a similar one-room plan, their interiors being subdivided with partitions and box beds. The hind's cottage drawn near Wooler in 1871 (top) also had a sleeping loft over the entry end. The farm cottage designed in 1824 by John Green of Newcastle for the Beaufort estate was a 16 x 22ft (4.8 x 6.3m) room divided into;

1. entrance porch	5. hind's bed
2. out-bye or store	6. kitchen
3. bondager's bed	7. fireplace with 15ins diameter oven,
4. bondager's bed	17ins grate & 8 gallon side boiler

finery ... The press-beds form a partition, behind which is a small space [the out-bye] containing in one part a bed for the Bondager, and in another, a little dairy and pantry containing stores of meat, flour, etc., [From the matted ceiling hangs] the plentiful supply of bacon ... together with hanging shelves containing a supply of cheeses, pot-herbs, etc., and in other parts bunches of yarn ready for making into stockings or blankets. [There is] *white loaf* which the women always have, and the dainty *white-cake* for tea, [nodden cake], kneaded with butter or cream, when a friend comes to visit them, [and] the fat things which their cows and their pigs provide overflow the larder. [They are] always milking a cow, and frequently churning and making cheese, making great profit of their butter, about £5 a year.[6]

This was the opinion of the wife of a major landowner's agent. Mr Thomas Dodds, a surgeon, expressed a contrasting, but well informed view. To him, these cottages were worse than stables, earth-floored, single-roomed, dark and insanitary, the cow housed in the out-bye behind the bed contaminating the room with its manure and urine.[7] Examples of these extremes certainly existed, the majority probably lying somewhere inbetween. Given the quantity and range of foods received as wages, the farm worker and his family enjoyed milk, butter, cheese, home-fed pork and bacon, vegetables for boiling and cereals for porridge and bakery. In his report on *Food of the Poorer Labouring Classes of England* of 1863, Dr Edward Smith found that with more than 15lb/6.75kg of bread per week, the Northumbrian workers were the best-fed in the whole country. Further reports of around 1870 confirmed that the wages in this region were unusually high, an agricultural day-labourer in Durham receiving 20s 6d/£1 and 2p a week, the national average being 14s 8d/73p and in Dorset only 10s 4d/52p.[8] As a result, the farm workers and shepherds were considered to be a 'splendid race'. William Senhouse of Wark confirmed the reason for this;

> A man should eat the food of the country in which he is born ... Bannocks made of barley and peas made a man as hard as a brick. Men would take a lump of bannock out for the day, and drink water.[9]

Some rural families continued to eat in a similar way well into the twentieth century, except for having more beef and wheaten bread. At Mrs Henrietta Clark's house at Ponteland, a pig was killed for winter and in early spring, the sides being dry-salted or brined for bacon. Beef joints were also brined, while mutton was air-dried for preservation. Dinner, usually boiled in the pot, included a large suet pudding often eaten separately as a first course, while for tea etc. there was home-baked white bread, teacakes, brown bread sometimes with caraway seeds, along with rock cakes, gingerbread, fruit cake and seed cake.[10]

	BREAKFAST	DINNER	TEA	SUPPER
Sun.	Porridge or crowdy	Roast beef, potatoes & veg.	Scones, tarts etc.	hard cheese & bread
Mon.	„	cold „ in gravy „ „	toasted teacake	„ „
Tues.	„	minced beef „ „	„ „	„ „
Wed.	„	stew „ „	„ „	„ „
Thurs.	„	stew „ „	„ „	„ „
Fri.	„	sausages „ „	„ „	„ „
Sat.	„	fried bacon „ „	„ „	„ „
To drink;	milk	water	tea	cocoa

The crowdy which was still served here for breakfast was;

> Made by filling a basin with oatmeal, and then pouring in boiling water. A vigorous stirring is required whilst the water is being poured; and, when the two ingredients are thoroughly mixed, the 'hasty pudding' is ready. It is served with a little butter, dripping, or other flavouring, according to taste, or it is taken with milk. 'He' ye had yor crowdy?' is said of any repast whatever; and 'That man is not worth his crowdy!' is equivalent to saying he is not worth his keep.[11]

As described by the last operator of Felton Mill, the oats intended for crowdy were lightly toasted on a crowdy iron. This was an iron plate about five feet/1.5m diameter with a three to four-inch/7.5-10cm upstand all round, heated from below by a low fire, a rotating iron blade continuously turning the oats and preventing them from burning on. This gave a pleasant slightly toasted flavour to the final, finely-ground crowdy meal. He made lots when he was young, but the trade fell off in the 1920s–30s.[12]

Crowdy
Mrs M.A. Taylor, Catless Farm, North Tyne.[13]

6-8 tbs fine oatmeal *½pt/300ml boiling water*

7. On coming into the farm kitchen, each man found a place set with a mug covered by a bowl, with a spoon to one side (right). He then scooped fine oatmeal and a pinch of salt into his bowl from the communal supplies on the table, poured in boiling water from the kettle on the fire, and stirred it briskly to make crowdy. This was eaten with a mugful of skim milk ladled from the communal bowl.

> Follow the instructions given above, but stir *very* vigorously and allow to swell for a few minutes before eating, otherwise it causes painful indigestion.

This recipe was for a communal bowl of crowdy, but in most farms it was made individually. When the farm men came into the kitchen at six a.m., each place was set with a pint pot with a basin up-ended over it, with a spoon alongside. At the centre of the table stood a tin of crowdy-meal, a bowl of skimmed milk, and a salt cellar, while the kettle of water sat boiling on the top bar of the kitchen range. Each put oatmeal and salt into his basin, and then poured on the boiling water while stirring vigorously. This should form a smooth, porridge-like mixture, but those lacking the necessary experience usually produced a lumpy mass. By the time the pint pot had been filled with milk the crowdy had swollen and softened, so that a little could be taken in the spoon, dipped into the milk, and the two eaten together. Alternatively a little treacle or butter and sugar might be added to the crowdy, while

28

in Northumberland, if eaten with dripping, it became 'fat crowdy'.[14]

By the 1890s there had already been a gradual progression from wages in kind towards wages paid in cash. This greatly reduced the keeping of cows and pigs, and hence of home-produced milk, butter, cheese and bacon. Since porridge made without milk was comparatively unpalatable, it too fell out of fashion.[15] As a result, the hinds and their families experienced 'a falling off in strength and stamina ... The children are being brought up on tea instead of milk and, without it, porridge is disliked and given up ... Men ... now eat white bread and drink tea, and ain't half so hard.' Cow's milk was no longer available for feeding babies, mothers preferring to give them tinned condensed milk imported from Switzerland, as a substitute.[16]

In addition to the meals eaten at home, the farm workers also needed snacks to keep them going when out in the fields. These would be made up of the mixed-corn bannocks baked on the girdle hung over the fire, or breads baked in the oven, with a piece of cheese and probably a drink of water. When time was short, and everyone thronged the fields during the harvest, some farms provided everyone with porridge. A large cauldron of water was heated by a fire lit inside a shed, the oatmeal sprinkled in, and the mixture stirred with a huge stick or thible which hung from the roof. When ready, it was tipped into a number of 'fivesome boys', wooden tubs large enough to serve four shearers and the binster, and carried out together with five tins full of milk and five wooden spoons. Each of the reapers then lay down around it and ate out of the same vessel. On the last day of harvest apples were concealed in the pot, each person trying to find one, since this would bring them luck.[17]

HARVEST

On all the arable farms in the north-east, the end of the harvest was marked by a celebration called either the kern or the mell. In the eighteenth century the sheaf formed part of 'an Image apparelled in great finery, crowned with flowers, a sheaf of corn placed under her arm, a scythe in her hand, carried out of the village in the morning of the conclusive day of reaping, with musick and much clamour of the reapers, into the field, where it stands on a pole all day, and when reaping is done is carried home in like manner. It is called the Harvest Queen'. The alternative names were Harvest Doll or Kern Baby. It was also described as 'an image gaily dressed like a female child, and carried by a woman on a pole, in the midst of a group of reapers, as they go dancing and screaming to and from the fields on "a shearing out day". These parties generally consist of women, but after the day's work is done the mell-doll ... graces the board where the swains partake with their female partners in reaping a plentiful meal, and the evening concludes with mirth, music and dancing.'

When all the corn had been stooked, the last remaining sheaf was reaped and 'shouted', the farmer's head man or some other elderly harvester cried out rhymes such as;[18]

> *Blest be the day Christ was born,*
> *We've gettin't mell of Mr -------'s corn,*
> *Weel bound and better shorn,*
> *Hip! Hip! Hip! Huzza! Huzza! Huzza!*

or;

> *Blessed be the day our Saviour was born,*
> *For Master ------'s corn's all well shorn,*
> *And we will have a good supper tonight,*
> *And a drinking of ale, and a kirn!*
> *all then shouting 'A kirn, ahoa!'*

The mell doll or kern baby was then displayed at the supper. Around 1900 it could still be made of a sheaf in a white dress, with ears of corn sprouting out as a head and hands, and perhaps stuck with flowers, or be a cross formed from a few stalks of wheat.[19] It was still considered to be important, the *Newcastle Weekly Chronicle* reporting that 'If there is no kern baby, the next harvest will be bad.'[20] By this time, however, the lively mell and kirn suppers, with their dancing, food and drink were already in decline, as the churches converted them into sober harvest festivals.

By the later nineteenth century the age-old practice of threshing the grain from the corn by beating it with a flail had come to an end. Barn threshing machines driven by horse wheels, here known as 'gin-gans', had been introduced around 1800, these in turn being supplemented by mobile threshing machines powered by traction engines on many farms. Instead of providing weeks of barn work for the cold winter months, threshing now usually took no longer than one single, hectic day. Everyone was busy, but the family, visiting helpers and the threshing team still had to be provided with substantial quantities of food, in a form which was easily prepared. To meet this need farmer's wives developed something like a Christmas pudding which could

8. Here at Low Waskerley Farm, Shotley Field, the sheaves are being removed from the ricks, tossed up to the women on the threshing machine, and fed inside. The straw then emerged at the back, and the separated grain down a chute into sacks. This was intense, hot and dusty work, the workers then looking forward to a meal which featured Threshing-Day Pudding.

be made weeks in advance, and then only steamed or boiled to heat through when needed.

Threshing Day Pudding [21]

5oz/150g plain flour	5oz/150g currants
5oz/150g sugar	5oz/150g raisins
2 tsp ground mixed spice	5oz/150g dates, chopped
4oz/100g fresh white breadcrumbs	5oz/150g suet
1 egg, beaten	5oz/150g grated carrot
milk to mix	5oz/150g grated apple
3oz/75g candied lemon peel, finely chopped	

Mix the dry ingredients, make a well in the centre, drop in the egg, and mix in sufficient milk to form a stiff mixture. Steam or boil for 3 hours, as for a Christmas pudding (see p. 240), if stored boil for 2 hours before use, and serve with a sweet white sauce.

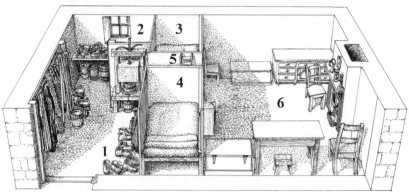

9. The shepherd's cottage (top), drawn near Wooler in 1871, shows the papered walls, canvas ceiling, box beds, range with oven and side boiler, and hanging ham and sides of bacon typical of Northumberland. The cottage below stood at Middleton, just south of Wooler, where it housed seven shepherds when visited by William Howitt in 1840. It featured;

> 1. entrance serving as a cloakroom for outdoor clothes, plaids, crooks and a cheese-press.
> 2. dairy, also serving as a pantry and a store for the small coopered 'bickers' from which food and drink was consumed.
> 3. & 4. box-beds with sliding doors
> 5. ladder to loft with further beds and a store for fleeces.
> 6. kitchen, with a matted ceiling and chinty cornice.

SHEPHERDS

The status of a Northumbrian shepherd was quite different from that of other farm workers. He enjoyed a far more independent position, particularly since he received no wages in the form of money. Instead, he ran a large number of his own sheep within his master's flock, and was also allowed to keep geese and poultry for his own profit. This frequently enabled him to accumulate capital, and perhaps take on his own farm in due course. At work, his hours were long, and his life solitary, moving and feeding the sheep, tending them throughout lambing, supervising their washing and shearing, and protecting them from blizzards, floods, dogs and, particularly up to around 1830, from sheep-stealing. The shepherd's cottage was therefore a combination of a home and a workplace. [22]

In the 1830s William Howitt visited one of their 'very snug and curious' cottages at Middleton, at the foot of the Cheviot. It housed several shepherds, but probably reflected the layout of individual shepherds' homes. The first room was filled with outdoor clothing, shears, crooks, etc., and a press for ewes' milk cheeses, prepared in the adjacent dairy. Within, the main living room resembled those of other farm cottages, with a fireplace and two box beds, with a ladder to the loft which had three or four stump or wicker-work beds, along with lots of fleeces. This was quite a basic arrangement, shepherds on the larger farms often being provided with good-quality two-storeyed houses. [23]

Richard Heath's visit to a shepherd's cottage near Wooler in 1871 presented a very similar impression. The ceiling was of stretched canvas, the wind flapped the wallpaper as it penetrated the rough stone walls, and the range, with a square oven on one side and a boiler on the other, had been put in by the shepherd. He ran forty-two sheep with his master's flock, these bringing a cash income from the sale of their wool and lambs, along with a cow and pigs provided by his master. His only other income was in kind, comprising thirteen six-bushel barrels of corn, 1500 yards of potatoes, his rent, and the carting of his coals, which he paid for with his own money. He also kept a few chickens to provide fresh eggs and the occasional 'old boiler' for the pot. [24]

The lifestyle was similarly basic in 1928, when Ms Ruth Stuart worked for a shepherd and his two sons at High Blakehope, Powburn, near Alnwick. Here a pig was killed every March and November, a beef came from the butcher twice a year, and half a sheep in autumn.

Along with fresh fish, most of this was salted down for future use. All the vegetables were grown on the allotment, some being cooked in the stock left over from boiling the bacon to provide soup three times a week. All the bread was home-baked in an oven, but the scones were still baked on an iron girdle over a peat fire. Taken together, these virtually self-sufficient resources provided a very good basic diet:[25]

	BREAKFAST	DINNER	TEA	SUPPER
Sun.	bacon & egg	meat or boiled bacon, potatoes & veg.	brown fadge, cake bread & scones	boiled egg; bread
Mon.	„	cold meat or bacon with boiled rice	bread, cake,cheese scones	bread, scones, butter
Tues.	„	fried bacon, dumpling, potatoes & veg	fudge, cake, bread, scones	bread, pickles, cold meat
Wed.	„	hot boiled bacon, potatoes, veg., pudding	„	scrambled egg on toast
Thurs.	„	cold boiled bacon, potatoes, veg., pudding	„	cold meat & bread
Fri.	„	boiled fish, vegetables, pudding	„	boiled eggs & bread
Sat.	„	fried bacon, vegetables, boiled pudding	„	tinned meat & bread

Even so, with bacon appearing at every breakfast and up to six dinners each week, it must have become monotonous over the years.

CHAPTER FOUR

THE LEAD MINERS

The high Pennine hills of western County Durham were one of the world's most important sources of lead, a metal essential for the roofing, plumbing, bullets, shot, paints and numerous other products necessary for Britain's industrial expansion. The ore-bearing veins usually ran vertically through the hard rock, requiring completely different methods of working to those of the coal mines. They were of uncertain size and shape, and worked by partnerships of between two and ten miners who collectively agreed a price with the management for each 'bing', or eight hundredweight of ore they produced. Once extracted, boys aged about seven to eleven picked the waste stones from the ore or 'bouse' before it was crushed either by women using a heavy, flat, iron-headed hammer called a 'bucker' to the 1840s or by crushing machines powered by large waterwheels. Sieving in a tub of water separated the lighter waste from the heavy lead ore, which was then crushed into finer fragments and flushed with a rapid flow of water by boys on large dressing floors. Skilled smelters then heated the ore on specially-designed hearths until the metallic lead finally ran off into moulds. These formed it into ingots, ready to supply leadworks around Newcastle, or for export further afield.

Since the lead-mining region was one of largely high, desolate hills and narrow valleys, with a very sparse farming population, the expansion of the industry from the early eighteenth century required numerous new houses and cottages for the miners and their families. Most took the form of miniature farms or small-holdings, with their living accommodation, barn and hayloft all under one roof, set within a few closes of land. Here they could grow both cereal crops and vegetables, keep a few animals, etc., in order to produce much of their own food at a subsistence level. New mining villages were also built, Allenheads and Carrshields by the Blackett-Beaumont Company, and Nenthead and Garrigill by the London Lead Company, each cottage being provided with its own garden plot.

The ability to produce much of their own food certainly gave the mining families a degree of independence, but it was never sufficient to meet all their needs. As a result, the relationship between their pay and their acquisition of essential foods was more complex than in other industries. The wages were paid at bargained prices per fathom for the 'dead-work men' who drove the new shafts and levels, and by the 'bing' of ore produced by each partnership of miners. Most of the others, the dressers, smelters, etc., were paid either by the day or shift, or on piecework. However, the mining companies only paid their employees either once a month, or once every three months. This made it difficult to manage the domestic budget, particularly when prices of lead and of food could vary considerably. In 1795, for example, the lead miners of Stanhope were so angry at having to pay 16–20 shillings (80p–£1) per boll of four bushels of wheat that they went to Wolsingham market, took the wheat from the farmers selling there, sold it at 10/6d–12 shillings (52–60p) the boll, and gave the money back to the farmers. They also smashed the flour cylinders at the town's two mills. To prevent similar riots, the London Lead Company then ordered its agents to buy grain at the Newcastle and Alston markets, and sell it to the miners at cost price.[1]

In 1799/1800 the current situation caused the bargain rates to be changed from the price of lead, to the price of food, the Company buying in £500 worth of wheat and rye and converting a lead mill at Tynebottom into a steam-powered corn mill so that they could supply the miners at Newcastle prices. At this time the weekly advances against the due wages was raised from 10s to 12s (50–60p), in order that the miners could feed themselves. Later in the Napoleonic wars this rose to 16s–20s (80p–£1), then dropping back to 12s–14s (60–70p) as the prices of both corn and lead became depressed. Corn continued to be issued in lieu of wages in times of shortage up to around 1840. Then the London Lead Company advanced an extra month's wages to each man so that they could set up their own co-operative 'Corn Associations', such as that established at Middleton in Teesdale in 1846. For other foods, the miners could use local shops, such as the 'Ready Money Shop' set up at Nenthead in 1816, its tenant being prohibited from extending credit to any of his customers. Where credit was available, the miners took full advantage of it, especially when wages were high and they had just been paid, and when hard-up before the next pay-day. This made them frequently fall into debt to the shopkeeper, who, to protect his own business, had to keep all his prices high. As Thomas Sopwith, manager of the Beaumont mines in Allendale and Weardale reported in 1846;

I do not consider that goods can be safely furnished on the precarious credit which the miners now possess for 30-35% profit, hence 8d or 9d in hand will buy as much as could be bought for a shilling (12d) on credit.

In effect, credit was reducing the spending power of their wages by about 25%[2].

The range of foods bought by a miner, his wife and two children is given in this account, collected from John Longstaff for the 1842 *Commission ... into the Employment of Children in Mines*;

Bread, two stones	4s	0d
Potatoes, one peck	0	6
Bacon, 2lb	1	4
Coffee, 2oz		2
Sugar, 1lb		8
Milk		7
Butter, half pound		6
	7s	9d[3]

The way in which these were prepared and eaten when living at home were described by one of the seventeen-year-old washer-boys, William Salkeld;

I take with me to the pit milk and brown bread and white bread; the brown bread is made of rye; it is very black, but not as black as your hat; it tastes pretty well. When we come home we get boiled potatoes, and sometimes butter, and sometimes a piece of bacon. We have a rather better dinner on Sundays, and have some meat to it.

and another twelve-year-old, William Whitfield of Nenthead;

I get crowdy and milk to breakfast; I get tatoes to dinner, and salt, sometimes butter; I get tea for supper, and eat bread with it; I drink beer sometimes; I get a sup when I can; I like it.

The Commission similarly confirmed that;

A great many men have oatmeal crowdy to breakfast, which is cheaper than bread. Men who have no cow have no milk to the crowdy, they have only a bit of butter. There is not much beer drunk now by the miners; the temperance societies have made a great change. A miner generally does not eat so much as a working man in the open air; the foul air takes away the appetite.

The combination of home-grown potatoes, probably other vegetables, home-fed bacon and offal from the pig, milk and butter from the cow, and bought-in oats, rye and wheat flours, tea and coffee, provided one of the most basic of diets. The bread, whether of rye or rye and wheat 'maslin', was baked as flat cakes on the girdle, until ovens became available, while the butcher's meat purchased for Sunday dinner was usually oven-baked in the form of a meat and potato pie. As Thomas Sopwith noted;

> They have meat, which is frequently put into pies of pastry, of a more dense consistency than I would like. I have often been sorry to see young children in the school eating pies, that, I am afraid, any of us would require a very good appetite indeed in able to manage ... they sometimes have fruit pies and sometimes meat; they are very well fed.

Since Sopwith was a prosperous manager, he would have been used to delightfully short, crumbly pastry to his pies, this requiring plenty of butter, lard or dripping which the miners would have found prohibitively expensive. These would have been reserved for making the special knead- or ned-cakes which were baked on the girdle for important visitors. He had;

> sometimes when, ... in extensive mineral surveys, been extremely glad to go in and have a cup of good tea and what they call knead cakes, a flat cake baked on the girdle, and buttered and cut up into small squares. I have enjoyed it in a miner's cottage and have thought it as great a luxury as one could have in any place.[4]

The distance a miner might have to walk to work could be several miles, but if the journey became too long to be performed every day, he would stay at the mine for the whole week, or even longer. For this

10. These drawings of lead miners on Alston Moor around 1820 show (above) "Monday Morning", as they walk from home to the mine, each carrying his wallet or poke of food for the coming week. Below, they celebrate November 5th by drinking as on a pay-day. The mine lodge or shop shown here was built about this period at Manor Gill Mine, Middleton Common.

purpose the company provided a lodging called a mine shop. One at a mine some nine miles south of Stanhope had a large ground-floor living room which had;

> a great fire burning at the east end. Along one side, that next the window, was a deal table extending the whole length of the room, and alongside it was a form, and there were two other forms in the room. Along the other side on the wall were little cupboards 48 in number, in four tiers above each other, six of the cupboards with the doors off, but most of the rest carefully locked with padlocks, and in which the several miners had deposited their wallets, with their provisions for five days.[5]

Here too were a pitcher, a pan for boiling potatoes, two pans for frying bacon, fire-irons, a besom, and a large box containing the protective clothes which the masters put on when inspecting the mines. A ladder gave access to the bedroom above. Here were seven bunk-beds, each with two tiers of 6ft x 4ft 6ins/183 x 137cm beds, each of which might hold three men with a boy sleeping across their feet.

As a washer-lad explained in the lead-mining song 'Fourpence a Day', early on a Monday morning;

> Mi mother rises oot o' bed, wi' tears on her cheek,
> Pats mi wallet on mi shoulders that hes ti last a week

The wallet resembled a pillowcase slit along one side, in which his week's supply of oatmeal, bread, potatoes, cheese, bacon and milk could be carried, slung across his shoulders.[6] As one boy at Bentifield mine reported in 1842, he made his own breakfast of crowdy with milk at the fireside of the mine shop, then having his potatoes boiled for dinner, this being included in the 6d a week he paid for his lodgings.

Living on crowdy, bread and boiled potatoes, with a little cheese and bacon, is a poor diet for a man constantly employed in hard-rock mining. In 1862–4 the *Kinnaird Report on the Condition of Mines* commissioned doctors to report on the general health of a number of lead miners. A 37-year-old from Ireshopeburn;

> has worked all his life in the mines in Weardale, and is now working at Burtree Pasture. In some places the mine is very bad. The candles sometimes will not burn unless held on one side. They feel the bad air in the chest, and get sleepy, and have headache, and some men say it takes all the strength out of their limbs. Delicate, thin-looking and pale. He has a poor appetite, and his food does not agree with him. He suffers from pain in the bowels.

Another from Middleton-in-Teesdale;

> Has worked in some bad places, and some very bad from air and 'stour after blasting' … It causes cough … Their appetites also fail, and sometimes their food does not agree with them. Pale, sallow and thin. Appetite defective. Bowels regular.

11. "Washers at Dinner 1819" on Alston Moor. The central man in the upper group is eating a pasty with a boldly-crimped crust. A further seventy years were to pass before this savoury pastry, made in many parts of the country for at least 700 years, was ridiculously claimed as a solely Cornish product. The lad below appears to be eating his bread and cheese in the traditional manner, holding it in his left hand, while using the pocket knife in his right hand to cut it up and carry it to his lips, the handkerchief on his lap catching the crumbs.

Dr Ewart, the London Lead Company's surgeon also confirmed that the miners all had delicate appetites, and could only eat simple, insipid foods, all tasty, highly-seasoned foods being avoided. The combination of bad air, meagre food, lead poisoning and hard labour took a hard toll on their lives. Around 1840 the average age of death was only 47½ years, three-quarters that of someone living in a town like Carlisle.[7] As the century progressed conditions degenerated even further as the rapid expansion of new mines in America and Spain greatly reduced the price of lead. By the 1880s wages had fallen to starvation level, the entire industry virtually disappearing by 1900.

CHAPTER FIVE

FISHERFOLK & SAILORS

T he sea made a considerable contribution to the food supply and overall prosperity of Northumberland and County Durham.[1] It was extremely rich in fish and, before the development of railways, provided the sole means of exporting the region's coal, lead and fish in bulk, and of importing all manner of basic and luxury goods. Whether catching fish or carrying cargoes, seamen required a degree of hardiness, traditionally transferred skills and domestic support which led to the formation of very close communities. The families living in coastal villages and ports had little in common with those inland, and maintained their own distinctive lifestyles throughout the late nineteenth century. Only then did they begin to welcome strangers into their midst, as coastal settlements developed a new role as holiday resorts.

The wives of the fishermen operating off the north-eastern coast played an essential role in the industry by collecting mussels, limpets, crabs and sand-eels as bait. These they stuck on the 240–300 hooks, each on its 30ins/90cm horsehair 'snood' spaced along a 200–240 fathom long line, and carefully wound it onto an oval wickerwork 'rip'. The lines were then taken out in cobles, the local deep-bowed, square-sterned clinker-built open fishing boats, shot across the tide and held in place with a combination of anchors and floating buoys for about six hours. Their harvest of haddock, whiting, cod, ling and turbot was then returned to shore and transferred to great wicker creels so that the fishwives could carry three or four stone of fish up to ten miles along the roads to the main market towns.[2]

This trade continued in the smaller fishing villages, but the larger ports, with their quays, began to be used by trawlers from the south coast from the 1830s. These were succeeded by steam-powered trawlers in the 1870s, so that the Sea Fisheries Report of 1879 reported that they had made line-fishing unprofitable.[3]

The herring fishery started in early summer, when the Berwick boats set off for the Forth estuary, then, joined by those from the other fishing communities, followed the shoals as they passed down the coast and departed towards Yarmouth about the middle of September.

12. Sarah Cromarty and Bessie Morris, better known as 'Lang Sal and Fat Bess' were Holy Island fishwives in the 1880s. They used their pannier-laden donkeys to hawk fish around local villages.

It was also in the 1870s that the Scottish boats began to join this fleet, bringing with them the herring girls who rapidly gutted, salted and packed the catch into barrels to serve both local and overseas markets. The catches landed in the ports of Berwick, North Shields, Sunderland and Hartlepool were truly massive, totalling over 13,000 tons in 1903.[4]

There was also an extensive shellfish trade, the expensive lobsters and crabs being caught in creeves over the summer months. These were frames some 2-3ft/60-90cm long with semicircular ends some 1ft 6ins/45cm high each having a trap/entrance in its covering of netting.[5] The catch was then kept in a perforated box called a hully until ready for sale.[6] Oysters, mussels, cockles, prawns and shrimps were also taken, most being sold in the markets, although landowners such as Lord Tankerville at Chillingham Castle had his oysters delivered by the local oyster-keeper.[7]

The north-east coast, and the mouth of the Tweed in particular, were one of Britain's finest sources of salmon. As described around 1800, the season ran from 10th January to 10th October each year, the salmon returning from the sea being netted by the hundred, some reports claiming even five or seven hundred per draught.[8] At sea they were taken in drift nets, while bob nets, or ring nets, long rectangular

43

nets fastened between a stone or anchor in the river and a post or ring on the shore, were the main methods of fishing.[9] There were also stake nets – long, deep and rectangular and hung on vertical posts on the shores to take salmon on the ebb-tide.[10] Barbed, three-pronged fish spears or leisters to take salmon attracted to lamp-light on dark evenings, or click-hooks, three large salmon hooks bound together on a line, thrown beneath a salmon and then jerked upwards, were often used by poachers.[11]

At first the fresh Berwick salmon were taken down to the Tyne for pickling 'The Newcastle Way', before being shipped to London. The Berwick traders then discovered that they could gather sufficient ice over the winter months to enable the salmon to be carried to London without any other form of preservation. This trade started in 1788, and by 1799 over 7,600 cartloads of ice were being stored in Berwick ice-houses solely for this purpose.[12] During the season some 75 single-masted vessels called smacks, each between 70 and 120 tons and crewed by a dozen men, made about fourteen voyages to London.[13] By creating some 900 jobs for sailors, along with 300 more for salmon and general fishermen in Berwick, this trade brought great prosperity to this part of the region.

Most of the traditional cottages occupied by the fishing families have now been demolished. Some around Spittal at the mouth of the Tweed were single-storey, with one room or bothy used for accommodation, and the other for storing the tackle.[14] Others, such as Fisher Square in Beadnell, built around 1776, were thatched with bents, the long, coarse grass of the sand dunes. The larger middle cottages had large lofts used for bedrooms, the ground-floor room having a fire, later with an oven to one side and a boiler at the other, and the space under the stairs used as a pantry.[15] Many of the cottages had just a single room, those at Brown's Buildings built at Cullercoats in 1836 had four-poster beds, a table, chairs, a mantelpiece decorated with 'pot dogs', brass candlesticks, etc., and walls hung with cheap prints.[16] The door and windows were always kept open throughout the day, since the floor was in regular use in preparing fishing gear.

The interior of one Cullercoats cottage is shown in Frank Holl's painting 'No Tidings from the Sea' of 1870. It depicts a wife who entered the cottage in which he was working, with her, 'hair dishevelled, and wild eyes, muttering and moaning distractedly, wandering from door to window, window to door, half-mad with suspense and misery', since her husband had not returned after a terrible storm. It also shows the typical flagged floor, wide fireplace, and the hangings of a four-poster

13. The rare view of the interior of a fisherman's cottage at Cullercoats (top) was painted there by Frank Holl in 1870. As he was drawing the fireplace and four-poster bed a woman 'with hair dishevelled, and wild eyes, moaning distractedly ... half mad with suspense and misery' entered. There had been a terrible storm while the boats were out, and her husband had not returned.

Many of the traditional fishermen's cottages were simple single-room structures, like these seen at Newbiggin around 1900 (bottom), while the long lines were being baited.

bed.[17] In other cottages along the coast the box-beds were preferred, providing extra protection from the cold north-eastern winds.[18]

For fisherfolk there was usually no shortage of fish for the table, but living in a totally fishy environment meant that it could become far too much of a good thing. For this reason other foods were more welcome, such as meat, which could be purchased, and rabbits and ducks, which could be poached.[19] Few vegetables were grown, but greengrocery was either carried back from the markets in the empty fish baskets and creels, or bought from traders who came round with supplies on a 'flat' cart pulled by a donkey.[20] When setting out for a day's fishing in the cobles – the traditional open, square-sterned coastal vessels of the North-East – some fishermen took no food, but chewed tobacco to ward off hunger, while others took sandwiches and cold tea drunk out of a flat tin pitman's bottle. Out on the trawlers there was usually fried bacon for breakfast, while corned beef and onion sandwiches often appeared for dinner with monotonous regularity.[21]

If there were prolonged storms and the boats could not get out, the families risked starvation. If this happened they were sometimes forced to catch starlings, as at Newbiggin, or gulls to eat. As Thomas Bewick observed in his *Water Birds* of 1804, some people who lived near the sea, presumably including fishing families, commonly ate various kinds of seagull. The gulls were said to be perfectly edible, 'when they have undergone a certain sweetening process before cooking, such as burying them in fresh mould for a day, or washing them in vinegar.' Seaweed called slawk was also eaten. As early as 1562 it was recorded that 'The bryon thalassion of Theophastus and Pling is called in Northumberland slauke; which ... the poor people sethe, and that with lekes and oyniones. They put it in a poot, and smoze it, as they call it, and then it looketh blake, and then put they onyons to it and eat it.' Slawk, the Gaelic name for the green laver, *Ulva lactuca* and *Ulva latissima*, was also collected and eaten in Scotland, Ireland and Cornwall.[22] The other edible seaweed, purple laver *Porphyra lacunista* or *Porphyra vulgaris*, was similarly gathered, quantities being sold in Newcastle for both boiling and pickling. The Irish community of the town also collected it for sale at the Sunday 'rag-fairs'.[23] Another collected food was gull's eggs, these being harvested from the cliffs of the Farne Islands by fishermen of the north Northumberland coast.[24]

Along with a basket of herrings salted down as a winter standby, the other dishes particularly associated with the fishing communities were the poodler of Tynemouth and North Shields, and the sun-dried skate of Holy Island. The former was a small coalfish caught near the river mouths in later summer and boiled whole, being as tasty as mackerel.[25] The latter, dried on the tiled roofs of the cottages, was eaten by the fishermen when drinking their ale, being 'much in demand by the sailors of scotch vessels that are driven here for shelter. They are eaten either without any preparation, or simply toasted on the fire.'[26]

The diet of the sailors involved in the coal trade had to be substantial in order to provide them with the energy required to sail their vessels.

14. Euphemia Scott was the Queen of the Newcastle fishwives in the mid 1820s. Songs of the period describe her as 'Euphy, the Queen, singing *Maw canny Geordie*,' and how it was 'fine indeed to hear ... Euphy Scott fight or bawl fresh heerin'.' In contrast, on hearing of the death of her friend Judy Dawney, a local songster told how;

> *Alang wi' Heufy Scott aw cried,*
> *Till byeth was owt o' breeth,*
> *For, greet and sma', fishwives en' a'*
> *Luck'd up tiv her wi' veneration.*

Each keelman who manned the keels that carried the coal from the quays out to the large collier vessels never went on board till their baskets were stored with a good joint of meat, which, with a bottle of beer, formed his usual diet. The meat, which was of the fattest kind, was sliced, laid upon a piece of bread, and then cut into convenient bites with a knife.[27] They also carried ships' biscuits with them, as an alternative to the bread.[28]

The collier brigs involved in the coastal trade usually weighed about 260 tons, with a capacity of some 400 tons of coal. Traditionally powered by sail, each required a crew of twelve to fourteen men and boys to undertake up to ten voyages to London and back every year. They were usually owned in shares divided into 64ths, and each made its own purchases of the food and drink needed to feed its crew, recording these in its voyage accounts. Those of the Whitby-owned *Benjamin & Mary* returning from London to South Shields in 1807 include;

	£	s	d.
Beef at Greenland Dock		19	0
Soft Bread 10/8, Oxhead 4/6 Greens 8/-		18	2
Grocer 7/6, Cheese 1/3		8	9
Mr. Turner for Pork got in 1805	6	0	0
Butter &c £2/7/0, Liquor £2/12/0	4	19	0
Butcher £10/1/11	10	1	11
Fresh meat at Grays		8	6
Mutton at Bridlington 12/6, Greens 5/-		17	6
Water Cest 1/1		1	1

On other voyages there were purchases of sheep, mutton, bacon, fish, eggs, potatoes, greens, vegetables, sugar, and rice, along with casks of water, 'liquor' (i.e. beer), and tea. Veal, fowls and ducks were clearly intended for the captain, mate and carpenter in the cabin, while wine, brandy and gin were probably used to fortify the whole of the ship's company in cold and stormy passages. There are also payments for firewood for the ship's stove, and £2 10s/£2.50 to the ship's cook.[29] Such records show that the sailors had a plain but very well-balanced diet, with red meat, fish, potatoes and fresh vegetables for their dinners. The accounts of other ships also include oatmeal, ideal for porridge and crowdy, barley for stews, dried peas for peas pudding and flour for pastry, dumplings and sea pies.[30]

The victualling and chandlery trade brought a good income into the local ports. Just one ship, *The Three Sisters*, spent almost £6,000 in the north-east over 27 years in the late eighteenth century, for example, dealing with 250 separate suppliers.[31] A search through the trade directories of the Victorian period provides ample evidence for the expansion of this trade. By 1851 James M'Cartney of Sunderland was supplying ships with beef and pork, mild-cured for preservation, along with Cumberland hams, bacon, butter, cheese and lard. In Stockton-on-Tees Clapham & Co. made soda, cabin and ship's biscuit by machinery, delivering them free on board at Stockton, Middlesbrough and Hartlepool. Thomas Young of Hartlepool similarly made ship bread and ship's biscuit.[32]

There were numerous recipes for cooking at sea, the following being typical:

Sea Pie [33]

1lb/450g stewing steak	For the pastry;
1 onion, peeled	6oz/175g flour
1 carrot, scraped	3oz/75g suet
1 tsp salt	½ tsp baking powder
½ tsp pepper	¼ tsp salt

Cube the meat, cut the vegetables into rings, put in a saucepan with the salt, pepper and water to just cover them, and bring to the simmer. Mix the pastry ingredients with sufficient water to make a stiff dough and, roll out ½ins/12mm thick to fit in the top of the pan. Skim the ingredients in the pot, lay the pastry on top, cover, and stew for 1½ hours. To serve, cut the pastry into 6 or 8, remove these onto the upturned pan lid, pour the stew into a deep dish, and arrange the crust on top.

Biscuit Hash [34]

6lb/2.7kg ship's biscuits	1 cooked turnip
2lb/900g cooked salt beef or pork	1 tsp mixed herbs
2 onions	salt & pepper
1 cooked carrot	2oz/50g dripping

Soak the biscuits until soft, then squeeze out all the water. Mince the meat and vegetables, mix in the remaining ingredients except the dripping, and put in a baking tin, smoothing the top with a knife or the back of a spoon. Pour the melted dripping on top, mark in squares, and bake at 180°C, 350°F, Gas mark 4 for about 30–40 minutes until browned. Cut into squares and serve hot.

Mutton Pudding [35]

1½lb/675g lean mutton, cubed	For the pastry:
1 small onion, chopped	*12oz/325g plain flour*
½ tsp salt	*6oz/175g suet*
¼ tsp ground pepper	*¼ tsp salt*
1 tbs plain flour	

Make the pastry by mixing the dry ingredients with about 8fl oz/225ml cold water, to form a soft dough and roll out on a floured surface to about 14ins/35cm diameter. Cut out a quarter, to form the lid, and use the rest to line a 3pt/1.7l pudding basin.

Mix the salt, pepper and flour, roll the pieces of mutton in it, then layer with the onions in the basin, and half-fill with cold water. Cover with the remaining pastry, sealing the edges. Cover with pleated greaseproof paper and steam for 3½ hours, then turn out and serve.

Dried salt fish kept well at sea, some being made at Beadnell.

To Boil Salt Fish [36]

Remove the outer skin and fins, keeping the under skin intact, while cutting the flesh into small squares. Soak for several hours in plenty of water, then put into a fish kettle of boiling water to poach for 45 minutes. Lift the fish out of the water without breaking the squares, dish, and serve with or without parsley sauce.

On returning home, the sailors looked forward to the region's greatest delicacy, a rich home-made singing hinny. This is described in the local song 'Liberty to the Sailors', which was written after many impressed sailors came back after the end of the Napoleonic wars. It was sung to the tune of the carol 'I saw Three Ships Come Sailing By.'

Lasses, call your lads ashore,
lads ashore, lads ashore,
Lasses, call your lads ashore.
There's liberty for the sailors.

Our bairns shall all be dressed so nice,
Our girdle cakes be black with spice,
With a pound of butter in every slice,
All for to please the sailors!

CHAPTER SIX

THE POOR

Real poverty and starvation were a constant threat to many working families before the introduction of the Welfare State and Old Age Pensions. The death of a breadwinner through industrial accident or disease often left women and children virtually destitute, while illness and old age left many alone, vulnerable and unable to support themselves. Even those in regular employment were subject to unexpected financial problems totally beyond their control. The loss of wartime production, the discharge of thousands of soldiers and sailors, and the drop in trade with a disfunctional Continent led to six years of depression and unemployment after the end of the Napoleonic wars in 1815, for example. Further severe depressions in the 1830s, 1840s and 1880s caused similar periods of unemployment and misery. Even attempts to improve wages and working conditions took their toll on local communities. The pitmen who struck for some ten weeks in 1831, sixteen weeks in 1832 and twenty weeks in 1841 received virtually no income, no poor relief, and no credit from shopkeepers, while some faced eviction from their homes. Any savings were soon used up, and hunger followed.

As the Industrial Revolution progressed, many families left the countryside and moved into the mushrooming industrial towns, where the populations increased at an unprecedented rate. The conurbation of Newcastle and Gateshead multiplied almost tenfold, from some 37,000 in 1801 to 325,000 in 1901, for example. This rapid growth brought numerous problems, particularly regarding the supply of food. Despite the enclosure of thousands of acres of common land and their conversion to productive farmland, the region was frequently unable to feed itself, especially if bad weather led to a poor harvest. In the years 1795, 1800, 1801, 1809, 1815, 1816, 1837, 1838 and 1845 the harvests failed, leading to a scarcity of corn, and a consequent rise in prices. A single wheaten loaf cost 1s/5p in Newcastle in 1816, for example, where many families were receiving a total weekly income of 1s 10d/c.9p as poor relief. In the same years rioters pillaged the provision shops of Sunderland, burning one of them to the ground, replicating the riots which took place at many other market towns during the famine years.[1] Only the repeal of the Corn Laws in 1846

15. As the major towns expanded, the great demand for accommodation led to many houses being divided into numerous single-room houses, such as this one (top) at 11 Magnesia Bank, North Shields, which had only a basic grate, a bed recess and a tiny window. Access to the upper floors was frequently gained by external wooden galleries, such as those at Providence Place (left) and Bowl Alley Bank (right) in Gateshead. Major slum clearances only started in the mid 1930s.

enabled the import of cheap foreign grain to end such nation-wide shortages, but poverty remained a constant problem.

There was poverty and hardship in the countryside, but the worst levels of deprivation were to be found in the overcrowded streets, yards and chares (side-streets or alleys) of the largest towns. Here, those in regular work might occupy just a single room, but still have a good diet of meat, potatoes, pies, dumplings, etc. to fuel their eleven- or twelve-hour days in the nearby factories and works. Their poorer neighbours were in much worse circumstances, however. In the 1840s as many as nine people could be living in a single two-bedded room, with minimal cooking facilities, and no water supply, drainage, sanitation or ventilation. There were also common lodging houses to accommodate a combination of newly-arrived workers, vagrants and the criminal underclass. A visitor to one of these described its

> room not more than 14 feet square [in which] from 15 to 20 men, women and children lodges, the men and children completely naked, with the exception of a small rug, and the women with nothing more than a shift, which, from the length of time and filthy habits of the wearer, had the appearance more of oil-cloth than the undergarments of a female.[2]

The diet of these people was usually little more than bread and the very cheapest of foods, washed down with beer, spirits, or the contents of the 'poverty-engine', the regional name for the teapot.[3]

Since poverty had been accepted as a brutal fact of everyday life for centuries, its relief was seen as the Christian responsibility of those who were able to rise above it. Frequently lands and investments had been left to parishes to fund the regular distribution of bread, etc. Such small-scale resources were totally inadequate to meet the needs of the larger industrialised communities of the late Georgian and Victorian periods, however. When mass starvation brought a threat of riot and disorder, committees were formed, subscriptions raised from the local gentry, industrialists and shopkeepers, and soup kitchens opened. One built at the back of the Holy Jesus Hospital in the Manors area of Newcastle in 1880 still survives today. Using a recipe provided by the local prison governor, the ingredients were first chopped, cooked in a digester, then steamed in eight boilers and finally poured down a chute into a trough on the ground floor. Up to eight hundred-gallon batches were sold each day at a penny a pint to those holding a ticket from either a subscriber or the local parish authorities. The soup was so good that its recipients, 'the deserving poor', began to sell it at a profit to the keepers of Newcastle lodging houses. On discovering this, the committee closed it down in 1891. In Gateshead, meanwhile, the poor had been able to obtain a penny ticket from certain shops which entitled the bearer to receive a quart of soup from the kitchen during the harsh winter of 1800-1801.[4] This then became a necessity over most of the succeeding years. In 1895 a soup kitchen here was still serving 1,000 quarts of soup each day. In addition, there was a Poor Children's

Sunday Morning Breakfast Fund, and the School Board's children's Dinner Fund, to ensure that the youngsters were adequately fed.[5] Such charitable works made substantial improvements to the quality of life of the poor, but were never able to cope with the increasing problems of mass poverty.

Ever since the sixteenth century every parish had been obliged to levy a rate on property-owners in order to maintain those unable to support themselves. This relief might take the form of payments in cash or kind called 'outdoor relief' made to those living in their own homes, or else full-time care and housing in an almshouse or poorhouse, where some kind of work was usually demanded. The ablebodied who refused to work were sent to houses of correction, where they were imprisoned and given laborious tasks until they changed their ways. This system was still in operation in the early nineteenth century, every parish using its poor-rate to maintain a workhouse for the poor. To its inhabitants, this was a place of last resort, for few were willing to give up their own homes and their personal liberty unless they had absolutely no alternative. As a result, many of the inmates were young children, unmarried mothers and the elderly, none of whom were able to work effectively to offset the cost of their keep, as originally intended.

Despite their poor reputations, the workhouses usually provided better and more plentiful food than that available to many of the poor living in the outside community. At the South Shields workhouse, for example, the following meals were being provided in 1797;[6]

Breakfasts	hasty pudding [porridge]	
Sunday	Dinner	beef etc.
	Supper	broth & bread
Monday	Dinner	peas soup
	Supper	boiled milk
Tuesday	Dinner	barley boiled in milk
	Supper	bread & milk
Wednesday	Dinner	beef etc.
	Supper	broth & bread
Thursday	Dinner	pease soup
	Supper	boiled milk
Friday	Dinner	suet dumplings
	Supper	cold milk
Saturday	Dinner	barley boiled in milk
	Supper	bread & milk

This gave boiled beef twice in a week, served with vegetables, but the remaining meals were of broth or milky 'slops'. Other workhouses were able to provide a better diet by cooking larger joints on two days, so that there was sufficient left to be served cold or hashed on the following days. In 1827 at St Andrew's Poor House in Newcastle the diet comprised;[7]

Breakfasts		hasty pudding [porridge] and new [whole] milk, with coffee or tea for the old and sick
Sunday	Dinner	round of boiled beef with peas, potatoes or vegetables, broth and suet dumplings
	Supper	Children: bread & milk. Old people: tea
Monday	Dinner	cold or hashed meat, with potatoes
	Supper	broth, or new milk & bread
Tuesday	Dinner	suet dumplings or fish
	Supper	broth, or new milk & bread
Wednesday	Dinner	boiled beef or mutton, with broth & pease or potato pudding
	Supper	broth, or milk & bread
Thursday	Dinner	cold or hashed meat, with potatoes
	Supper	milk & bread
Friday	Dinner	suet dumplings or fish etc.
	Supper	milk & bread
Saturday	Dinner	frumenty sweetened with treacle etc.
	Supper	milk & bread

This shows how the workhouses cooked many of the regionally popular everyday dishes with which its inhabitants were very familiar. Experience had proved that boiled beef, fish, dumplings, pease puddings, frumenty, porridge and milk were both nutritive and economical.

The cost and efficiency of the parochial poor-houses began to be questioned in the 1830s, when the government appointed a Poor Law Commission to investigate the manner in which they were being operated. It concluded that;

> In-doors Relief, that which is given, within the walls of the Poor-Houses [or Workhouse] is also subject to great mal-administration ... in the absence of classification, discipline and employment, and the extravagance of allowance [of food etc.].[8]

To remedy this situation, the New Poor Law of 1834 transferred responsibility for maintaining the poor from the parishes to large union workhouses controlled by a locally elected Board of Guardians who were bound to carry out the orders of a central body of Poor Law Commissioners for England and Wales. The new workhouses were purposely designed to be as unwelcoming and impersonal as possible, permanently dividing families into separate wards for men, women and children, and treating poverty as a punishable crime. Unsurprisingly, they were soon re-christened as 'Bastilles' by the general public, taking the name of the Parisian fortress which symbolised the brutal oppression imposed by the French monarchy. In terms of their food, however, they largely continued the practical and economic principles of their parochial predecessors, but now had to submit their proposed diets to the national Poor Law Board and obtain its approval. The quality of the ingredients was certainly as good as that consumed by most working families, as demonstrated by the following request for tenders to supply the Teesdale Union Workhouse at Barnard Castle in 1855. It specifies;

> BUTCHER'S MEAT. Thick Breasts, Thick Flanks and Sloats [necks] of Beef, Loins of Mutton ... and suet.
> MEAL, FLOUR &c. Meal of the best Red Wheat, Flour, and Oatmeal.
> GROCERIES. Tea, Coffee, Sugar, Pepper, Treacle, Salt, Soda, Starch, Blue, Candles, Soap, Rice.

These, together with fresh vegetables, would keep everyone inside better fed and healthier than many of their contemporaries living outside on the lowest incomes, even if entering the workhouse usually involved the abandonment of all personal liberty and dignity.

CHAPTER SEVEN

FUELS & FIREPLACES

The provision of heat for cooking was dependant on the availability of fuel. For heating ovens, boiling and roasting, timber was one of the best, but its felling, chopping and drying demanded a considerable amount of time and energy. An additional problem was the quantity required to serve a household throughout an entire year. As a result, wood tended to be used more for heating ovens and for kindling fires than as a major everyday fuel in most parts of the region. Fortunately nature had provided two good alternatives in massive quantities, these being peat, especially in the Pennine uplands, and coal, which could be mined throughout eastern Durham and up the eastern side of Northumberland up to around Alnmouth.

Peat-cutting was a seasonal occupation, starting at the end of May and continuing through to June. First the flaks or flaws, the top level of roots and recent vegetation, was pared off, cut into squares and dried for fuel.[1] The underlying rough, fibrous peat was then cut out using perhaps an ordinary spade or hay spade, or a peat spade with a broad blade. This type of spade, with a wooden shaft shod with an L-shaped iron blade so as to cut two sides of a peat at once, produced blocks about 12-15ins/30-38cm long, 8-9ins/20-23cm wide and 4ins/10cm thick, although they shrank considerably as they dried out. The deeper, denser and harder black peat beneath was cut with similar peat-spades, often working horizontally to give long blocks some 4ins/10cm square in section. By the close of 'the peatin' towards the end of July, just before the start of the hay harvest, the area around the peat beds would be covered with neat parallel rows of cut peats. These were then turned and stacked at intervals until perfectly hard and dry, ready to be carried back to the house in September. A horse and cart could be used for this purpose, but the soft nature of the moors usually made a peat-sledge mounted on metal runners a much more effective alternative.

Lighting a peat fire was easy enough, given plenty of kindling and experience, after which it burned on the flat hearthstone with little need for attention. Just raking off the fire ashes from the sides and adding new peats to the centre was all that was necessary, a covering

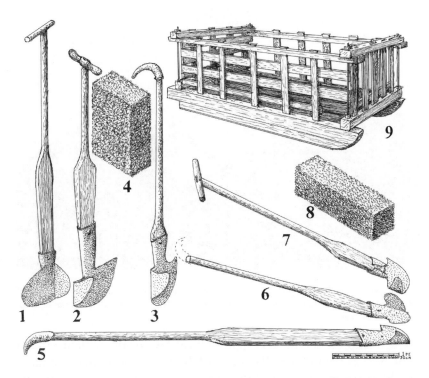

16. Peat was usually cut in two forms. The initial vertical cuts through the upper, rough, fibrous layer was made with broad peat-spades, such as these from 1. Frosterley, 2. Bolt Hope Farm, Blanchland, 3. Harwood, Teesdale, to produce large slabs, 4. The hard black peat beneath was then cut with narrower spades, as from 5. Hill Top Farm, St. Johns Chapel, 6 & 7, Weardale & Teesdale, to give long square-sectioned blocks, 8. As the moors were often too steep or too soft to take the wheels of a cart, the dried peats were often carried down to the farms in horse-drawn sleds, 9.

with fine peat mull (dust) keeping it smouldering overnight ready for reviving each morning.[2] In some parts of Northumberland flat cast-iron hearthplates with close-set central firebars and standing on short legs were sometimes used where peat was burned.

One of the most practical and efficient ways of improving the heat of the peat fires was to add a few 'cats'. These were a mixture of small coals and clay formed into balls and left to dry, a method invented before 1603 when Sir Hugh Platt published instructions for making them as *A new cheape and delicate Fire of cole-balles*. When placed on a peat fire they soon became incandescent and produced a hot, long-lasting glow. Descriptions such as 'I weel remember sitting opposite Molly in the kitchen, watching the red glow of burning 'cats' in the whitewashed fireplace' or of Burnhope in Weardale, where 'They pile

17. The whole region was provided with plentiful supplies of coal from the mines of County Durham and south-eastern Northumberland. This is Blue Bell Pit at Backworth, near Whitley Bay.

the cats in peats the higher' show that they were still popular around 1900, just as the industrially-produced 'briquettes' were in later years.[3]

The north-east was one of the first regions to use coal as a domestic fuel. The open hearths of the fourteenth-century great hall in the bailey of Warkworth Castle already had ashpits and provision for firebars for their coal fires. Unlike wood or peat, coal needs to be burned on a grate, for only this can give the essential under-draught and dispose of the ashes which would otherwise choke it.

Coal was readily available throughout this region, although it had to be carted from the mines in the coalfields to customers living in the coal-free Pennines and Cheviots, into the town centres, and down to the riverside and coastal quays to serve the more distant markets. Visitors found the use of coal here to be unusually widespread. Writing in 1698, for example, Celia Fiennes noted that most was 'small coale, though some is round coales, yet none like the cleff coales ... the small sort is as good as any, if it is black and shineing ... the sulphur of it taints the aire and it smells strongly to strangers'.[4] The local terms for the different sizes of coal as they emerged from the pithead screens were 'roondy coal' for the largest, then 'beans', then 'peas' and finally the fine dust called 'duff'.[5] Each had its own particular use as a domestic fuel, that from individual seams or collieries having its own reputation. In 1822, for example;

Hetton-Main coal is round and good,
It takes neither chips nor wood;
But makes a fire both brisk and braw.
Hetton coal it bangs them a'.[6]

Despite these claims, coals did need a little wood as kindling to set them alight, after which the use of the poker to dislodge the ashes and break up any coked masses usually kept them going. Fresh coal might be added from a bucket, but if possible it was dumped on a deep ledge on the fireback, so that lumps could be raked down as needed.[7] To keep the fire burning overnight 'the last thing the women did was to heap them up with as much small coal as the grates would hold, so that it was only necessary to thrust a poker into the smouldering mass to cause it to burst into a red flame.'[8] The alternative was to put a 'gatherin-coal', a large lump, onto the fire just before going to bed, this also producing a good fire when broken up in the morning.[9]

In rural areas during the eighteenth and early nineteenth century many fireplaces were built by fixing a large wooden beam across the kitchen at head height and a few feet from the gable wall. A partition to one side, the 'hallen' and its 'hallen-post', formed an entrance passage from the outer 'heck' door.[10] The space above the remaining space over the beam was occupied by a huge timber-framed pyramid, its surfaces coated in clay daub to form a smoke hood to carry the fumes upwards, and out of the chimney.

A lighter beam, often the branch of a tree with the bark stripped off, ran across the base of the smoke hood, this being called a 'galley-bauk', 'rannle bauk', 'barked branch', or 'peeled grain'.[11] Through its centre a shorter beam passed backwards into a socket in the gable wall. This was the 'reckin-tree', from which hung the adjustable iron pot-hook or 'reckin-crook' by which cooking pots, frying pans, girdles etc. were suspended over the fire.

On the flat hearth below, coal was burned in a wrought-iron grate, the iron firebars having 'end-irons', 'clamps' or 'niggarts' behind each end to hold in the fuel.[12] Sometimes these were adjustable so that the length of the fire could be increased or reduced as required. To either side a masonry hob might be built, its top finished with a slab of stone or wood. This was the 'hud', or 'hood-end' on which the cooking pots etc. were stored when not in use.[13] Over the years most of these open fireplaces were replaced by stone or brick chimney-stacks, but the general form of the firebasket and their hobs remained much the same until replaced by improved, multi-purpose kitchen ranges.

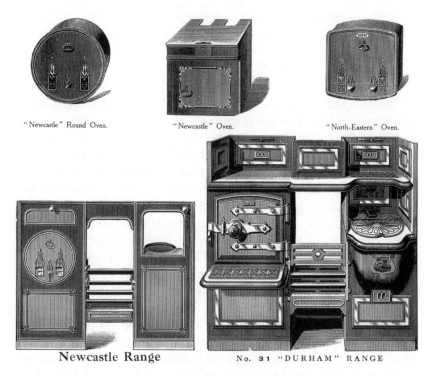

" Newcastle " Round Oven.

" Newcastle " Oven.

" North-Eastern " Oven.

Newcastle Range

No. 31 "DURHAM" RANGE

18. The cast-iron ranges of Northumberland and Durham had a strong regional character. By around 1900 local ironmongers were selling Newcastle round ovens from 14ins to 20ins diameter at 18s to 33s each, Newcastle square ovens from 12 to 24ins wide at 22s to 94s each, and North-eastern ovens from 14 to 20ins wide at 26s to 45s each. Each of these could be easily set into brickwork at the side of the firegrate.

Complete ranges, incorporating side boilers and face-plates were much more expensive. Newcastle ranges with inset boilers cast from 180s to 232s., for example, while Durham ranges with their projecting boilers cost between 299s to 428s, depending on their size.

Wood-fired stone or brick-lined 'beehive' ovens were in regular use in the region from at least the fourteenth century through to around 1900, since they were ideal for baking large batches of loaves etc. The idea of an oven made as an iron box heated by a coal fire was quite a revolutionary idea when introduced around the mid eighteenth century. One of the earliest illustrations of an oven of this kind is a drawing by Samuel Heironimus Grimm of the interior of the Prior's Kitchen at Durham Cathedral. Set to one side of a large roasting range, it took the form of a cylinder set horizontally in a casing of masonry, its flat, round door hinging down horizontally to form a convenient shelf when open. An open coal-burning fire burning on a grate beneath provided the heat, a small door above the oven giving access for both cleaning and for removing the soot which would accumulate there. Soon more fashionable versions were being cast by the Carron ironworks in Scotland. One installed in North Shields was octagonal, its door having the figure of Diana, goddess of the moon, virginity and hunting, set in an oval cartouche set between two of the Graces.

The original form of round oven continued to be the usual pattern throughout the north-east through into the early twentieth century, thousands being built into one side of working-class fireplaces here, particularly from the 1840s onwards. The vast majority were cast in local foundries such as Robert Heppell & Co.'s Pipewellgate Foundry in Gateshead, or W.H. Walker & Son's Percy Iron Works in Newcastle. The main reasons for their popularity was their cheapness, efficiency, and ease with which they could be set into their brickwork cases without either complex flues or superfluous expensive ironwork. Usually their only decoration was limited to ornamental hinges and door rest, but some also bore the name of the colliery company such as the Ridley Colliery Company, that had commissioned them for their own pit cottages. Around 1900 'Newcastle' round ovens were being made in various sizes from 14ins/35cm diameter at 18s/90p each up to 20ins/51cm at 33s/£1.65 each. The square 'Newcastle' ovens, box-shaped with integral flues to two sides and the top, and a door hinging from one side, cost 25s 6d/£1.27 each to 45s 6d/£2.27 for the same sizes, almost half as much again. 'North-Eastern' ovens, like the round ones but with vertical sides were even more expensive, these costings showing why the Newcastle round ovens were so popular.

In 1780 Thomas Robinson of London developed the first range in which the iron oven was heated by the main fire. Within a few years flues from the side of the fire were being directed around the oven before being drawn up the chimney. Newcastle round ovens were ideal for this purpose, the standard form of setting now having the oven to one side, and the boiling copper to the other, all heated from the central fire. Their individual heats were adjusted by dampers - sliding shutters which controlled the draught in their flues. Such ranges, their brickwork either painted or whitewashed, remained in use in many homes well into the 1970s and '80s.

For the better-off, the ironfounders began to produce ornamental face-plates which completely sheathed the exposed masonry, their ranges, polished to a high gloss with black lead, being both impressive and efficient. Many retained the local arrangement of round oven to one side and open-topped boiler to the other, this pattern being known as the Newcastle range. They represented a considerable

19. Foundries in the larger towns, including W.H. Walker & Son of the Percy Ironworks, Newcastle, made and supplied numerous Newcastle, Durham and Yorkshire ranges. Those sold by local ironmongers and bearing their screwed-on nameplates (below) might have been made locally, or else bought in from leading foundries such as the Carron Ironworks in Scotland.

investment, however. One of average size, with an 17ins/43cm round oven, 17ins/43cm wide grate and an 8-gallon pot or boiler cost £10 around 1900, about five times the price of the individual round oven, grate and boiler.

Other varieties of cast-iron range were also used in the north-east. Some were of the 'Yorkshire' pattern, with a large square oven to one side of the grate, an enclosed boiler below a hob to the other, and a long hotplate for both gentle cooking and plate warming running the whole width above. 'Durham' ranges were a useful combination of the best Yorkshire and Newcastle features, essentially being of Yorkshire pattern, but with an open-topped side boiler, its front bowing forward to increase its capacity. These were the main varieties of local range, but many others were readily available, ironmongers in every market town holding the catalogues of range manufacturers in every part of the country. Those calling at Moffatt Brothers in 18-24 High Street in Gateshead, could order models entitled the 'Hotspur', 'Dunelm', 'Durham', 'Newcastle', 'Borderer', 'Yorkshire' etc. However, even if cast with the name of the local supplier, many such ranges might easily have been cast anywhere between Scotland, Yorkshire, the Midlands or London, once the railways could provide cheap long-distance transport.

The range might be largely self-sufficient for cooking and heating purposes, but it still needed a whole selection of ancillary equipment to make it work efficiently. Pokers, tongs, hearth-shovels and bellows were all essential, as was a blazer, a rectangle of galvanised sheet iron fitted with a handle. This stood on the top firebar and blocked the space above, forcing a strong underdraught to rapidly turn a smouldering fire into a fiercely flaming inferno. Some used a sheet of newspaper propped against a hearth shovel for the same purpose, but unless carefully watched it would catch fire and either disappear up the chimney, causing a chimney fire, or cover the hearth with dirty, smoking ash.

Beneath the fire, a 'tidy Betty' covered the front of the ashpit, retaining the ashes, while a fender around the hearth stopped any falling coals or embers tumbling onto the hearthrug. In pitmens cottages it was often made from part of the rim of a wheel from a chaldron railway wagon. The spokes and hub were broken away, and a blacksmith-made frame riveted across the top to form a useful stand for pots and pans.[14] Commercially-produced iron fenders were readily available, but the finest, not only in this region, but in the entire country, were those made by colliery and factory smiths and engineers for their own homes. Made of magnificently forged, turned and pierced polished steel set against 'Berlin' blacked iron plate, they were displays of amazing skill and ingenuity. They may incorporate brackets at each end to hold the fire-irons, or individual stands for pans or kettles. To complete the whole scheme, both tidy betties, pot hooks or brackets to fit on to the firebars were sometimes made to matching designs.[15]

Open coal fires, especially when used for cooking, generate an enormous amount of dirt, dust and ash. The housewives therefore took an enormous pride in keeping their fireplaces as spick and span as possible. Especially at the Friday-morning cleaning, the hearth was washed and finished with a rubbing of white scoury-stone, this probably being exchanged for jam-jars by the local scoury-stone man.[16]

At the same time, as described by J.C. Sinclair,

> The women were morbidly ambitious about a perfect glitter on their fireside utensils ... where the brasses and the copper ornaments shone with such lustre that you would see your image reflected in each shining object. The fender, fire-irons, spit-boxes, and the brass dogs that glowered in their places, were all kept beautifully polished.[17]

20. Housewives always took great pride in keeping both their ranges, their associated brassware and their steel fire-irons as clean and highly-polished as possible.

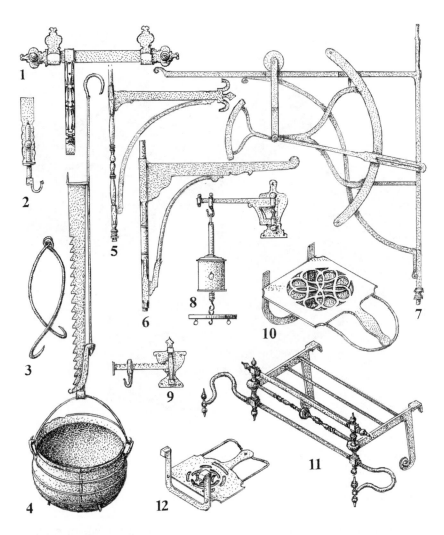

21. Each fireplace required a number of iron fittings to support cooking pots, kettles, girdles etc. over the fire. These examples comprise;

1. reckon, from Leasing
2. reckon – hook
3. potkilps, to support a cauldron
4. a reckon hook from Baldersdale supporting a kail-pot (cauldron) From Houghton-le-Spring.
5. A local chimney-crane
6. Chimney crane from Balder Head
7. chimney crane from Heydon Bridge
8. jack-crane from Eggleston, with a bottle-jack
9. a local jack – crane
10. a 'winter' for holding pans etc. before the fire. From North Shields, its brass top is pierced by a Lovers' Knot
11. - 12. local 'winters'. (11 from Annfield Plain).

22. Polished steel fenders, magnificently forged, pierced and turned, were made by highly-skilled engineers and smiths as displays of their creative abilities and as decorations for their domestic fireplaces. The top set of fender, 'tidy betty' and 'winter' came from Seaham, while the lower fender and reckon are from the Darlington area.

Today, when everyone has access to central heating, gas or electric cookers, bathrooms and plentiful hot water, it is almost impossible to appreciate the importance of the range and its utensils in supplying most of the necessities of life for all working families. It cooked all their food, boiled kettles for tea and coffee, heated water for bathing and laundry, and bricks to be wrapped in flannel to warm their beds. Its radiant light, heat and life made it the centre of every daily activity from cooking to conversation and relaxation. Although it demanded constant attention and cleaning, it is easy to understand why housewives took such an enormous pride in its appearance.

CHAPTER EIGHT

OF MEAT

Meat was probably the most important and valued of all traditional foods, its flavour and texture, its nourishment, and the stomach-filling satisfaction it gave all being greatly appreciated. Perhaps equally important, it was a visible indicator of a family's status and prosperity, since it was never cheap, and the most tender joints always commanded high prices.

The north-east was ideally situated for obtaining good supplies of beef, being the first place in England where the Scottish cattle drovers sold off their beasts at the great seasonal fairs and markets, before continuing down into the Midlands. Most were Kyloes from the Highlands, easily recognised by their thick and furry black coats

23. The Durham Ox, bred by the Colling brothers, was six years old in 1802, by which time it had grown to 11ft long, 5ft 6ins tall, and 171 stones in weight. The painting by John Boultbee was engraved by I. Whessel in 1802 and then appeared on a blue-and-white Staffordshire dinner service, as seen on this meat-dish.

and fine white horns and weighing around forty stones. Fine oxen had also been bred by the Blackett family, but major local improvements took place from the late eighteenth century with the introduction of new breeds. In 1789, for example, Edward Hall of Whitley fed a Holstein ox measuring almost ten feet/3m from nose to rump and six feet/1.8m high and weighing 187 stones without its offal.[1] It was the Colling brothers, Charles and Robert of Darlington, who made the most significant improvements to the local breed, the Shorthorn, from around 1800. By selective in-breeding they produced hardy animals which were good breeders and gave excellent yields of both meat and milk. They soon became the most important breed not only here, but throughout England and in many places overseas.

The native breeds of sheep were the Blackface, the Cheviot and the Teeswater. These were all improved by introducing Robert Bakewell's New Leicesters from the Midlands. Bakewell's friend George Culley moved to Fenton in Northumberland where his crosses converted the Teeswaters to the New Border Leicester breed. This produced fine early maturing lambs which fattened quickly.

From the late eighteenth century local farmers began to introduce new varieties of pig. Arthur Mowbray of Sherburn near Durham made crosses between the larger English pig and the Chinese black pig, for example, while George Baker of Elemore near Easington produced small Chinese pigs to give the best pork and roast sucking pigs. From the 1850s the Yorkshire Large White and Middle White pigs began to predominate, since they produced good bacon and ham, fattened well, and were good breeders. The Small White pig, meanwhile, was created by Mason of Chilton and Robert Colling of Bampton.

These new breeds continued to provide the bulk of the meat consumed in the north-east, but the need to provide cheap food for its growing urban populations saw the importation of various preserved meats from around the 1880s. These included tinned or refrigerated beef and mutton from Australia, New Zealand, America and Canada, as well as bacon from Denmark. These were convenient and affordable by most families and were particularly useful as a stand-by for a quick meal, as most could be prepared in minutes rather than hours. As a result they were stocked by most grocers, including the Cooperative Societies established in every town.

At working-class level, while the coal industry was at its most profitable, the greatest meat-eaters were pitmen. The physique and physical energy they needed to hew coal, their uncertain futures, which made it important to live well while they could, and their high

DURHAM PRIZE PIG.

24. The Durham Prize Pig was bred by Luke Seymour of Woodhouse Close and fed by William Reed of Durham. In 1805, when only 17 months old, it already weighed 36 stones.

wages, all combined to make meat a major part of their diet. Unlike others, they also had free coal, and so could well afford to keep up the fires needed for roasting and baking. As a result, there might be large daily roasts in many mining families. Those in similarly demanding and well-paid jobs might eat to the same high standard, but for many others meat was much less abundant. The very poor might have virtually no meat in their diet, or only occasional cheap cuts and offal. The majority lay somewhere between these extremes, many working families buying a roasting joint of beef, mutton or pork to eat hot at their Sunday dinners, when it would be served up with potatoes and vegetables, and perhaps accompanied by a Yorkshire or a seasonal pudding.

As described in poems such as Thomas Wilson's, *The Pitman's Pig*, late Georgian miners liked their meat spit-roasted in front of the fire. Here, cooked only by radiant heat, with a draught to carry off the coarser flavours, it was 'roasted to a single roun' [turn] ... Not brunt but beautifully brown'. This was a long and tedious task, constantly turning the cranked handle at the end of the spit for perhaps hours on end. In the houses of the better-off mechanical substitutes were available. Clockmakers such as Thomas Pearson of Newcastle were making smoke-jacks in the 1770s-80s. These had a propeller mounted inside the breast of the kitchen chimney, the hot air and smoke rushing up from the fire causing it to spin round. By means of a worm-gear on the propeller shaft the power was transferred to a set of pulleys protruding from the chimney breast. Here their brass bearing-box was usually engraved with the name of the maker, a task once performed by Thomas Bewick during his apprenticeship as a wood-engraver. Loops of rope descending from the pulleys then turned the spits without any further trouble, except for regular basting. Good examples of these smoke-jacks can be seen in the kitchen of Raby Castle. Other mansions used a waterwheel instead, an example being in the collections of the Bowes Museum at Barnard Castle, while smaller households relied on clockwork jacks powered by either weights or springs.

A further device employed a dog-wheel, a giant version of the exercise wheels found today in hamster cages. One of these at Mitford measured 3ft 6ins/1.07m in diameter by 10¼ins/26cm wide, and was mounted close to the ceiling in a recess by the left side of the kitchen fire.[2] Once the small dog within began to run forward, it rotated the wheel and a pulley which then turned the spits. It required a special breed to do this efficiently, as illustrated and described in Bewick's *History of Quadrupeds* of 1790;

THE TURNSPIT

Is generally long-bodied, has short crooked legs, its tail curled upon its back, and is frequently spotted with black upon a blue-grey ground. It is peculiar in the colour of its eyes; the same Dog often having the iris of one eye black, and the other white.

It is a bold, vigilant, and spirited little Dog. At present, however, its services seem but little attended to; a more certain method of doing the business of the spit having superseded the labours of this industrious animal.[3]

He was, of course, referring to the newer kinds of jack.

A simpler method of turning the roast was to do away with the jack and spit, and to hang it vertically on a twisted skein of cord. One of S.H. Grimms watercolours of the Prior's kitchen at Durham

THE TURNSPIT

25. Dog wheels, such as this one from Mitford, were powered by a dog which was placed inside, and ran forward, a pulley transferring its movement to rotate the spitted meat roasting before the fire. The special breed developed for this purpose was called the Turnspit, and is seen in this engraving by Thomas Bewick.

Cathedral shows a huge baron of beef hanging in this way before the fire, with an old lady sitting a few feet behind holding a string tied to the bottom of the skein. As the joint turned in one direction, it wound up the string, and as she pulled the string, it would accelerate it in the other direction. In this way a piece of meat weighing perhaps 50 or 60lb/22.5 or 24kg, could be turned for hours with virtually no effort. The same method could be used in any cottage, being very cheap and effective. By the mid nineteenth century the skein was being encased in a brass or tinplate case, complete with a clockwork motor to replace the pulled string. These 'bottle-jacks' could turn hanging roasts with only occasional winding up. Priced from 5s 3d/26p in the 1890s, they were affordable by working families who preferred to roast their joints before the fire.

The alternative way to 'roast' the meat was to put it in a roasting tin and enclose it in a hot oven, actually baking it. The results were not so good, but it was a lot less troublesome, used less fuel, and was perhaps more reliable for an inexperienced housewife. This is the 'roast' which most families prepared regularly, especially for their Sunday dinners. Some nonconformists preferred to roast on Saturdays, however, thus reducing the Sunday workload, and leaving more time for their Sabbath 'meetings'.[4]

One of the most economical ways of obtaining roast meat in the towns was to buy it ready cooked from a shop. Joe Wilson describes a number of these in his poems. At one it was possible to obtain sandwiches of beef or leg of pork, sausages, pies, saveloys, black puddings, white puddings, pig's tripe, pig's fry and potted pig's head. At another;

> Iv'ry day at twelve o'clock
> Ye shud only see them flock
> Roond the counter, for the canny man to serve them:
> Frae the joints that's smokin het
> If a smell ye only get
> It'll pleas yor eyes an' nose te see him carve them
> Ye shud see them feast their eyes
> On the soop, the meat, an' pies,
> For such hungry-luckin customers surroond him;
> But he's ower wide awake
> Te myek ony greet mistake,
> His auld-fashin'd fyece 'ill show they'll not confound him.

Meanwhile, at one at the end of New Grainger Street in Newcastle, late Victorian diners could be served with a good dinner for 1s–1s 6d/5–7.5p;

> *Thor's soup, an' ham, roast beef, an' tea,*
> *Pies, pork, an' puddins ye may see*
> *At this most famous cook-shop,*
> *as well as mutton, peas-pudding, apple tart and cheese.*

Roasting

Pre-heat the oven to 180°C, 350°F, Gas mark 4. Melt 1oz/25g of dripping or lard in a roasting tin, and cook for the following times, basting from time to time.

Beef	15 minutes per 1lb/450g	+ 15 minutes	(rare)
	20 „ „ „ „	+ 20 „	(medium)
	25 „ „ „ „	+ 25 „	(well done)
Lamb	25 „ „ „ „	+ 25 „	
Pork	30 „ „ „ „	+ 30 „	
Veal	25 „ „ „ „	+ 25 „	

For beef, the internal temperature of the cooked meat should be 60°C/140°F rare, 70°C/160°F medium, and 80°C/180°F well done.

Lamb should always be cooked to 80°C/180°F, and pork to 90°C/190°F. Remove from the heat, cover, and leave to rest for 20-30 minutes before carving.

As a rough guide, allow 4-6oz/100-175g boneless meat, or 6-12oz/175-350g meat on the bone, for each person.

In addition to the roast or boiled potatoes and the seasonal vegetables, the joint might be accompanied by either a Yorkshire pudding or a seasoned pudding, as was customary on Tyneside. Those in County Durham followed the true Yorkshire tradition of having them as a first course, served on their own except for plenty of gravy.[5]

Yorkshire Pudding

4oz/100g plain flour	*½pt/300ml mixed milk & water*
pinch of salt	*1oz/25g dripping*
2 eggs	

Mix the flour and salt in a basin, make a well in the centre, break in the eggs and beat with a fork, gradually adding the milk and water and working in the flour from the sides to form a smooth batter. Leave this to rest for 30-60 minutes. Heat the oven to 220°C, 425°F, Gas mark 7, put in the dripping in a large rectangular dripping tin and leave for about 10 minutes until smoking hot. Pour in the batter, and return to the oven for 40-45 minutes. It should then be crisp, risen and browned around the sides, and thinner in the middle, but good results are rarely obtained in a fan-assisted oven. Remove, cut into large squares, and serve immediately.

Variations. At Byers Green near Spennymoor thin slices of show leeks, the white parts, were scattered over the raw batter, to give a savoury flavour, while at Barnard Castle snow replaced the water in the batter, which apparently gave very light puddings. Others put raw minced onion into the mix.

Seasoned, or Savoury Bread Pudding [6]

4oz/100g stale white bread, broken into lumps	
1 large onion	*½ tsp sage*
4oz/100g fine oatmeal	*¼ tsp mixed herbs*
4oz/100g suet	*¼ tsp ground pepper*
½ tsp salt	*2 eggs, beaten*

Soak the bread in water, and leave in a sieve to drain. Boil the onion in salted water, drain, and chop finely. Squeeze the surplus water from the bread, put into a bowl, and beat smooth with a fork. Stir in the onion and remaining dry ingredients, then the egg, and pack about ¾ins/2cm deep as a level layer in a well-greased dripping tin. Bake at 200°C, 400°F, Gas mark 6 for 30 minutes, until the top is crisp and browned, then serve with the roast. These puddings were especially good with both pork and duck.

Stepney Pottery

Newcastle upon Tyne

26. The potteries of Sunderland and Newcastle made very practical ovenproof baking dishes called trays. The top one, deep and on four short feet, is a bread-pan for baking loaves, and was made at the Stepney Pottery in Newcastle. The plain and partitioned trays below were made in various sizes, from 9 to 21ins long, both decorated and plain, the largest costing only 1s 9d (9p) each in the 1880s.

Towards the middle of the week, when the Sunday meat had already been served hot and cold, its dry remains needed to be slowly cooked with vegetables and stock to produce further hot, delicious and satisfying dinners. North-eastern housewives developed an interesting range of suitable recipes which were easy to prepare, and needed no attention when baking in the oven.

Shepherd's Pie[7]

8oz/225g chopped cold meat   *salt & pepper*
1 small onion, chopped   *2lb/900g mashed potato*
½pt/300ml thick gravy   *1oz/25g beef dripping*

Mix the meat, onion and gravy, season to taste, lay in a pie dish, top with potato, mark its top with a fork, dot with the dripping, and bake at 170°C, 325°F, Gas mark 3 for 45-60 minutes.

Tuesday Hot Pot
Mrs. A. Robson, Whiskershield Farm, Elsdon[8]

Lay the sliced cold meat in the bottom of a dripping tin, cover it with layers of cubed raw or cooked vegetables, top with sliced potatoes, season with salt and pepper, and pour over sufficient gravy or stock to half-cover the contents. Bake at 170°C, 325°F, Gas mark 3 for 1½-2 hours.

Mince Savoury
Mrs Steel, Haydon Bridge[9]

4oz/100g cooked meat, minced	pinch of salt
½ large onion, finely chopped	½pt/300ml milk
2 eggs, beaten	1oz/25g butter
4oz/100g plain flour	

Sift the flour and salt into a bowl, drop in the eggs, and beat continuously, adding the milk little by little to form a smooth batter. Heat a 2pt/1l pie dish in the oven, lift out onto a heatproof surface, add the butter and spread it across the interior. Pour in half the batter, cover it with the cooked meat mixed with the onions and a little salt and pepper, cover with the rest of the batter and bake at 180°C, 350°F, Gas mark 4 for 50 minutes until risen, browned, and cooked through.

One of the other popular ways of using stewing beef was to blend it with bacon to produce a tender and finely textured roll which could then be sliced and served cold with salad, in sandwiches, or with hot vegetables.

Beef Roll
Ms A. Law, Burdon Mill[10]

8oz/225g minced stewing steak	½ tsp mixed herbs
8oz/225g minced bacon	½ tsp parsley & sage
4oz/100g fresh white breadcrumbs	1 egg, beaten
pepper & salt, to taste	

Mix the dry ingredients, bind with the egg, then either:

1. Roll in a rinsed and floured cloth, tie the ends and boil for 2 hours
2. Roll in greased greaseproof paper and steam 2 hours.
3. Pack into a greased basin, cover, and steam 2 hours.
Leave until cold, before slicing.

Potted meat could be made in a similar way, but at its best was thickened using the gelatin of pig's trotters instead of egg and breadcrumbs. In Stocksfield Mrs Stokoe simmered pig's cheek, stewing steak and trotters with salt, pepper and herbs for up to three hours until tender, then removed the remaining bones etc. before putting it through a mincer and leaving it in bowls to set firmly. Another version was;

Ox Tail Brawn
Mrs Winston, New Shildon[11]

1 ox tail, chopped into pieces	*1 tsp salt*
1 large slice of ham	*½ tsp pepper*
3 cloves	*½ tsp ground nutmeg*

Simmer the tail, ham and cloves in 1½pt/900ml water in a covered pan for 3 hours, leave it to cool a little. Remove all the meat from the bones and retain the stock. Coarsely mince or finely chop the meats, mix with the seasonings, pack into basins, cover with the strained stock, and leave to set in a cold place.

BOILED BEEF

Today the traditional ways of boiling beef have virtually disappeared, but this used to be a popular method since it required little trouble, kept the meat moist, and produced lots of nourishing broth.

Boiled Beef & Broth
Miss A.M. Dent, Barnard Castle area[12]

3lb/1.75kg silverside or brisket	*2oz/50g pearl barley*
1 each, turnip, onion, carrot	*6pts/3.6l water*
1 tbs salt	*½ tsp pepper*

Chop the vegetables very small. Truss the meat and put

into a large pan with the water. Add the vegetables, salt, pepper and barley when it simmers, then remove any scum from the surface. Cover and simmer without boiling, for 3 hours. Remove the beef from the stock, cover and leave it to rest for 20 minutes before cutting some of it into cubes and serving with the hot broth, leaving the remainder to cool so that it may be sliced later and eaten with pickles.

If the boiled joint was to be eaten cold, especially around Christmas when it provided an excellent stand-by for unexpected visitors, it was prepared by a preliminary pickling either by dry-salting or immersion in brine.

Pressed Beef [13]

4lb/1.8kg lean beef or brisket joint	2 tsp ground allspice
5oz/150g mixed salt & sea salt	2oz/50g muscovado sugar
½oz/12g saltpetre	4 tbs water

Place the beef on a large dish. Combine the remaining ingredients and rub in for 5 minutes each day for 9 days, keeping it in a cool place.

OR:

Immerse the joint for at least the same time in a pickle of;

12oz/325g mixed salt & sea salt	4oz/100g muscovado sugar
½oz/12g saltpetre	1 tsp black peppercorns

THEN:

Truss the joint, put into a pan, cover with cold water, slowly bring to the simmer, remove any scum, cover, and simmer for some 2 hours, until tender. It may be served hot, with vegetables and pease pudding, or pressed overnight between two plates with a weight on top, and served cold over the next few days.

If to be served hot, dumplings could be added to the same pot, providing an ideal hot and filling accompaniment.

Dumplings
Darlington area, c. 1852[14]

8oz/225g plain flour	*4oz/100g suet*
½ tsp salt	*8 tbs water*
¼ tsp white pepper	

Mix the dry ingredients, make up to a dough with the water, divide into 6 or 8 balls, roll in flour, and add to the boiling stock 20-30 minutes before serving.

Savoury Balls
Mrs Strong, Low Fell, 1910[15]

8oz/225g plain flour	*1 small onion, finely chopped*
1 tbs each parsley, thyme, & marjoram	
2 tbs suet	*1 tsp baking powder*
½ tsp pepper	*1 tsp salt*

Mix all the ingredients with water and cook as in the recipe above. Alternatively stew in gravy and serve with roasts.

The best way of dealing with the coarser steaks was to cube them and make them into stews.

Irish Stew
Darlington area[16]

2lb/900g rump or stewing steak	*½ tsp salt*
1 large onion, chopped	*½ tsp black pepper*
12 small potatoes, peeled	

Cube the meat and put into a casserole with the onion, salt, pepper, and 4pts/2.4l cold water. Cover, and cook at 170°C, 325°F, Gas mark 3 for about 2 hours, then add the potatoes and continue cooking for a further 30 minutes until they are tender.

Shin beef, which always required long and slow cooking to bring out its rich flavour, was ideal for making broths such as this, its original quantities being given to show how many it once fed.

27. The stew-pots made in the Sunderland and Newcastle potteries were decorated with bands of white slip-trailing and covered in a hard-wearing glossy yellow glaze. One 10ins in diameter, suitable for a large family, only cost 1s (5p) in the 1890s.

Scotch Broth
Mr. J. Reid, Gateshead[17]

1½lb/625g shin beef	2-3 sticks celery
1 small ham shank	8oz/225g pearl barley
8oz/225g soaked dried peas	1 turnip
1 parsnip	1 tbs chopped parsley
2-3 leeks	2 tsp salt, ½ tsp pepper
2 large carrots	8pts/5l water

Cut the meat into small pieces, and the vegetables into small dice, and simmer with all the remaining ingredients for 2½ hours. Dumplings may be added 30 minutes before serving.

The best parts of the beef offal were the tongues and the tripes, particularly the honeycomb from the second stomach. Spiced tongue made a good dish for Christmas, being ideal for slicing for light meals and teatime sandwiches.

Spiced Tongue
Mrs E.M. Birkett, Newbiggin, Hexham[18]

1 ox tongue	2oz/50g allspice
8oz/225g brown sugar	½oz/12g saltpetre
2oz/50g crushed black pepper	½ tsp ground mace
4oz/100g salt	½ tsp cayenne pepper

Wash & dry the tongue, put into a bowl, rub with the sugar and saltpetre for 10 minutes, leave for a few hours, then rub in the rest. Turn and rub in its juices every day for a week. Drain the tongue, put into a pan of warm water, slowly bring to the boil and simmer for 5-6 hours. When tender when tried with a skewer, drain the tongue, trim off any waste, pack tightly into a cake tin, put a weighted plate on top and leave in a cool place overnight. Next day pass a knife around the inside of the tin, turn out and use.

Tripe was usually stewed tender, drained, cut in pieces, stewed with finely-chopped onions, and thickened with milk, flour, salt and pepper just before serving. The following recipe gives better flavours and textures.

Tripe[19]

1lb/450g honeycomb tripe	1 onion, finely minced
1pt/600ml milk	1 egg, beaten
6oz/175g stuffing (or sausage meat)	
mashed potato as accompaniment	
either breadcrumbs, fat for frying, and tomato & onion sauce	
or 1pt/600ml rich white or brown sauce.	

Stew the tripe in the milk until tender, drain, and cut in 3-4ins/7.5-10cm strips. Mix the stuffing with the onion and half the egg, spread this on the tripe, roll up, and hold in place with a skewer (or cocktail stick). Then either coat in egg, then breadcrumbs, deep fry, and serve with tomato and onion sauce, or stew slowly in the white or brown sauce for about an hour.

LAMB & MUTTON

The region's enthusiasm for lamb and mutton was best described by Hedley Purvis, a road-mender of Ryton-on-Tyne. Writing in the late 1870s he expressed realistic opinion of most carnivorous country Christians:

> *'I love to see the gambling lambs in Springtime sunny splendour,*
> *Better still to dine on one when it is young and tender!*
> *To see them running in the fields, does many people please,*
> *But as for me, I'd rather eat them, nicely cooked with mint and peas!'*
> *For while I like to watch them, and never am a glutton,*
> *God sent them to us to be eaten, either lamb or mutton.'*

Both lamb and mutton joints were roasted just as they are today, except for the boned and stuffed shoulder, which was known as 'mock duck' around Haydon Bridge.[20] Thomas Bewick was a great connoisseur of northcountry mutton. He found that the old native breed, 'the long-legged, black faced kind [of which] the Mutton eat like dark juicy Venison' was far better than that of 'the *improved breed* with their fatting qualities [which] put one in mind of blubber'.[21] In many homes, the best and cheapest part of the sheep was its head. Unused today, the head was both cheap and reputed to provide a good dinner for six people with its combination of meat and broth. The tongue was used for sandwiches, while the brains were either mixed into the broth, or eaten on toast. It was celebrated in a poem describing three jolly, brisk women of Durham;

> *There's three sheeps' heads i' the pot,*
> *A peck o' peasemeal in the pudding,*
> *They jump'd, laugh'd, and skipp'd at that,*
> *For the joyfull days are coming.*[22]

This recipe is given just as it appears in a manuscript book from the Barnard Castle area.

Sheep's Head Broth [23]

1 sheep's head, 1 turnip, 2–3 onions, 3 sage leaves, ½ teacup rice, 6 pts cold water, 2 small carrots, 3 potatoes, 2 tbs oatmeal, salt & pepper

Wash the head well in salt & water. Take out the nose bones &
let the head soak for about 1 hour in cold water. Now take out
the brains and tie them with the sage in a bag. Put the head into
a pan. Pour on the water. Bring to the boil & skim. Cut up the
vegetables, add them & add to the broth & simmer for about 3
hours. The brains should be boiled about 1 hour [in the same pot].
Mix oatmeal with a little cold water & stir it into the soup & let
it boil 20 minutes. The head is served separately.
Take all the meat from the head in as nice pieces as possible. Skin
the tongue & split it & into this stir up the brains chopped &
seasoned. Serve with parsley sauce, ½ milk ½ water.

The other traditional stewed mutton dish was;

Mutton Broth

2lb/900g scrag end	*1oz/25g pearl barley*
1 carrot	*salt & pepper to taste*
1 turnip	*3pt/1.8l water*
1 onion	

Joint the mutton, rinse it, and simmer with the salt, pepper
and water for 2 hours, skimming off all scum. Cut the
vegetables in large dice, tie in a piece of muslin, add to
the stew with the pearl barley, and continue stewing for
another hour. To serve, skim off the grease and remove the
vegetables.

There were various ways of using up the sheep's offal, too. Mrs E.
Birkett of Newbiggin, Hexhamshire, could remember the heart being
oven-baked with sage and onions, and the lights [lungs] stewed,
minced, and oven-baked with minced onions before being served
cold for breakfasts and suppers. The liver, meanwhile, was fried with
onions in the usual way.[24]

Roast mutton or lamb were always considered to be a particular
delicacy, perhaps reserved for Sundays, or for entertaining a special
guest. The way in which it was prepared and served in the 1780s
occurs in a colourful description of a dinner given by Betty Allen of
Shiney Row to Mr Hampson, a visiting Methodist preacher. To give
him a proper degree of respect it was agreed that the family would
'stand back' and let him help himself to a fine leg of lamb, green peas

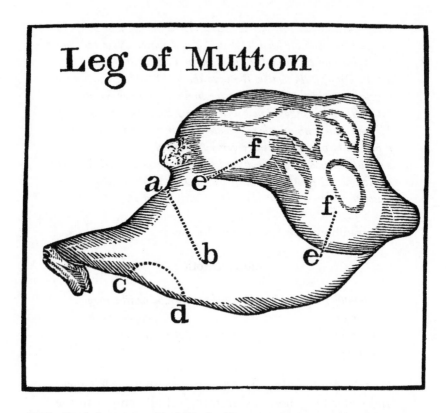

28. John Trusler's *Honours of the Table* of 1788 instructed ladies and gentlemen to carve a leg of lamb from the centre, on line a – b, and the fat from lines e – f. In contrast, economical northcountry housewives carved across the thick end, and proceeded towards the knuckle.

and a 'fadge'. As a socially skilled gentleman, he followed the detailed instructions given in manuals such as John Trusler's *Art of Carving* of 1788, and plunged the knife directly into the centre of the joint. To the economical and practical Betty, this was more than she could bear;

> What a piece of extravagance! Did you ever see a leg of lamb cut before? If these are your gentlemanly ways I have done with them – Come Wally and Charley, sit up, and let us have our dinners!
>
> Snatching up the knife and fork, she then started at the broad end and carved 'in the wholesale, not the retail fashion', like the sensible woman she was.
>
> The appearance of the 'fadge' as a second course

completely baffled Mr Hampson – he had never seen anything like it before. The exasperated Betty then forcefully explained;

It's a fadge to be sure. Did you never see a fadge before? Your Lord and Master had a worse dinner. Ye need not stare at it!

A fadge is a kind of flour pudding with suet, without eggs, and worked to the consistency of paste for bread, about an inch thick, baked under the meat, which sometimes rests upon it, well browned, and enriched with gravy.[25]

Roast lamb and fadge makes a very heavy and substantial meal. The fadge absorbs the fats and juices from the joint, but its surface bakes extremely hard and crisp, a real challenge to the teeth. In the original version below, there is no raising agent, but it may be improved for modern tastes by adding 2 tsp baking powder.

Leg of Lamb & a Fadge

1 leg of lamb	*12oz/325g suet*
1½lb/675g plain flour	*½pt/300ml water (approx)*
1 tsp salt	*1oz/25g dripping or lard*

Mix the flour, salt and suet, and mix in just sufficient cold water to produce a medium dough. Line a small roasting tin with the fat, and cover the base with an even layer of the suet pastry. Pre-heat the oven to 180°C, 350°F, Gas mark 4. Weigh the leg of lamb, place on top of the 'fadge' and bake at 25 minutes per lb/450g plus 25 minutes, then carve both the lamb and the fadge directly from the roasting tin.
Serve with gravy, mint sauce and vegetables.

The fadge was also known as a pan-soddy in the North-east. While on a rough voyage from Newcastle to London, one inhabitant remembered how, off Flamborough Head:

To cheer wor hearts in vain they brought
The porter, grog and toddy -
My head swam round when ere I thought
Upon a fat pan-soddy.

Following the usual practical and economical tradition, the ends of roasted mutton joints often appeared on the table a few days later in the form of delicious, succulent pies.

Re-cooked Mutton
F.H., Haydon Bridge[26]

4-6oz/100-175g sliced cold mutton	*4oz/100g plain flour*
1 medium onion, finely chopped	*½pt/300ml milk*
1oz/25g dripping or lard	*salt & pepper*

Arrange the mutton in a pie dish. Fry the onions in the fat until golden brown. Stir in the flour, then the milk, salt and pepper, and stir until thick and boiling. Pour this over the meat and bake at 150°C, 300°F, Gas mark 2 for 45 minutes.

Legs of mutton were made into mutton hams in the north-east through to the early to mid twentieth century, this recipe coming from Berwick upon Tweed in 1769.

Mutton Ham [27]

1 large leg of mutton, cut like a ham   1lb/450g salt
1oz/25g saltpetre

Mix the salts, rub well into the ham and lay it skin-side down in a deep dish. Turn and baste the ham with its own juices for 2-3 weeks, then drain, press under a heavy weight for an hour or so, dredge it with flour and hang up in a dry, cool, well-ventilated place until needed. It may be sliced and fried, but is best soaked in lukewarm water for 3-4 hours and then either roasted or preferably put into cold water slowly brought to the boil, simmered until tender, and served hot.

PORK PRODUCTS

> *Byeth sausages, pies, an' saveloys,*
> *sink law i' maw esteem,*
> *Black puddins an' white puddins tae,*
> *aw eat them in a dream;*
> *Pig's tripe, an' fry, an' potted heed,*
> *may stand the public test*
> *But i' the shop, an aw'm a judge,*
> *the pork-shop lass's best.*[28]

Roast pork, with crisp crackling, sage and onion stuffing, apple sauce, potatoes, vegetables and gravy, makes a very fine dinner. It only uses the best parts of the fresh pig, however, but still leaves a wealth of other joints and so on, ideal for preserving or converting into all kinds of rich, tasty and economical savouries. In the north-east, they boasted that they used every part of the pig, except the squeal. Claiming even greater efficiency, Yorkshire folk said they could use that too – selling it to the Scots to put into bagpipes!

The relationship between a family and its pork was completely different from that which it had with any other meat. There were many reasons for this. Firstly, most pigs were usually home-bred and home-fed, being treated with a care and concern at least equal to that bestowed on a beloved family pet. Secondly, they provided a uniquely useful and economical source of fresh and preserved meats, fats, etc., and, through the sale of their hams, a valuable injection of cash. Thirdly, they were home-killed, most other cattle and sheep going to the slaughterhouse. The importance of pigs, and the role they played in everyday life, is reflected in numerous stories of their characters, their escapes, and their final ends, which many people still remember in detail. The escapades involved in killing black-market pigs during periods of wartime rationing are particularly notorious and hilarious. They provided Alan Bennett with a rich source of humour for his play 'A Private Function', but it would require another book to do them full justice.

From a practical point of view, pig-killing was an extremely busy time, as remembered by Mrs Agnes M. Clark of Presson, Cornhill-on-Tweed, back in 1923;

The pig was killed in the middle of the day (dinnertime) [after which it was] scalded and the hair scraped off, then

29. Pig-killing at Rookhope. Once Tomlinson the Polis had stunned the pig with his pole-axe, its throat was to be cut by Tom Oliver (in the bowler hat), and the blood caught by the man with the pot, ready for making black puddings. Meanwhile Fred Lowery (right) holds the rope, ready for hanging up the carcase for butchery.

it was hung on a tripod until evening to cool off. Then the shepherd and the men from next door came along to cut the carcase up and salt it away in a tub. It was kept for two or three weeks in the salt to cure, then hung up to mellow a bit before it was used.

The day after the pig-killing was a busy time for the housewife, there was the fat to cut into cubes and render down for lard and put in earthenware jars, and that was used to make scones for the rest of the year. Then all but the little bits and pieces of meat were put in a large pot with the trotters and the head and kidneys and heart and boiled to make the potted meat; and pudding meat (which was some lean meat minced then mixed with equal quantity of cooked pot barley), it was lovely fried.

My mother always made oatmeal puddings, which was fine oatmeal and fat rubbed together with black peppers and some salt. There was always spareribs for stovies and fried liver and braised liver. Needless to say, in those days there were no freezers, so the spare bits were always shared with the neighbours and friends, which was quite handy as they shared theirs when they killed a pig. We were always sure of a nice dinner after a pig-killing, it was a real treat. The men all had a cup of tea or beer and a nice supper after the pork was in salt and finished off the evening, with a good chat and a smoke and a glass of beer.[29]

The first culinary task at a pig killing was to collect the fresh blood and keep it stirred, otherwise it formed clots or 'strings', as it cooled. Every family appears to have had its own particular recipe, but most in the northeast included milk and fine oatmeal, along with salt, pepper and mint. To these basics, some added suet, boiled rice or barley, soaked bread, flour, or finely-chopped 'crappins', the crunchy 'pork scratchings' left after rendering the lard. These mixtures might then be packed into skins, leaving plenty of room for expansion, the ends tied with thread and twisted into the shape of an 8. When hung on sticks, one end could be poached for 10 minutes, and then the other, after which they were turned onto a bed of hay or straw on a table to cool.[30] This form of black pudding was sold at mid-day to Newcastle pitmen when they had just been paid, as described by Henry Robson's poem 'The Collier's Pay Week.'

> And now for black puddings, long measure,
> They go to TIB TROLLIBAG'S stand,
> And away bear the glossy rich treasure
> With joy, like curl'd bugles in hand ...
> And now a choice house they agree on,
> Not far from the head of the Quay;
> Where they their black puddings might feed on,
> And spend the remains of the day.[31]

They were also sold around the streets by women, crying out; 'A fine black puddin', hinny, A fat 'n and a gud 'n hinny' at North Shields, or 'Fine black puddin' hinny smoking hot' at Newcastle's Bigg Market. Tommy Armstrong also described them in his lively song about 'Stanla Market';

> Thare's black puddings, neerly wite,
> Thor muaid to suit yor appetite
> One 'il sarv freh six tiv hite
> Thae suit e chap thit's rither tite ... [32]

30. North-eastern black puddings were either boiled in loops or large guts, or else baked in large earthenware trays. The best trays, elaborately decorated in multicoloured bands of trailed and feathered slips, were made at Harwood's Clarence Potteries, Stockton-upon-Tees, from around 1850 to 1895.

The alternative way of making black puddings, one particularly associated with County Durham and Tyneside, was to bake the mixture in a rectangular earthenware dish, so they set as a solid slab about 2ins/5cm thick. A number of local potteries made these dishes in brown earthenware, sometimes decorated with trailed sprays of white slip, all beneath a yellow lead glaze. If 'plain trays', John Patterson's Bridge Pottery at Monkwearmouth offered them from 9ins/23cm to 21ins/53cm long at a shilling (5p) each in 1883, as did Ambrose Walker & Co's Stafford Pottery at Thornaby-on-Tees in 1894, 20% extra being charged for slip decoration. The finest of all were called 'Welsh trays', and made by Thomas Harwood and his successors at the Clarence Potteries, Norton, Stockton-on-Tees. Although the same shape, these were made in finer white earthenware, their interiors decorated with extremely narrow parallel bands of pale blue, buff, dark brown and white slips. While still liquid, the bands were combed through at right-angles to produce an extremely beautiful and refined over-all pattern, the finest slip-trailing of its kind ever produced. Their clear glazes ensured that they remained extremely practical, even after numerous bakings in both domestic and professional butcher's ovens. Production ended after the First World War, but by this time their place had been largely taken by trays made of white enamelled pressed steel.

Black Pudding
Mrs O.B. Bannister, West Auckland[33]

fresh pig's blood	*2 loaves white bread*
1pt/600ml lukewarm milk	*2-4pt/1.2-2.4l milk*
a handful of salt	*1½lb/675g suet*
2-3lb/900-1.35kg fine oatmeal	*saucerful plain flour*
pepper, dried mint	

Stir the blood to prevent thickening, take out any 'strings', slowly stir in the lukewarm milk, salt and oatmeal, and leave overnight. Next morning soak the bread in water, squeeze dry, and mix into the blood etc. with the remaining ingredients. Pour into a greased dripping pan or pie dishes, then bake at 140°C, 275°F, Gas mark 1 until firm to the touch, then remove to a cool place, and use within the next few days.

While the blood was being made into black puddings, other parts of the offal were being prepared as white puddings, a regional speciality still sold by many butchers and ready to be sliced and fried.

Farmhouse White Pudding[34]

pig's heart, kidney, tongue and any trimmings from the carcase	
1lb/450g pearl barley	*pepper, salt, pinch of ground cloves*

Tie the barley in a cloth bag [or piece of muslin] leaving room for it to expand. Place in a pan with the heart, etc., barely cover with cold water, cover, and gently simmer until all is tender. When cooked, remove all the skin, bones and gristle, mince finely, then mix the seasoning with most of the barley, for there should always be more meat than barley, mix in the meat and sufficient of the stock to produce a soft mixture.

Pack the mixture into sausage skins, tying each end and

twisting them in a figure-of-eight before poaching until cooked through. If hung from the dairy ceiling, they lasted up to six weeks. To serve, slice and fry until brown on both sides.

The liver was good fried on its own, with bacon, or made into a savoury pudding.

Liver & Bacon [35]

8oz/225g liver, sliced	*¼ tsp salt*
2oz/50g bacon	*pinch ground pepper*
2 tsp plain flour	*¼pt/150ml stock or water*

Fry the bacon, put into a hot dish. Mix the flour with the salt and pepper, dip the liver in it, and fry in the bacon fat until lightly browned and add to the bacon. Stir the stock in the pan until thick and boiling, then pour over the liver and bacon. For more flavour, fry sliced onion rings in the pan just after the liver, and add to the dish.

Savoury Patties
Mrs G.I. Jones, Medomsley [36]

8oz/225g liver	*1lb/450g mashed potatoes*
¼ of a large onion	*2 tbs white breadcrumbs*
¼ tsp sage	*2 tbs plain flour*
1 slice cooked bacon, chopped	*salt & pepper to taste*
fat, for frying	

Simmer the liver and onion for 15 minutes, drain, and retain the stock. Finely chop or mince the liver and onion, mix into the remaining ingredients, adding just enough of the stock to form a firm mixture. Form into flat round cakes, dust in flour, and fry in boiling fat.

Oatmeal & Pig's Liver Pudding
Mrs A.W. Dickman [37]

8oz/225g liver	*4oz/100g pearl barley*
8oz/225g dripping, lard or suet	*1lb/450g medium oatmeal*
1 tsp salt, pinch of pepper	*a little grated onion (optional)*

Simmer the liver, barley and salt in 1½pt/900ml water for about 1 hour, remove the liver, and continue cooking the barley until very tender. Grate the liver. Pour the barley, its water, the liver and the remaining ingredients into a bowl and mix together. Pack the mixture into a greased pudding basin, tie a piece of buttered and pleated greaseproof paper over the top, and steam for 2 hours.

Serve with potatoes and vegetables. Leftovers can be fried with bacon.

The leaf, the inner fat of the pig, was next cut into dice, put into a dripping tin with a sprinkling of salt and baked in a moderate oven until all the lard had liquefied. It was then given a good boil, strained into stoneware jars, tied down with a few layers of brown paper, and stored in a cold larder ready for making bread, pastry, etc.

As the carcase was butchered, the trimmings and part of the fresh pork were used to make pork pies, sausages and 'mock goose', the local version of the faggot.

Pork Pie[38]

2lb/900g fat and lean pork, minced	Pastry:1lb/450g plain flour
1 tbs salt	5oz/125g lard
¼ tsp ground black pepper	½ tsp salt
2 tbs water	1 egg, beaten

Mix the pie filling and set aside. Rub the lard into the flour and salt, then mix in about 9fl oz/250ml boiling water, knead until smooth, cover, and leave until tepid. Use two thirds of the pastry to raise a pie crust within a strong paper collar, or use to line a greased 6-7ins/15-18cm cake tin, and fill with the pork. Roll out the remaining pastry, to form a lid. Dampen the edges, set in place and seal and crimp the edges. Cut a hole in the centre, and use any trimmings to apply decorative leaves etc. Brush the top with beaten egg, and bake at 220°C, 425°F, Gas mark 7 for 30 minutes, then reduce to 180°, 350°F, Gas mark 4 for a further 2½ hours, protecting the top with paper.

If available, pig skin was boiled in water for 3 hours until its stock jellied when a sample was cooled. Today this may be replaced by stirring 2 tsp gelatin into ¼pt/150ml cold light stock, soaking it for 10 minutes, then heating gently, without boiling, until dissolved. Pour this into the cooling pie and leave to chill before serving.

In the hillside farms a local version of the true Bologna sausage was made by packing just meat and a little fat into sausage skins and hanging them up for some four months to dry and develop a coating of green mould. Peggy Hutchinson ate them at ten weeks old, just washing off the mould and frying them for a delicious meal.[39] This should not be tried today, but the following recipe produces good sausages to be used fresh, even if local farmers kept them for up to two months!

Pork Sausage [40]

> 1lb/450g equal parts fat & lean pork, minced together
> 4oz/100g fresh white breadcrumbs, soaked in cold water & squeezed dry
> ¼ tsp pepper   ½ tsp dried sage or marjoram
> ¾ tsp salt   sausage skins

Mix all the ingredients thoroughly, pack into the skins, and twist into links (or form into cakes) and fry or grill.

Burtergill Mock Goose [41]

> 1lb/450g sausage meat   1 tsp dried sage
> ½lb/225g mashed potatoes   ½ large onion, grated
> 1 egg, beaten   pepper & salt to taste
> 1oz/25g oatmeal

Mix all the ingredients, except half the oatmeal and press into the form of a roast goose. Rub the surface with the remaining oatmeal. Put in a greased dripping tin and bake at 180°C, 350°F, Gas mark 4 for 45 minutes. Serve cold with apple sauce.

Pig's heads were used to make rich, glutinous brawns, while the cheeks, stuffed with parsley stuffing, rolled and baked, were sliced cold to provide breakfasts over the Christmas period.[42] The cheeks and trotters were also seasoned, boiled, boned and minced to make delicious potted meats.[43] The remaining parts of the fresh carcase

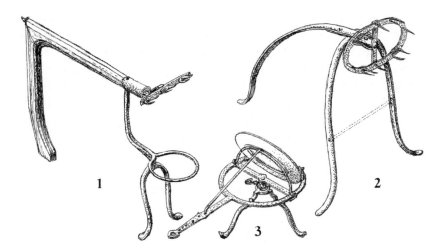

31. Bacon, chops and steaks were held before the fire on toast-dogs (1 & 2), that on the left having a ring to hold a dish or a stotty cake to catch the falling fat. The stand below (3) stood on the hearth to either warm a plate before use, or keep food hot.

were then butchered, either into roasting joints such as the leg, loin, neck, and rolled stuffed belly etc., or into pieces for preservation.

The sides of fat hogs were the prime source of salt pork joints. Having been cut into pieces small enough to be packed into large earthenware pans or coopered tubs, they were first rubbed with saltpetre, then rubbed again with a mixture of half common salt and half large-crystal sea salt. A layer of these salts was then put into the bottom of the container, followed by alternating layers of pork and the salts until it was full, leaving no vacant spaces. As the salt settled down and turned into brine more salt was added, ensuring that the pork was always covered. A piece of cloth was then set on top, followed by a board and a weight to ensure that the pork was always submerged. Stored in a cool place, this provided a constant source of salt pork ready for boiling.[44]

The sides were also cured as bacon, and the legs as hams, using a mixture of coarse salt, saltpetre and brown sugar. Everyone who kept a pig was familiar with the process, using their own particular blend of ingredients and method. Today, however, it is much more convenient to buy good-quality dry-cured ham and bacon, either 'green' and unsmoked (often preferred in the North) or smoked. The hams and sides of bacon hanging from the ceiling-beams of every cottage and farmhouse were a visual sign of security for all the inhabitants. So long as they were present, meals of boiled or fried ham or bacon were always available. In the border regions, where constantly troublesome times had developed practical methods for making emergency departures from the house, great care was taken of these foods. In 1804, for example, when Mrs. Elizabeth Ferguson's mother heard of an impending French invasion, she had her side of bacon taken down from the joists, roasted, and carried up into the hills on Simonside.[45]

Since bacon was such a popular food, it is not surprising to find it being cooked in a number of quite different ways, including;

Bacon Fritters
E.N. Danby, Darlington area[46]

1 tbs bacon, minced	*2 eggs, beaten*
4oz/100g mashed potatoes	*½pt/300ml milk*
4oz/100g plain flour	*lard for frying*

Mix the dry ingredients, beat in the eggs, then the milk. Drop tablespoonfuls into boiling lard and fry brown.
The same mixture, minus the bacon, was poured into the pan after frying bacon or ham, fried brown on both sides, then cut in pieces and served.[47]

Stovies
M.L. Alder, Alnmouth[48]

6oz/175g bacon, in thick slices	*about ½pt/300ml milk*
8oz/225g leeks, chopped	*½ tsp salt*
1oz/25g lard	*1 tbs cornflour*
8oz/225g potatoes, peeled & sliced	

Dice the bacon and fry with the leeks in lard until tender, but not coloured, then stir in the salt and cornflour. Spread the potatoes on top, pour in the milk, cover, and simmer gently for about 30 minutes until the potatoes are tender.

Bacon Cake[49]

A few slices of boiled bacon	*8oz/225g short or puff pastry*

Roll the pastry as a large round on a baking tray and cover one half with the bacon. Moisten the edges, fold the vacant half over the bacon, pat down and roll to exclude the air, then seal the edges. Prick all over with a fork and bake at 200°C, 400°F, Gas mark 6 for about 30 minutes.

This was served for 'ten o'clocks' in Durham farms.

Ham Savoury [50]

a few slices of ham, sugar, pepper, milk, grated cheese

Lay the ham in a fireproof dish, sprinkle with a little sugar and pepper, half cover with milk, sprinkle with grated cheese and bake at 180°C, 350°F, Gas mark 4 for 30 minutes.

POULTRY & GAME

Neither poultry nor game figured largely in working-class diets, as they were too expensive, unless it was an old boiling fowl, or the result of poaching. There were plenty of grouse, etc,. on the moors, as well as pheasants, hares and rabbits on the farms and estates, and wildfowl on the Northumbrian coast, but these were preserved for the nobility and gentry. Depending on personal resources, a chicken, a turkey, or, best of all, a goose, might be bought in for Christmas Day or some other celebration. The way of roasting the goose is fully described in Thomas Wilson's verses;

> We're gawn to get a geass te morn,
> There's nought aw get aw like se weel
> After they've grown, wi' stubble corn,
> As fat an plump as ony seal.

> Aw like her stuft wi' onions best,
> An' roasted to a single roun',
> A'nicely scrimpt frae back to breast -
> Not brunt, but beautifully brown ...
> She myeks a real royal dish,
> On whilk a king meet myek a myel -
> Aw wadn't for a better wish
> Were aw to-morn a king mysel.

The oddments, te, beath boil or fry
Provided geassy be a gooden -
Eat famous in a giblet pie,
Crib'd roun' wi' coils of savory pudden.

Such a roast and its accompanying pie were always held in the highest regard, their appearance on the table an eagerly anticipated treat. However, those who had a delicious-looking pie set down before them might have been less than enthusiastic had they known the true nature of its contents. As in other parts of the country, pies could be used as a way of disguising bad food so that it could be sold at a profit. Apparently this was the practice at the fast-food takeaway cook-shop described in Joe Wilson's poem 'Her Feythur keeps a Keuk Shop'. Here the prospective son-in-law explained how;

The mysteries of the pies, an' the sassages aw'll prize.
Aw heh ne call te tell the neybors what we trade on;
"Where ignorance is bliss, information brings distress,
So it's best for folks te know nowt what thor made on.

Pies provided great scope for practical jokers, for which songs of Tommy Armstrong provide two excellent examples. When a grand supper was being prepared at the inn at Street Gate near Gateshead, it was decided that a hedgehog should be killed for the rabbit pie. Since both a mallet and a knife failed, it was eventually drowned and prepared, after which;

Th' landlady's sister made up the pie crust
We th' best e beef fat en sum dumplin' dust.
She nickt it aul rooned, made it tender en thin,
Th' yuven wis hot, en she put th' pie in.[51]

The deception worked well, and apparently brought no complaints. Meanwhile at Slentey, 'not far frae Skeel Row ... ';

Tiv a hoose ivory Sunda' sum chaps used to gan
An' eat all th' meat thit was boil i' th' pan
These chaps used to gan an' sit doon on a steal,
They knew thit Jack alwis had plenty i' meal;
But Coxon an' Charlton went oot for to try
To catch an awd cat te make them a pie.

32. As Thomas Bewick's engraving shows, large hot meat pies were extremely popular, even if it might be best if the diners had no knowledge of the true nature of their contents!

Having been killed and prepared, 'pussy' was shoved into the pastry and baked, after which part of the pie crust was removed to make it look as if its makers had already eaten their share. To their delight, the others;

> *thowt 'twis a rabbit, an hoo te makes thares,*
> *Charlton got Coxon to run up th' stairs*
> *Bob Whitfield then thowt a grand trick wed he try*
> *So he into the pantry an' off wi th' pie.[52]*
> *little suspecting that he was about to feast on pussy-cat!*

Sometimes a pie was served to a guest who found it to be most excellent, tender and delicious, only his own sensibilities causing him later regrets. This was certainly the experience of a Durham draper who lost his way when returning one evening from St. John's Chapel in Weardale. Finally approaching a lonely farmhouse, he stopped his horse and trap, knocked at the door, accepted the welcome hospitality of 'the gudewife', and sat down to dinner. Then;

The Piggy Wiggy Pie he now does try,
He finds the flavour rare.
'Tis plainly seen his appetite is keen,
Braced by the fellside air.

The traveller ate with enjoyment great,
His face glowed with content;
That Piggy Wiggy Pie, he made it fly
Till appetite was spent.

After returning home next day, and for some time afterwards, he remembered the pie with relish, and so decided to return to the farm once more. This time he took a friend with him, with the promise of a champion pie for dinner. On entering, he asked;

'We should like to try – that Piggy Wiggy Pie
In the making you excel
'Tis a very great treat, so crisp and sweet
With such an exquisite smell.'

'This time' she said, 'the pigs were not dead,
But all born alive, you know.
That's the reason why we didn't make a pie,
It would be a waste to do so.'

As the travellers heard these dreadful words
Their appetite shrank away;
A deadly chill did their spirits fill,
They could eat no more that day ...

What appeared to be a perfectly acceptable source of delicious, tender meat to the hill-farming family was disgusting to the townsman - but only after he had discovered its source.

Pies were not the only way of serving unwelcome meats to the unwary. When Jack Nicholson, a carrier, had his dinner of bread and beef stolen by the lead-smelters at Blackton in Baldersdale, he made no fuss, but quietly planned his revenge. Finding the carcase of an old, skinned horse lying by a barn, he cut two steaks from its flank, and, wrapping them with his bread, went back to the mill. As before, the smelters stole it and ate it greedily, until he told them what it was. Much groaning and vomiting followed, but no-one ever stole his dinner again.[53]

My grandfather had similar feelings after enjoying the hospitality of a Chinese sea captain delivering iron ore to Bradley Williams' Dunstan Metal Works around 1911. On asking what kind of meat he had just eaten, he was told that it was the chow he had petted, and therefore selected, when he had come on board that morning to take samples for analysis. He thought that the dogs were pets, but the Chinese crew saw them as food.

CHAPTER NINE

OF FISH

Dance to thy Daddy, sing to thy Mammy,
Dance to thy Daddy, to thy Mammy sing.
Thou shalt have a fishy on a little dishy,
Thou shalt have a fishy when the boat comes in.

Having such a long coast lined with fishing villages and ports, Northumberland and Durham were well-supplied with fresh fish. Much of it was sold by the fishermen's wives, who carried their heavy loads around their immediate hinterland and into most of the region's markets, where they were easily recognised by their distinctive dress, smell, and street-cries.[1]

Those from Cullercoats carried their fish into nearby villages and onto the Newcastle quayside, using large creels slung on to their backs. In the herring season their cry was;

> Caller hern, fresh hern! Here's yo'r noble hern!
> Fower a penny, fower a penny!

Or even;

> Fine codlins, hinny; cheaper for hyem consumption thin butcher's meat. There's fine mackerel; come mister, ye shall hae them at yor own price, but the sea's up. Aw's sure fish just noo's as bad to catch as husbands, and a great deal worse ti sell!

'Caller' was the northcountry word for fresh, newly-gathered and seasonable. The North Shields fish-women and men carried their smaller fish in baskets, the larger ones being piled on well-scrubbed boards some 2-3ft/60-90cm square. These they placed on a 'weeze', a pad of cloth worn on top of the head, so that they could be carried around while leaving both hands free. Their usual cry was a simple 'Buy fish!' but others included;

33. In the early nineteenth century oysters were harvested along the Northumbrian coast to provide a popular delicacy in the region's country houses, ordinary homes and, as seen here, in its inns and taverns.

> New boil'd crab, New boil'd crab!
> Caller oyster!, or
> Cockles a-live, all-a-live!

In Newcastle the fish-wives had occupied numerous stalls on the Sandhill, but in 1823-6 John Dobson designed a fine new covered fish market within a semicircular Doric colonnade at the east end of the Guildhall.[2] Described as 'one of the handsomest ornaments of the town', it had lead-covered stalls irrigated with cold running water.[3] Despite their initial misgivings, it was soon ringing to their cries of;

> Will ye buy any fish! Caller hern, fresh hern, caller hern!
> Fresh crabs, new boil'd crabs!
> Ye buy lobster, fresh boil'd lobster! (usually meaning prawns!)
> Ye buy lobster! Fow'r-a-penny lobster!
> New boil'd sherimps! Fresh shrimps, new boil'd shrimps!
> Ye oyster loy!

Or;

> Buy kipper, buy new kipper!

34. In 1823-6 a fine new Fish Market was built at the east end of the Guildhall on Newcastle's Quayside, its elegant Doric design being provided by the town's leading architect, John Dobson. Its opening on 2nd January, 1826, was celebrated in verses commencing;

March! March to the Dandy Fish Market.
See what our Corporation's done for yoa.
By pillars and paling so nobly surrounded
And your stone tables all standing before you.

In 1835 the Corporation went on to replace its older food markets with a new market designed by John Dobson as part of Richard Grainger's massive redevelopment of the town. Originally the largest and finest covered market in the country, the Grainger Market still sells excellent fresh fish today. The region's other major towns also built covered markets later in the nineteenth century, removing the retailing of fish from their streets into cleaner, permanent shops. It was not until the early twentieth century, however, that the traditionally-dressed fish-wives finally ceased to heave their loaded baskets and creels of fish into the open markets and streets, just as they had done over many previous generations.

Being relatively cheap and plentiful, both fresh and preserved fish were regularly eaten in most homes. They varied in price, however, according to their species, their quality and their freshness. Salmon, for example, was always considered to be a special and costly delicacy, rarely eaten by most working families, unless illegally poached.

SALMON

It is frequently claimed in Newcastle, and many other historic cities too, that salmon was once so common that the apprentices refused to eat it more than three times a week. The only problem with this is that no-one has ever found a scrap of evidence to confirm it. In actual fact, salmon has always been one of the most exclusive and expensive of fish, certainly not to be wasted on apprentices. This region had a nation-wide reputation for its salmon, as Daniel Defoe recorded in the early eighteenth century;

> We receive at London every year a great quantity of salmon pickled or cured, and sent up in the pickle in kits or tubs, which we call Newcastle salmon; now when I came to Newcastle, I expected to see a mighty plenty of salmon there but was surprised, on the contrary, that there was no great quantity, and that a good large salmon was not to be had under five or six shillings. Upon enquiring I found, that really this salmon, that we call Newcastle salmon, is taken as far off as the Tweed, which is three-score miles, and is brought by land on horses to Shields, where it is cur'd, pickle'd, and sent to London, as above; so it ought to be called Berwick salmon, not Newcastle.[4]

This description fails to recognise the importance of the Tyne's salmon fishery. Its scale may be judged by a description of 2,400 salmon being taken above Newcastle Bridge on 12th June, 1755, individuals weighing up to 54lb/24kg being recorded about this time. In the later eighteenth century it sold for about 1d/25p a pound, but then increased due to a combination of a growing demand and a decreasing stock caused by poaching and pollution. In 1807 salmon could bring 3s 6d/17p a pound, continuing to be an expensive fish for the remainder of the century.

The preservation of salmon created a considerable coastal industry in the late eighteenth century, when twenty-eight pickling families worked in Berwick, and a further six in Newcastle. Mrs Gardiner's recipe of 1763 'To Pickle Salmon the Newcastle Way' records the process as practiced at this time. Having been scaled, split down the back and the backbone removed, it was washed clean, cut into pieces about 4-5ins/10-12.5cm thick, boiled in brine, allowed to cool, and packed into a cooper-made keg. A pickle made by boiling 2oz/50g each of allspice and black pepper in 8pts/4.8l vinegar, leaving it to cool, and stirring in a handful of salt, was then poured on, and left to stand overnight. Next day any oil was skimmed off, presumably more brine added, and the head of the keg sealed down tightly, ready for transport or long-term storage. By 1799 this trade had finished in Berwick, as the use of natural ice as a preservative from 1787-8 enabled the raw salmon to be delivered in London while still fresh. In Newcastle, however, the last salmon picklers appeared in the local directories of the 1830s. However, the Georgian cookery writers of Berwick and Newcastle still published recipes for boiled, baked, collared, potted, dried or kippered salmon, salmon pies, olives, collops and ragoos, and 'How to Pickle Salmon the Newcastle Way'. These were all intended for the fashionable upper classes, however, not for general use. Some families still potted local salmon in a traditional way, however, using this recipe;

To Pot Salmon [5]

> 1lb/450g salmon steaks or fillets, skin & bones removed
> 2 tbs salt   4oz/100g butter
> ½ tsp ground black pepper, ¼ tsp ground mace, ¼ tsp ground
> nutmeg, pinch cayenne pepper all beaten together

Put the salmon in a deep dish or tray, rub the salt into the fish, and leave in a cool place for 12 hours, turning frequently. Wash the salmon, wipe it dry, dust with the mixed spices and pack into a buttered straight-sided oven-proof vessel, with slices of butter between each layer. Cover and bake at 180°C, 350°F, Gas mark 4 for 1 hour.

Remove from the oven. Pour off all the liquid into a transparent jug, strain off the clear melted butter into a saucepan, add a little water, boil together for a few minutes, then skim and leave to cool. Pack the drained salmon into straight-sided jars or pots, pour in sufficient clarified butter to cover it, then store in a cool place until needed.

As an alternative, the cooked salmon was pounded to a smooth paste with a little of the clarified butter, packed tightly into jars, and sealed with a layer of clarified butter.

If fresh salmon was available, it was usually poached, any left over being used to make dishes such as;

Salmon Pudding
Mrs S. Moore, Haydon Bridge[6]

8oz/225g cooked salmon, flaked	*½ tsp baking powder*
2oz/50g fresh white breadcrumbs	*salt & pepper*
1oz/25g suet	*1 egg, beaten*
about ½pt/300ml milk (or fish stock)	*1oz/25g plain flour*

Mix the dry ingredients, except the salmon, make a well in the centre, mix in the egg and sufficient milk to make a soft dropping mixture. Gently stir in the salmon, pack into a greased basin, cover with a piece of pleated greaseproof paper, tie down and steam for 2 hours. Turn out and serve with parsley sauce.

WHITE FISH

Cod, haddock, plaice and other white fish were all readily available either directly from the fishwives who hawked them from their coastal homes, from the markets, or from various fishmongers. They were usually either grilled at the fire using simple gridirons called spits or 'speets', or else poached, but since the coal-fired ovens were usually hot, they were also baked.

35. The popularity of fish and chips as major take-away meals developed in the late Victorian period. These 'Newcastle' frying ranges could be purchased from the Newcastle showroom of their manufacturers, Mabbott & Co. of the Phoenix Iron Works in Manchester, in 1904.

Stuffed Haddock
Mrs H. Symes, Brockmill, Beal[7]

1 small, whole haddock, gutted, rinsed and wiped dry
2 tsp salt   *salt & pepper*
¾pt/450ml fresh white breadcrumbs
½pt/300ml warm milk   *1oz/25g suet*
plain flour for dusting   *2 tsp chopped parsley*
2oz/50g butter

Rub the salt down the inside of the haddock's backbone. Mix the breadcrumbs, suet, parsley and salt & pepper, and mix in sufficient milk to form a firm mixture. Stuff this into the haddock, and either tie up with tape or sew up the belly. Lay in a greased ovenproof dish, dust with flour, dot with the butter, and bake at 170°C, 325°F, Gas mark 3 for about 20 minutes. Serve with sprigs of parsley and slices of lemon.

Stuffed Plaice
A. Porlock, Hepscott[8]

6 medium fillets of plaice	*½ tsp chopped parsley*
1½oz/35g bacon, fried & chopped	*1 egg, beaten*
1½oz/35g fresh white breadcrumbs	*salt & pepper*
¼ tsp mixed chopped herbs	

Wash & dry the fillets. Mix the remaining ingredients and spread on the skin side of each fillet, roll up, and stand on end in a greased fireproof dish, so as to just fill it. Cover the dish and bake at 190°C, 375°F, Gas mark 5 for 20 minutes, and serve with parsley sauce.

Fish Pudding
Miss Addison[9]

12oz/325g cooked cod	*salt & pepper*
2oz/50g butter	*1 egg, beaten*
3oz/75g fresh white breadcrumbs	*a little stock or water*
pinch ground nutmeg	

Remove all bones, etc. from the fish, pound to a smooth paste, and mix with the remaining ingredients, adding sufficient liquid to form a dropping mixture. Put into a buttered baking dish, and bake at 190°C, 375°F, Gas mark 5 for about 20 minutes. Serve with a white sauce well-flavoured with anchovies or anchovy essence.

This recipe may also use left-over cooked fish instead of the raw cod.[10]

1lb/450g cod	*2 tsp salt*
3oz/75g fresh white breadcrumbs	*pinch ground pepper*
3oz/75g suet	*2 eggs, beaten*
2 tsp dried parsley	*½pt/300ml milk*

Skin and bone and mince the fish, mix with the remaining ingredients, pack into a greased basin, cover with pleated greaseproof paper, tie down, and steam for 1 hour. Serve covered with parsley sauce.

Fish Head Soup

Having boiled a large fish head, use the stock to make soups. Scrape off the flesh, mash with potatoes, season with salt and pepper, make into fishcakes, and fry.

HERRINGS

Herrings were a very popular food in the north-east, every part of them being used according to the Northumbrian song 'The Herrin's Heed';

Oh, what'll we dee wi the herrin's heed?
Oh, what'll we dee wi the herrin's heed?
We'll maak it into loaves o' breed, an' aal manner o' things

Of all the fish that are in the sea
The herrin' is the one for me.
Hoo are ye the day? Hoo are ye the day?
Hoo are ye the day, me hinny, oh?

Cheap and plentiful throughout the summer, fresh herrings made a delicious and nutritious meal when coated in oatmeal and either simply grilled or fried, baked, or perhaps preserved by bottling.

Grilled Herrings [11]

2 herrings, the head, guts and backbone removed
1 onion, peeled   *1oz/25g butter*
6 black peppercorns   *1 tsp mustard powder*
¼pt/150ml malt vinegar   *½oz/12g plain flour*

Simmer the onion and peppercorns in the vinegar in a covered pan for 15 minutes. Meanwhile grill the herring 4 or 5 minutes each side, having slashed them diagonally a couple of times on both sides if plump. Melt the butter in a pan, stir in the mustard and flour, strain in the vinegar, stir until boiling, then pour over the herring and serve.

36. The processing of fish was a distinctly female speciality. During the herring season the Scots fisher lasses who followed the fleet down the coast first cleaned and gutted the catch, as seen here at Newbiggin, before packing it into barrels with salt.

Baked Herrings [12]

herring fillets	*salt*
ground black pepper	*malt vinegar*

Highly season the herrings with the pepper and salt, lay in a baking dish, cover with a half water/half vinegar mixture, and bake at 190°C, 375°F, Gas mark 5 for about 25 minutes.

Bottled Herrings [13]

herring fillets	*salt & pepper*
brine made by boiling 2 tsp salt in 1pt/600ml water	

Dust the inside of the herrings with pepper and salt and roll up, skin outermost. Pack on end into a buttered casserole, cover, and bake at 180°C, 350°F, Gas mark 4 for about 30-40 minutes, then leave to cool. Pack the fillets into glass jars, cover with the cold brine, seal down, and store in a cool place for up to six months.

RED HERRINGS

Red herrings have been prepared in England from at least the thirteenth century, their manufacture at the east end of Tweedmouth starting in 1797. They were left whole, dry-salted, mounted on long sticks thrust through their heads, and smoked for a few days. The result was a red-brown almost leathery fish which could be stored almost indefinitely, had a strong flavour and scent, and was ideal for creating a raging thirst before a heavy drinking session. Today they are still sold by shops serving the Afro-Caribbean community. They were usually prepared by soaking in warm water for an hour, cutting across the fillets two or three times, and grilling before the fire.

KIPPERS

The practice of preserving herrings by splitting them, soaking them in brine for three or four hours and then lightly smoking them in a chimney was already in use in England in the early seventeenth century. They were called bloated herrings, and there are watercolours showing them being hung up to smoke in Whitby in the autumn of 1837.[14] In 1843 John Woodger, a native of Hampshire who had recently moved to Newcastle, where he kept *The Plough* in Union Street, invented kippers. These were herrings, lightly dry-salted, then split, gutted and de-gilled, before smoking them overnight.[15] The resulting variety of the old bloater (a whole, lightly-salted herring), was re-christened the 'kipper', adopting the well-established term for the local salted and air-dried fillets of salmon. His 'Newcastle Kippers' were first sent to London in 1846.[16] From that time kippers were made at most of the main fishing ports along the north-eastern coastline from May to August each year. Craster still has an excellent reputation for its kippers, which are brined for about twenty minutes, stretched open on rows of hooks or pegs and hung in smokehouses over smouldering oak sawdust for about twelve to sixteen hours. Larger ports developed extensive kippering facilities as the demand for kippers expanded in the later nineteenth century. Hartlepool had nine smokehouses close to its fish quay, their operators following the herring shoals down the coast to extend the curing season into early autumn.[17]

Being easily and quickly cooked, and a tasty, savoury cheap meal, kippers were popular in all working families. In his poem 'The Kipper'd Herrin' Edward Corvan described how Jim Farrins, a hewer;

... yen day bowt a cask o' the best kipper'd herrins
To eat tiv his coffee, his taties, and breed,
Determined a' winter te hev a cheap feed.[18]

The usual method of cooking the kippers was to grill them before the fire, but they could also be jugged by being stood tail-up in a jug, covered with boiling water and left for five minutes before draining and serving.

SHELLFISH

Crabs, lobsters, prawns and shrimps were usually sold ready-boiled by the fish-wives, and so only needed to be cleaned, picked and dressed for the table. For this reason, there are very few ordinary family recipes for cooking them. One exception is the following, which pots the ready-boiled shrimps to convert them into a long-keeping and finely-flavoured delicacy.

Potted Shrimps [19]

1pt/600ml fresh boiled shrimps   *½ tsp anchovy sauce*
2oz/50g butter   *pinch cayenne pepper*
1 small blade of mace

Heat the butter in a pan until just boiling, set aside to cool and set, and remove the whey, etc. to produce clarified butter. Pick off the shells, etc. and pound with most of the clarified butter, the mace, anchovy and cayenne. Transfer to a pan, heat gently for 6-8 minutes, and rub through a sieve into a clean pan. Add the tails, heat until quite hot, pour into small pots, allow to set, then melt the remaining clarified butter and pour on top to form a seal. Store in a cool place. Serve cold, with bread and butter, or hot, with fresh toast.

CHAPTER TEN

OF VEGETABLES

On the allotments around mining villages, on the large plots provided for farm workers, and in numerous back gardens, vegetables were home grown to the highest standards. Some were intended to win prizes at the local show, but most added great, fresh flavours and nourishment to everyday meals. For those without a garden, or who needed to supplement their home-grown supplies, fresh, seasonal vegetables were readily available from the local markets. In November, for example, the streets rang to the cries of;

> Will ye buy ony large new taties!
> Will ye buy ony new green peas!
> Raddish and scallions [spring onions], two bunches a penny![1]

And;

> Onions! Onions! Who'll buy my onions! (This from the traditional Breton onion-seller, his bike supporting long strings of large, mild French onions.)[2]

Among all the different vegetables which formed part of the 'meat and two veg.' dinners which most Victorian and Edwardian housewives made every day, two were of particular local importance, the leek and the onion. The leek was the national emblem of Wales, but nowhere was it grown with such skill, and with such a competitive spirit as in the north-east. The weeks before the flower and vegetable shows saw them being carefully tended, fed with secret mixtures, and guarded against that most evil and despised predator – the leek-slasher intent on destroying competition for his own produce. Easily cooked and prized for their delicate texture and flavour, the leeks were prepared to various recipes, only a selection being given here. The leek pudding is particularly good, and those who wish to try them ready-made may still buy them in Newcastle's Grainger Market.

37. Leek clubs were particularly popular in the coal-mining districts, the competition for prizes at the annual shows being extremely fierce.

Leek Pudding
Mrs Edna Copman, Howdon[3]

8oz/225g plain flour	*4oz/100g suet*
2 tsp baking powder	*6oz/175g chopped leeks*
1 tsp salt	*salt & pepper*

Mix the flour, baking powder, salt & suet, and stir in some ¼pt/150ml cold water to form a dough that just leaves the side of the bowl. Roll out as a large rectangle, spread with the leeks, sprinkle with salt and pepper, and roll up. Rinse, wring and spread out a square of cloth or muslin, dust it with flour, roll the pudding in it, tying each end tightly with string. Plunge into boiling water or stock, boil gently for 2 hours, then turn out and serve with minced beef.

Leek Dumplings
Mrs Odd, Scremeston Town Farm, Berwick[4]

Make suet pastry as in the recipe above, and roll out. Trim the leeks, cut into 6ins/15cm lengths, roll each one in a piece of pastry, sealing the joints and ends. Roll each in a piece of cloth or muslin, prepared as above, and boil in water or stock for an hour.

Boiled Leeks (1)[5]

Trim off the root and green ends, cut in 2ins/5cm lengths, boil in salted water for 10-15 minutes, or steam for about 10 minutes, drain, and serve with white sauce.

Boiled Leeks (2)
Mrs D.A. Gallon, The Temperance Hotel, Stannington[6]

Cook as above, drain, then stir in ½pt/300ml milk mixed with 2 tsp cornflour, 1-2oz/25-50g grated cheese, and a little salt and pepper. Bring to the boil while stirring, and serve when thickened and the cheese has melted.

Boiled Leeks (3)

Trim off the root and green ends, cut into two or four pieces, soak in water with a little vinegar for 30 minutes, then simmer for 15-20 minutes in milk and water. Drain, and serve with white sauce.

Fried Leeks

Trim the leeks and cut in 1in/2.5cm lengths. Fry fat bacon in a pan, remove the bacon, add the leeks, and a cup of hot water, top with the bacon, put a plate or lid on top to keep in the steam, and leave to sweat slowly until tender. The leeks and bacon, accompanied by tea, was a favourite Saturday night tea-cum-dinner in the north-east.

Onions have always been one of the most popular and useful of all English vegetables, sometimes being added to soups and stews to give a fine flavour, and sometimes finely chopped and fried to produce rich savoury/caramel tastes and golden-brown colours in various dishes. They were also plain-boiled, or roasted with joints of meat, to appear as a vegetable in their own right. There are numerous recipes for cooking them, the following including only those collected from the north-east.

Onion Pudding

Follow the directions for Leek Pudding (p.118), replacing the leeks with onions.

Baked Onions [7]

Peel and quarter the onions, put into a pan, half-cover with water, cover, and simmer very gently until tender. Drain off the liquid, put the onions into a pie dish, dust with flour, salt and pepper, almost cover with milk and bake at 170°C, 325°F, Gas mark 3 for 30 minutes.

Onion Pancakes
Mrs Rodgers[8]

12oz/350g onions	*1 egg*
5oz/125g plain flour	*¼pt/150ml milk*
salt & pepper	*fat for frying*

Peel and finely chop the onions. Mix the salt and pepper into the flour, make a well in the centre, drop in the egg and beat in the flour, adding the milk little by little to form a batter. Mix in the onion and drop spoonfuls into the hot fat in a frying pan. Once it is seen to have set around the edges, turn over and fry the other side golden brown.

Onion Puffs[9]

6oz/175g onion, grated	*1 egg, beaten*
12oz/350g mashed potato	*a few tbs milk*
salt & pepper	*1oz/25g butter*

Mix the onion, potato, salt and pepper and egg together, adding a little milk if necessary to form a soft mixture. Heat the butter in a dripping tin at 200°C, 400°F, Gas mark 6 for 5 minutes. Remove from the oven, drop in spoonfuls of the mixture and bake for 30 minutes. The puffs are light and absorbent, and are good with roast meats and gravy.

Onion Savoury[10]

8-12oz/225-325g chopped onion and about the same quantity of mashed potatoes

1oz/25g dripping	*salt & pepper*

Fry the onions in the dripping until golden brown. Stir in the potato with a little salt and pepper, and continue stirring until the potatoes begin to brown, then serve for supper.

Onion Dumpling[11]

For each person; 1 large peeled onion   *½ tsp salt*
1oz/25g ham or bacon, in small dice   *4oz/100g suet*
8oz/225g plain flour

Mix the flour, salt and suet with 8 tbs cold water, and knead lightly until smooth. Cut the onion in half vertically, remove the central layers, pack with the ham or bacon, put it together again, and totally enclose in the pastry. Tie in a square of thin cloth or muslin which has been rinsed, wrung, layed flat and dusted with flour. Plunge into boiling water and cook for 2½ hours.

Another regional speciality was the pea. The pitmen and lads used to celebrate the ripening of the first of the fresh crop with an unofficial holiday called pea-mornin'.[12] The peas were boiled in their pods, tipped into a sieve on a table, and a saucer of butter arranged in the centre. Once salt had been sprinkled on, each person took a pod, dipped it in the butter, shelled the peas into their mouth, and then pelted their companions with the empty pods. As a result this 'scalding' of peas became known as 'peas and sport'.[13] The twelve bushels of peas given to Northumbrian farm workers as part of their annual pay were dry grey peas, which would last indefinitely if kept dry. To cook them they had to be soaked overnight and then boiled for hours, this being the origin of the continuing taste for pease pudding in the region. It was made from field peas left in their pods, threshed out, dried and split, then becoming the yellow split peas still used to make it today. It can be bought ready-made or in tins, or made to one of these traditional recipes, the second one being the best.

Pease Pudding
Miss A.M. Dent, Barnard Castle, 1883[14]

6oz/175g split pease   *1 small egg, beaten*
1oz/25g butter   *a few dry breadcrumbs*
salt & pepper

Soak the peas in at least 1½pt/900ml water overnight, then simmer for about 2-3 hours until tender. Drain, rub through a sieve to give a smooth pulp (today, use a food processor) with a little salt and pepper, the butter and egg, and pack into a basin which has been thickly greased and lined with the breadcrumbs. Bake at 150°C, 300°F, Gas mark 2 for 45 minutes, then turn out and serve.

Pease Pudding [15]

This used to be made with the salt pork, which was used both on land and at sea, but can now be replaced by a ham shank. Use the recipe above, but add the shank and an onion to the boiling peas, then remove it, pulp the peas, pack them into a basin and leave them to cool and set firm. It can then be sliced and eaten with cold meat with pickles, or in sandwiches.

Pea Soup [16]

12oz/325g split peas	3oz/75g butter
1 onion	2oz/20g plain flour
small piece of bacon, or a ham shank	¾pt/450ml milk

Soak the peas overnight, drain, put into 2½pts/1.5l cold water with the onion, bacon or ham shank, cover, and simmer for 3 hours, then rub through a sieve, including all the liquid. Melt the butter in a pan, stir in the flour, add the milk, stir over a gentle heat until it has dissolved and thickened, then mix in the pea purée, season to taste, and bring to the boil just before serving.

Lentil Soup [17]

8oz/225g lentils	2oz/50g dripping
1 carrot in small dice	1 tsp each parsley & thyme
1 turnip in small dice	2 cloves
1 onion, finely chopped	salt & pepper

Soak the lentils overnight, then boil for an hour and leave them in their cooking liquid. Meanwhile fry the vegetables in the dripping. When both are ready, make up the liquid to 4pt/2.4l, add the vegetables, the herbs tied in a piece of muslin and the cloves, cover, and simmer for 3 hours. Rub the soup through a sieve, season to taste, bring to the boil, and serve.

Other vegetables were usually cooked by being boiled in salted water in the usual way, but some were made into more interesting recipes:

Celery Pie
Mrs Dawson-Walker[18]

1 head of celery	2oz/50g grated cheese
½pt/300ml milk	1 egg, beaten
1oz/25g plain flour	salt & pepper
2oz/50g fresh breadcrumbs	1oz/25g butter

Cut the celery into short lengths, barely cover with water and cook for some 20 minutes until tender. Meanwhile beat the flour into the cold milk in a saucepan, until smooth, add the butter and stir continuously until boiled and thickened. Dip the base of the pan into cold water to stop it cooking. When cool, beat in the cheese, egg and drained celery (keep the stock for soups), with ½ tsp salt, and a little pepper. Pour into a 2pt/1l baking dish, cover with the breadcrumbs and bake at 170°C, 325°F, gas mark 3 for 1 hour.

Potato Floddies
Mrs E.M. Danby, Darlington area[19]

8oz/225g potato, grated	salt & pepper
4 tbs plain flour	fat for frying

Coarsely chop the grated potato to reduce the length of the strands. Stir the flour into the potatoes with salt and pepper to taste and mix with a little water to produce a stiff batter. Drop spoonfuls into the hot fat in a frying pan, pat flat with the back of a spoon and when browned turn over to fry the other side. They go well with a 'Full English' breakfast.

38. During the nineteenth century potatoes became a major source of nutrition, including Vitamin C, in most working households. Ralph Hedley painted this group of Northumbrian potato pickers in 1903, when there was a typically good harvest. However, a potato shortage in 1917 led to an outbreak of scurvy in Newcastle.

Potato Cake [20]

4oz/100g plain flour	*1oz/25g butter*
2oz/50g lard or dripping	*1-2 potatoes, peeled*
1 tbs bacon, finely chopped	*salt & pepper*

Mix the flour with a pinch of salt, rub into the fat, stir in 4 tsp cold water and knead lightly to form pastry. Roll out thinly as a large square, and place half at the centre of a baking tray. Cover with a single layer of potato cut into ¼in/6mm slices, dot with butter, and dust with salt and pepper and a sprinkling of bacon. Cover with the remaining pastry, seal the edges and bake at 180°C, 350°F, Gas mark 4 for 30 minutes. Try the potatoes with a skewer and if not tender bake a little longer, then serve for supper.

Vegetable Soup [21]

2 medium onions, finely chopped	1oz/25g lard or dripping
2oz/50g pudding rice or pearl barley	5pt/3l meat stock
2 carrots, diced	2 tbs fine oatmeal
1 turnip, diced	salt & pepper

Fry the onions in the fat until starting to brown, add to the stock, along with the vegetables and rice or barley, cover and simmer for 2 hours. Mix the oatmeal with a little water, stir into the soup, season to taste, return to the boil & serve.

The first references to the Northumbrian dish of pan haggerty describe it as a dish made largely of potatoes and onions, once common at Winlaton-on-Tyne. Its curious name appears to come from the Norse and Scots word 'Hagger', to chop roughly and unevenly. [22] It has survived as a dish of sliced potatoes and onions layered in a deep, heavy frying pan, some families frying it, others adding liquid and stewing it until tender.

Pan Haggerty (1) [23]

2lb/900g potatoes, sliced	1 tbs dripping
1lb/450g onions, sliced	salt & pepper
3oz/75g grated cheese	

Layer the potatoes, onions and cheese over the dripping in a deep, heavy saucepan, seasoning each layer. Cover with a lid or a plate, and cook over a minimal heat until tender, which should take about 30 minutes.

Pan Haggerty (2) [24]

Make as above, but replace the dripping and cheese with 4oz/100g coarsely chopped lean bacon or corned beef, and sufficient water or stock to half-fill the pan just before cooking.

CHAPTER ELEVEN

OF PUDDINGS

Originally all puddings were savoury rather than sweet, Pudding Chare off the Bigg Market in Newcastle taking its name from the black or white puddings once made there. By the seventeenth century sweeter puddings of flour, suet, dried fruits and sugar were boiled in skins prepared from the longer intestines of cattle. Later on, these were replaced by cloths to produce large, spherical suet puddings very similar to 'spotted dicks'. Before potatoes became popular in the later eighteenth and early nineteenth centuries, they were served with meat and vegetables, their spongy consistency enabling them to absorb all the gravy. Such puddings were seen mainly as middle-class dishes, most working families only making plain, unsweetened suet puddings. These social differences were demonstrated by a meal served in the 1780s by Betty Allen of Shiney Row to Mr Longridge, a visiting preacher, and his son William. Having been served with a portion of currant pudding, and seeing no sugar on the table, the boy asked for a little. Betty's response was explosive;

> 'Sugar! What! Sugar to pudding?! We may soon see how you have been brought up. No. No; if they have spoilt you at home, you shall not be spoilt here. Sugar to pudding! You must go without. It is very good as it is.'[1]

Plain suet puddings without any sugar or dried fruits were still being made here in the 1920s. In the 1960s, at the 'Cow Tail', The Dun Cow, Old White Lea, Billy Row, I was asked if I had ever had a blue dick, which I hadn't, or a spotted dick, which I had. It was then explained that, 'We often had blue dicks when it was cold; they were plain dicks, we couldn't afford currants.' But where did the "blue" come from? 'My mother used to boil them in a collier's sock, so they were pale blue, foot-shaped, and had a sort of knitted pattern on them when they were turned out!'

Suet puddings, which were richer and more palatable, eventually became more popular as a winter-time second course, these being typical northcountry examples;

126

Spotty Dick
Mr H. Anson, Haltwhistle[2]

8oz/225g plain flour
4oz/100g suet
2oz/50g sugar

4oz/100g currants
pinch of salt

Mix the ingredients and stir in some cold water to form a soft dough. Rinse, wring and lay flat a square of fine cloth or muslin, sprinkle with more flour, and shake off the surplus. Lay the cloth over a bowl, put the mixture inside, gather the cloth around it, and tie tightly with string. Plunge into boiling water, cover and simmer for 2 hours, topping up with boiling water as necessary to keep the pudding afloat. Finally lift the pudding out of the pan, plunge quickly in and out of a bowl of cold water, ensuring all has been submerged, then turn out onto a dish and serve.

Brown Bread Pudding
Mrs Sherwood, Snow Hall[3]

8oz/225g wholemeal breadcrumbs
4oz/100g suet
8oz/225g currants
1 tbs sugar
¼ tsp ground nutmeg & cinnamon

4oz/100g raisins
4 tbs cream
6 yolks, 3 whites of egg
4 tbs brandy

Mix the dry ingredients together. Stir in the cream, eggs and brandy, enclose in a cloth and simmer for 2 hours as in the recipe above.

Northumberland Currant Dumpling [4]

Half-way between a 'Spotty Dick' and a Christmas Pudding, this began to appear at farmhouse Sunday dinners from early November, being greeted with the riddle;

The flour of England and the fruit of Spain,
Met together in a shower of rain,
Put in a cloth and tied with a string,
'Twill make a plough-boy giggle and sing'

In answer to which, everyone pointed at the dumpling.

1lb/450g plain flour	*8oz/225g suet*
3oz/75g sugar	*8oz/225g currants*
3oz/75g candied lemon peel	*8oz/225g raisins*
milk, to give a stiff dropping consistency	

Mix all the dry ingredients, then stir in the milk, and boil in a cloth, as for the Spotted Dick above, but for 3 hours. Serve with either sweet white sauce or custard.

Batter Pudding
Peggy Hutchinson, Birtley[5]

4oz/100g plain flour	*2 eggs*
2oz/50g sugar	*about ¼pt/150ml milk*
pinch of salt	

Sift the dry ingredients into a bowl, make a well in the centre, drop in the eggs and beat in, adding the milk little by little, as if making a smooth batter for pancakes or a Yorkshire pudding. Rinse, wring, spread out, and dust a pudding cloth with a little flour, and lay over a basin. Have ready a large pan of boiling water, then pour the batter into the cloth, gather the sides and ends to the middle, tie with a string, and plunge into the pan. Boil for 1½ hours, topping up as necessary, then lift out, plunge into a bowl of cold water, turn out onto a dish, and serve with jam. This is a direct descendent of the 'Custard Puddings' of the Stuart period.

Fig Pudding[6]

8oz/225g chopped dried figs	*2oz/50g minced apple*
4oz/100g fresh breadcrumbs	*1 tsp baking powder*
4oz/100g plain flour	*pinch of salt*
4oz/100g suet	*about ½pt/300ml milk*
pinch ground nutmeg (optional)	*2 tbs sugar*

Mix all the dry ingredients and then beat in sufficient milk to produce a soft, dropping consistency. Pour into a greased basin, tie a piece of pleated greaseproof paper

39. This selection of the region's puddings shows, clockwise from the top, a Northumberland currant dumpling, a vanilla cream, Durham pudding, Northumberland pudding, and a fig-covered Hilton pudding.

over the top, and steam for 2 hours. Serve with a sweet white sauce.

Hilton Pudding
Miss A.M. Dent, Barnard Castle area[7]

8oz/225g figs　　　　　　　　*1 egg, beaten*
½pt/300ml milk　　　　　　　*1 tbs sugar*
3oz/75g stale white bread, in small cubes
pinch ground nutmeg

Flatten the figs, remove the stalks, and cut across to form two rounds. Grease a pudding basin, and line with the figs, skin-side to the basin. Put the bread inside, and pour in the sugar, nutmeg, egg and milk beaten together. Stand for 15 minutes to swell, then tie a piece of pleated greaseproof paper over the basin and steam for 45 minutes.

129

Lemon Dumplings [8]

1lb/450g fresh white breadcrumbs   *4oz/100g sugar*
4oz/100g suet   *2 eggs, beaten*
juice & grated zest of 1 large lemon

Mix all the ingredients, pack into buttered cups or small basins. Tie pieces of pleated greaseproof paper over the top of each and steam for 45 minutes. Turn out onto plates, sprinkle with more sugar and serve with Marion Sauce (see below).

Marion Sauce

2oz/50g butter   *few drops vanilla extract*
2oz/50g caster sugar   *⅛pt/75ml boiling milk*
1 egg, beaten

Cream the butter with the sugar, beat in the egg and vanilla, then beat in the boiling milk, and immediately pour over the puddings.

There were various other boiled or steamed puddings, such as ginger, treacle, jam, Eve's or half-pay sponges, just as in most other parts of the country. Since the oven in the kitchen range was usually hot, others were baked rather than steamed. Again, most were just like those made elsewhere, but the following were northcountry specialities.

Northumberland Pudding [9]

6oz/175g plain flour   *2 tbs brandy*
½pt/300ml milk   *4oz/100g butter, melted*
6oz/75g currants, ground smooth   *3 tbs sugar*
2oz/50g chopped candied lemon peel

Beat the milk into the flour and set aside for a few hours, then beat in the butter, then the remaining ingredients. Three-quarters fill a number of buttered ovenproof cups or moulds and bake at 150°C, 300°F, Gas mark 2 for some 30 minutes. Serve with a rum or brandy-flavoured white sauce. These miniature Christmas puddings are easy to make at short notice.

Durham Pudding[10]

10oz/275g puff pastry	*1pt/600ml milk*
3oz/75g fresh white breadcrumbs	*3oz/75g softened butter*
3-4oz/75-100g marmalade	*3 yolks & 2 whites of egg*
grated zest of ½ lemon	*1 tbs sugar*

Line a 2pt/1l baking dish with the puff pastry. Simmer the lemon in the milk for a few minutes, then bring to the boil, stir in the breadcrumbs, then the butter and sugar, remove from the heat and beat in the eggs. Spread the marmalade across the bottom of the puff pastry, pour in the mixture, and bake at 150°C, 300°F, Gas mark 2 for about 45 minutes. Serve either hot or cold.

BEASTINGS PUDDINGS[11]

The rich milk produced by a newly-calved cow, intended to support the calf for its first few days, was called beastings. It was frequently taken by the farmer's wife, either for herself, or to be shared out to her farm workers or friends to make a baked pudding or custard. The jug in which it was received had to be returned unwashed, a clean jug wishing bad luck to the cow. The beastings were usually mixed with half their volume of milk and baked in a greased pie-dish until set. They were then served with either milk and sugar, or a sweet white sauce. Alternatively ½pt/300ml milk and 3 tbs flour were mixed into each ½pt/300ml beastings and steamed in a basin for 2 hours, turned out, and eaten with treacle, white sauce or jam.

MILK PUDDINGS

As the British Empire expanded and steam-powered cargo vessels imported exotic ingredients in cheaper bulk, local shops began to stock a range of starchy cereals ideal for making milk puddings. These included ground and short-grained rice, semolina, sago and tapioca, all ideal for mixing with milk, sugar, a pinch of salt and a little nutmeg, and then left in a slow oven for two or three hours without any further attention. In many farmhouses they appeared as a second course at dinner throughout the summer months, eaten on the same plate as their accompanying fruit pies.[12]

JELLIES AND CREAMS

At first moulded jellies and creams were only seen on the tables of the middle and upper classes, for they needed long boiling, careful filtering and expensive ingredients to make them from raw materials. In the later Victorian period cheap, ready-made packet jellies were introduced, along with finely-ground cornflour, to enable everyone to enjoy jellies and blancmanges as special treats. By the 1860s C.T. Maling of Ford Potteries, Newcastle, were making attractive earthenware jelly moulds to meet this new demand, their range introduced in the 1920s being particularly attractive.[13]

Most people used the manufacturer's instructions to make these cold desserts, but the following individual recipes were also made here;

Vanilla Cream [14]

1pt/600ml milk	*2oz/50g sugar*
4 tsp gelatin	*2 eggs, separated*
[1 tsp vanilla essence]	

Sprinkle the gelatin into a quarter of the milk in a pan and set aside for 10 minutes. Beat the vanilla, sugar, and strained yolks into the milk, then add the rest of the milk, and stir over a gentle heat to 60°C. Remove from the heat, fold in the egg whites, which have been beaten to stiffness, pour into a freshly-rinsed mould, and leave in a cool place overnight before turning out.

Date Jelly [15]

8oz/225g stoned dates	*5 tsp gelatin*
grated zest & juice of 1 lemon	*3 tbs madeira*
pinch ground cinnamon	

Put the dates, lemon and cinnamon into a pan, barely cover with water, and stir 10-15 minutes until tender. Sprinkle the gelatin into ¼pt/150ml cold water. Set aside for 10 minutes, then stir into the dates with the Madeira. Heat and stir over a gentle heat without boiling for 5 minutes. Make up to 1pt/600ml with more water if necessary, then pour into a freshly-rinsed mould and leave to set in a cool place overnight before turning out.

Chocolate Oatmeal Mould
H.A. Bell[16]

This shows how resourceful housewives turned their traditional oatmeal into a moulded dessert.

4oz/100g oatmeal	*2 tsp cocoa*
1pt/600ml milk	*1 tsp vanilla essence*
1 tbs sugar	

Soak the oatmeal overnight in half the milk. Add the remaining milk and simmer for 10-15 minutes while stirring, until tender. Stir in the sugar and cocoa, continue cooking for a further 15 minutes, then stir in the vanilla, turn into a freshly-rinsed mould and turn out when perfectly cold.

The final 'pudding' is quite different from all the others, its Gaelic name 'sowens' revealing its largely Scottish ancestry, although it was regularly made in Northumberland. It was prepared by soaking the 'seeds' or inner husks of oats in water for a few days until they turned sour. The clear water was then poured off and replaced with fresh three separate times, and the resulting liquid strained, boiled until thick, then left to set in bowls. It eats with a yoghurt-like sourness, and is refreshing, if not particularly nourishing, on hot summer days. Some preferred it with a stronger flavour, this being achieved by the use of fish liquor and salt. A similar dish called 'lithics' was made by simply soaking fine oatmeal in water for a short time, without souring, then boiling up the strained liquid to form a Northumbrian baby food.

Sowens

Since oat husks are not generally available, this recipe uses oatmeal.

4oz/100g oatmeal	*2pt/1.2l water*

Mix the oatmeal into the water and leave in a warm place for about 4 or 5 days in summer, up to a couple of weeks in winter. Strain the liquid into a vessel, squeezing out as much as possible from the oats. Mix the oats with a little cold water, and squeeze again into the pan. Discard the oats, and leave the liquid to stand for two days more, then pour off and discard all the clear liquid, and pour the remainder into a saucepan. Boil, while stirring, until it runs off the tip of a wooden spoon 'as thick as a rat's tail', season with a little salt, and pour into freshly-rinsed individual bowls. Eat with cream or whole milk when perfectly cold.

CHAPTER TWELVE

THE DAIRY

Milking flocks of sheep had been a widespread practice in medieval Britain, but had died out in most places by the early nineteenth century, except in north-western Northumberland and into Scotland. Around 1812 'Mary and Bett' were seen milking ewes at Rockley Castle near Wallington, while in Liddesdale, just to the west of the Cheviots;

> They milk their ewes and make their cheese
> and makes fine butter plenty.
> They wash their face young men to please
> [in] cream both sweet and dainty.[1]

If milked two or three times after being separated from their lambs, the ewes continued to thrive, but not if this continued for up to ten weeks. Cheesemaking therefore tended to be an activity of late spring, early summer. It sold at 3d a pound, double that of ordinary cheese, and was renowned for becoming exceedingly pungent if kept for three or four years.[2] The 'very indifferent sorts of cheese, little things, looks black on the outside and soft sower things,' which Celia Fiennes found in Newcastle in 1698 may have included some of this kind.[3]

At this time Wooler had a reputation as a health resort, local people offering visitors whey made from the local herds of feral goats.[4] This was one of the places where, as Thomas Bewick noted, people resort to 'for the purpose of drinking the milk of the Goat; and its effects have been often salutary in vitiated and debilitating habits. The milk of the Goat is sweet, nourishing, and medicinal, and is found highly beneficial in consumptive cases: it is not so apt to curdle upon the stomach as that of the Cow. From the shrubs and heath on which it feeds, the milk of the goat acquires a flavour and wildness of taste very different from that of either the Sheep or Cow, and is highly pleasing to such as have accustomed themselves to its use: it is made into whey for those whose digestion is too weak to bear it in its primitive state'.[5]

In contrast, the use of cow's milk expanded to meet the demands of the north-east's growing population. From around 1800 the region's

THE COMMON GOAT.

(*Capra Hircus*, Lin.—*Le Bouc*, *La Chevre*, Buff.)

40. Thomas Bewick, who engraved this woodcut of a goat, found that its milk was sweet, nourishing, and medicinal, and highly beneficial in cases of consumption. For this reason, goat's milk and whey became a popular early nineteenth century health drink.

Durham Shorthorn cattle were greatly improved by pioneering breeders such as Robert Colling of Barmpton near Darlington and his brother Charles of Ketton Hall. They were the ideal breed for general farms, good producers of both meat and milk; as a result, their use was adopted throughout England and parts of America and Canada.

Dairywork was a female activity, whether for a single cow used by a farm labourer's wife, or a whole herd run by a farmer's wife and her dairymaids. Since they lived a healthy open-air life, had to keep clean and tidy, and, through the immunity of cow-pox, were completely free of disfiguring smallpox, the maids always drew crowds of male admirers, from gentry to the collier lads.

> '*Come now, my young collier, and rest here awhile,*
> *And when I have done milking, I'll give you a smile.*'
> *He kissed her sweet lips while milking her cow;*
> *And the lambs were sporting all in the morning dew ...*
> *Then she clapt her arms around him like Venus round vine*

'You are my jolly collier lad; you've won my heart,
I'll crown you with honour, and ever take your part.'[6]

Her work started when she went to milk the cows, in the pasture in summer or the byre in winter. Having looped a hair-rope tie around its back legs to prevent it from kicking or running off, she squatted at its side on a low stool, her skeel between her shins. A skeel was a cylindrical, coopered 6-gallon tub with one stave extending upwards to act as a handle, and, pressed back against the stool, to hold the skeel in place while milking. Some cows gave as little as 12 pints/7.2 litres a day, others from 20-30 pints/12-18 litres, and even as much as 60 pints/36 litres, depending on the season and quality of the pasture. In the opinion of Arthur Young, writing in 1770, a good cow around Belford gave 48 pints/29 litres a day, eight of these enabling a farmer to feed nine or ten pigs on their whey. One maid could tend ten cows.[7]

CREAM

The maid then carried the skeel back to the dairy on its circular pad, 'skeen' or 'weeze' on her head, with a circular floating wooden stillar on top to prevent spillage. Here it was poured through a sile, a wooden bowl-shaped funnel with a clean muslin sile-clout tied across its open base, in order to remove any grit, grass or bovine dandruff. The clean, fresh milk poured down into a broad, shallow tub with a handle at both sides, this being known as a kit. Left here in the cool overnight, the cream rose to form a layer across the surface. The old way of removing this was to tilt the kit until it was almost overflowing, and then take deep breaths, and blow the cream off into a jar or pot. This unhygienic method was later replaced by using large settling pans of lead or pottery and skimming off the cream with a shallow saucer-shaped wooden scale-dish.[8] In turn, later Victorian dairies purchased Alpha Laval or similar centrifugal cream separating machines which extracted 99.9% of the butter fat, within only a few minutes.

BUTTER

Similar improvements were made in the design of butter churns, the old vertical churns and the barrel churns rotating about the centre of their ends being replaced by more efficient end-over-end models. After the butter had formed, it was removed, rinsed, salted and often coloured to give a richer appearance.[9] Smaller quantities were sold at

41. After milking, the milk was strained through a muslin-bottomed wooden 'sile', mounted on its 'brig' over a milkbowl, and left to settle. Next morning the cream was lifted off with a skimmer (bottom left), and poured into a cream pot (top left) until there was sufficient for churning into butter. After washing and salting, the butter was either beaten into blocks using wooden 'Scotch Hands', or packed into a butter pot (top right) for bulk storage and sale. The butter-dish for table use was distributed to members of the Ryhope and Silksworth cooperative society at Christmas, 1895.

the local markets, larger ones to butter factors, for whom it was packed into coopered firkins such as those made in Cambo or Rothley.[10] These were then shipped out from ports such as Berwick.[11]

CHEESE

The virtually fat-free milk left after the separation of the cream was variously known as blown-milk, blue milk or skimmed milk. It was either used in the home as a drink or an accompaniment to porridge etc., sold into the towns, or made into hard cheese. To do this, it was brought up to blood heat in a large brass cheese-kettle, and then curdled by the addition of 'yearning', a rennet made from a cured calf's stomach known as reed, yearning or keslops in the northern dialects. In North Tynedale the juice of the butterwort, *Pinguicula vulgaris*, was used for the same purpose, also being called yearning.[12]

When the milk had set into a tender, junket-like curd, it was cut through with a knife and the sharp-flavoured whey run off. If flavoured with mint and sage, soured with a little buttermilk, boiled, cooled and

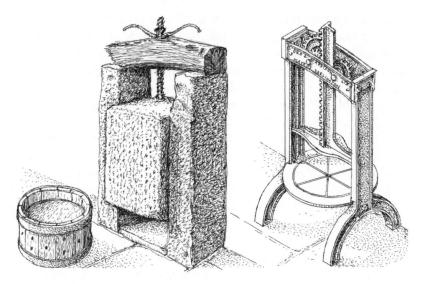

42. The traditional local cheese-presses, such as this example from Bardon Mill, relied on great stone weights, laboriously raised and lowered by an iron screw. Later on, Ord and Maddison of Darlington made improved cast-iron presses, easily adjusted and weighted by a short lever arrangement.

clarified, the whey became whig, a refreshing summertime drink.[13]

The remaining curds were next packed into a muslin-lined open-topped tub called a chesfit or cheesevat, pressed to expel all the remaining whey, and transferred to shelves to mature. This skim-milk cheese was extremely hard and strongly flavoured, its local names of aad-peg, blue-milk or half-nowt cheese hardly being complimentary. It was essentially a cheap, long-lasting everyday cheese for working people.

Better quality whole-milk cheese was also made, but those who could afford it bought in large mature Cheshire cheeses, these being mentioned in the fashionable cookery books published in Georgian Newcastle. The only cheese to have a really good reputation at this time was made in the Teesdale village of Cotherstone. On 12th June, 1792, the honourable John Byng dined at the Bull at Barnard Castle, finishing with 'an excellent cheese, made in Teesdale'. He was so impressed that he set off next morning 'to Cotherstone, where the excellent cheese is made', buying sufficient to pack the pockets of his servant and his local guide, along with bread and ale.[14]

Cotherstone cheese is still in production using unpasteurised milk. Having been left to rise overnight, the cream is skimmed off, heated, and returned to the milk, all then being heated and kept stirred as the rennet is added. After an hour the curd is cubed, milled, salted, lightly packed into lined moulds and pressed for some twelve hours. Ripening takes a further two to three weeks before the cheeses go off to the shops, but may continue for up to two months. The resulting cheeses are a pale creamy colour with a few small, irregular holes, the texture being smooth and the taste mildly acid.[15]

In 1894 Mr J.W. Annett of West Chevington, near the coast between Ashington and Warkworth, tried to find a profitable use for his surplus milk. Experiments with Cheddar cheeses brought little extra income, and so he tried soft cream cheeses similar to Camemberts. Samples circulated to knowledgeable neighbours were enthusiastically received, for they found it to be 'better than Camembert' being equally rich but without the strong taste. By 1896 he gave up the sale of new milk, as production had grown to over two hundred cheeses a week and he was forced to invest in more cows. Miss Annett converted the former turnip houses into a modern cheese dairy with a hot water system to bring milk with a 12-13% cream content up to 90°F/. After renneting it stood for three to four hours, was ladled into tin moulds, turned out after a further day, and then turned daily for six weeks. The result was a delicious, rich cheese, best when covered with a blue mould. In 1898 orders were being received from Berwick to as far as Devonshire, customers including the Home & Colonial Stores in London and H.R.H. The Princess of Wales.[16] A 'Chevington' cheese is still made today by the Northumberland Cheese Company at Wheelbirks, now using milk from a herd of Jersey cows.

On a smaller scale four or five cottagers used to contribute all their milk to each family in turn, so that they might have sufficient to make a cheese. In this way they might be able to prepare fourteen or fifteen ewe or cow milk cheeses each to feed them through the winter months. By around 1900 they had given up their cows, and so had to buy their milk and cheese.[17] A tradition of making fresh cheeses, ready in only a few days or up to a month, still continued into the 1930s, but then disappeared as unpasteurised milk and rennet both became virtually unobtainable.[18]

SUPPER DISHES

Today most people avoid eating cheese at bed-time, believing that it tends to induce indigestion and insomnia. Up to a couple of generations ago the reverse was thought to be true. Then, 'supper' still meant a snack at the very end of the day, rather than a heavy meal eaten in the evening, and cheese was its main ingredient. At its simplest it was just a strong Cheshire cheese, an even stronger English onion cut in slices, and dry white bread, but north-eastern housewives developed a whole series of hot cheese supper dishes, ideal for cold winter nights. They were usually called 'Supper Savouries', best made with a strong Cheshire or Cheddar cheese.

Supper Savouries
1. Mrs L. Richardson, Medomsley[19]

3 large potatoes, peeled and thinly sliced	salt & pepper
3oz/75g grated cheese	½pt/300ml milk

Grease a fireproof dish, lay in half the potatoes, then half the cheese, the remaining potatoes, and the remaining cheese. Sprinkle with salt and pepper, pour on the milk, and bake at 170°C, 325°F, Gas mark 3 for 1 hour. If preferred, a little chopped onion may be put in with the potatoes and cheese.

2. M. Willan, Haydon Bridge[20]

8oz/225g mashed potatoes	1oz/25g butter
2oz/50g grated cheese	2 eggs, separated
2 tbs milk	browned breadcrumbs
salt & pepper	

Mix together everything except the eggs and crumbs. Beat in the yolks, fold in the stiffly-beaten whites, and put into a greased basin lined with the breadcrumbs. Bake at 170°C, 325°F, Gas mark 3 for 30 minutes, then turn out onto a plate.

3. Mrs J.S. Davidson, Barmoor Bank, Morpeth[21]

3oz/75g fresh breadcrumbs	1 egg, beaten
2oz/50g grated cheese	½ tsp made mustard
1oz/25g butter	salt & pepper
½pt/300ml milk	

Put the bread and cheese in a basin, pour over the butter melted in the milk, mix, stir in the egg and remaining ingredients and bake at 170°C, 325°F, Gas mark 3 for 30 minutes.

4. Mrs L. Richardson, Medomsley [22]

8oz/225g onion, sliced	*1oz/25g butter*
8oz/225g grated cheese	*salt & pepper*

Pack the onion in a baking dish, sprinkling with salt and pepper, top with the cheese, dot with the butter, and bake at 170°C, 325°F, Gas mark 3 for 30 minutes.

Apple & Cheese Savoury
Mrs W. Little, Hat & Feather Inn [23]

1 large cooking apple	*4 slices hot toast*
1oz/25g butter	*4 slices cheese*

Peel and core the apple, cut in 4 rounds and fry in the butter for about 10 minutes until soft. Place a round on each piece of toast, top with the cheese and grill until melted.

Cheese Pancakes

4oz/100g plain flour	*½pt/300ml milk*
salt & pepper	*1 egg*
3-4oz/75-100g grated cheese	*fat for frying*

Sift the flour into a bowl with a little salt and pepper, drop in the egg and beat in the flour, adding the milk little by little to produce a smooth batter, then set aside for 2 hours. Stir in about half the cheese and fry as pancakes. When cooked on both sides sprinkle on some of the remaining cheese, roll up and serve.

Hot Cheese Spread
Mrs Graham[24]

½pt/300ml milk
2oz/50g grated cheese
½ tsp salt

½ tsp made mustard
1 egg, beaten
¼pt/150ml water

Stir all together continuously in a bain-marie until thickened, then pour over hot toast and serve immediately.

Cheese Sausages
Mrs J. Berwick, Sunderland[25]

6oz/175g plain flour
½ tsp baking powder
2oz/50g dripping, lard or butter
salt & pepper

2oz/50g grated cheese
a little milk & water
fat for deep-frying

Mix the flour with the baking powder, rub in the butter, stir in the salt and pepper, cheese, and just enough liquid to form a very stiff dough. Divide into pieces, roll as sausages and deep-fry until golden brown.

Whitley Bayweet

4 onions, peeled
2 tbs grated cheese

¼pt/150ml milk

Put the onions into cold water, bring to the boil, and simmer until tender. Drain the onions, chop them finely and season to taste. Put into a fireproof dish, pour in the milk, sprinkle with the cheese, and bake at 180°C, 350°F, Gas mark 4 for 15 minutes.

Cheese Stew[26]

onions, peeled and sliced
salt & pepper

milk
sliced cheese

Put the onions into a frying pan, almost cover with milk, season to taste, cover with a plate, and simmer until just tender. Lay the cheese on top, replace the plate, and simmer for a further 10 minutes before serving with thickly-sliced bread.

Hot cheese dishes such as these make very satisfying and savoury dishes, but in no way detract from the pleasures of eating simple, raw cheese. Their textures, the way their individual curds or even consistencies dissolve in the mouth, their variations in scent and flavour from their centres to their rinds, all create interest and pleasure. Added variety is provided by the traditional accompaniments of crusty bread, rye or oatmeal bannocks, crisp oatcakes, biscuits, pickles or apples.

When eaten in the fields, the piece of cheese, often as hard, mature and well-flavoured as Parmesan, was gripped between the thumb and first two fingers of the left hand, the two smaller fingers holding the hunk of bread against the palm. This enabled pieces of both to be cut off between the thumb and a pocket knife clasped in the right hand, and carried up to the lips, an efficient method of eating without a plate.

At table, the old rule of 'cut high, cut low, cut even', taking horizontal segments from the top, so that everyone got the same proportions of inner cheese and rind, was the general rule. Those who selfishly dug into the centre in the manner of the gentry faced severe reprimands from working housewives. In the 1780s Betty Allen took great pride and pleasure in setting a fine cheese before Mr. Bell, a visiting preacher. She had journeyed into Newcastle to find the best she could to serve at her Willy's funeral, but as he had unexpectedly recovered, it had been kept for a special occasion. Taking up the knife, the polite Mr Bell plunged it into the very centre, little expecting the inevitable explosion;

> 'Man, what are ye howking there for? Who learned ye to cut cheese that way?!'
> 'It is genteel to cut cheese in this way.'
> 'I like none of your genteel ways, sic fashions will not do here! Who is going to eat the crust after ye? Cut fair!'[27]

He should not have been surprised if the cheese was set before him bottom-up on his next visit, this being the cheesy equivalent of 'mooning' to show disrespect to the guest.[28]

CHAPTER THIRTEEN

OF BANNOCKS, LOAVES AND STOTTIES

The traditional breads of the region varied considerably from one locality to another. This was partly due to the influence of climate and geology on the kinds of grain-crops which could be grown, and partly on cultural differences which perhaps reflected the practices of various peoples who settled here over a thousand years ago. All the earliest breads were baked on a stone slab heated over a low fire, and therefore had to be relatively flat in order to cook through completely. Of these, the thin, crisp oatcakes called havercakes, from the Old Norse 'haver', meaning oats, were particularly associated with the south-western areas, around upper Teesdale, upper Weardale, and the south of County Durham. Not surprisingly, these were the major areas of Old Norse colonisation. Similarly the thick, leavened oatmeal 'jannocks' also made in Lancashire and Cumbria, appear to have had Old Norse origin.

Further north in County Durham and southern Northumberland, the main area of Anglian settlement, ryebreads predominated, this grain having been introduced into England with the Angles and Saxons about the 6th century A.D. The northern parts of Northumberland, meanwhile, preferred barley as their main breadcorn crop, perhaps reflecting a Scottish influence. Throughout all of these areas, wheat was usually considered to be the superior corn, especially when yeast-raised to produce light, spongy loaves. Even in the nineteenth century, individual communities still retained a strong preference for their particular kind of bread. When the pitmen were given barley instead of wheat in 1795, for example, they 'rioted and positively refused Barley even in mixture with other Grain, explaining that the Owners wished to feed them like swine' and that barley bread was 'as course and black as the coal'.[1] Those living in northern Northumberland would never have made such a complaint about their daily bread.

In the rural areas of Northumberland, where the farm workers received part of their wages in corn, and gleaned the ears of corn left in the fields after harvest, they had to arrange for it to be ground into meal.[2] Once threshed on the doorstep using a 'bittle', the corn was first tossed in a large sheepskin 'tambourine' called a wite, so that the wind could carry off the chaff.[3] It was then collected by the carter who took it to the mill, where it was ground between gritstone millstones. Instead of being paid for this service, the miller extracted a quart from every bushel, (one thirty-second part) as his fee, measuring this with a 7ins/18cm dish.[4] There was always a strong suspicion that the millers always took more than their due, and grew wealthy by cheating their customers. One of the songs in the Northumberland Minstrelsy tells the story of a miller who, on his deathbed, called in each of his three sons in turn, in order to decide which one should succeed him. On being asked how much meal he would take as his fee, the first answered a quarter, the second answered half, while the third;

"Father," said he, "I'm your only boy
For taking toll is all my joy;
Before I will a good living lack,
I'll take it all, and foreswear the sack."

"Thow art the boy" the old man said,
"For thou has right well learned thy trade;
This mill to thee I give", he cried,
And then turned up his toes and died.[5]

Usually the batches of wholemeal flours were carried back to each customer by a man called a 'poker', as he carried it in a poke or bag. Since he had a reputation for helping himself to its contents, he often attracted the chant of;

Millery! Millery! Moonty-poke!
Put in your hand and steal a loke!

For oats there was a different procedure, a messenger telling each household when their grain had been ground, and when they were to go to the mill to see it weighed. Usually it was the wives who attended, then selling some to the miller in return for either cash or the value in provisions. This was seen as an opportunity for a tea party, usually held in the house of the foreman miller, his wife being allowed one or two young pigs as payment.[6]

On returning home with the ground meal, it was first passed through a sieve to extract the coarse husks. One found in a barn at Broom House, Cambo, in 1918 was made of a wooden hoop 19ins/48cm wide by 2½ins/6.5cm high covered by a skin pierced by 75 quarter- to eight-inch/6·3cm holes.[7] If finer meal or flour was required, it was next passed through a temse. This took the form of a square sieve with a fine horsehair cloth across its base, which slid on two runners mounted on a frame over a table or meal ark. Batches were then put in the top and the sieve shaken rapidly backwards and forwards so that only the finer particles would fall through.[8]

FLATBREADS

Flatbreads, baked on a piece of flagstone heated over a small fire on the hearth, were the staple food of most working people in the northern counties. They were quickly made, required neither expensive equipment nor costly fuels, and had a very long shelf-life. Their main characteristic, when compared to modern bread, was their robust solidity; whether thin and crisp, or thick and dense, they exercised the teeth and provided a wide range of textures and flavours.

Whatever their main ingredient, their doughs were mixed in bowls and shaped on baking boards called 'backboards'. The hands were used to form them into loaves, or beat them into wafer-thin cakes, since most mixtures were so 'short' that a rolling pin cracked and broke them into pieces as they lacked the elasticity of wheat doughs.

For the actual baking, the traditional utensil was a slab of fire-resistant flagstone called a bakestone. It was often three or four feet in diameter so that it might hold a couple of cakes, and was fixed on three or four low pillars presumably on the broad hearth of inglenook fireplaces.[9] This was gradually replaced by the girdle, an iron plate usually about 12ins/30cm in diameter fitted with an arching bow handle and a swivelling loop for suspension. Hung from a reckon-hook over the fire on an open hearth, or over a low fire in a range, it provided a very convenient hotplate for baking, so long as the housewife knew how to control the temperature. The best fuels were cheap, rapidly burning waste products such as straw, heath, fern, furze or oat husks which could be fed beneath the bakestones or girdles to maintain an even heat, this process being called 'beeting'.

Today a girdle may still be used over gas or electric stoves on their lowest settings. On electric stoves it is best to raise the girdle a couple of inches above the ring on an iron trivet, meanwhile turning the oven on to its lowest setting to activate the cooling fan. Placing it directly on the ring causes hot-spots to develop on its surface and also reflects heat back into the stove, risking damage to its internal wiring.

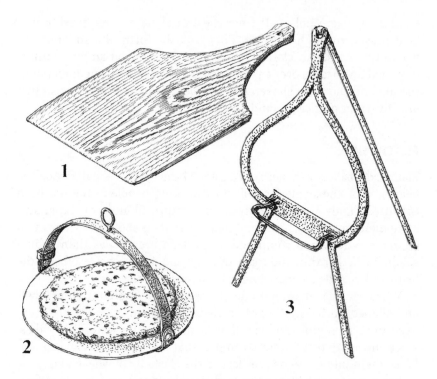

43. Baking various bannocks, oatcakes and flatbreads required only the most basic equipment, such as a cake-turner (1) an iron girdle 2) and a cake-stool, on which the thicker cakes were propped before the fire to finally cook through and dry out.

The traditional method of testing the temperature was to scatter a little flour across its surface, where it should slowly brown, rather than smouldering. For most flatbreads this is usually too hot. It should be just hot enough for the flour to cake and crack, or for a drop of water on the rim to boil away in a few seconds, rather than sizzle into steam. However, the only real solution is to gain practical experience by baking a few trial pieces. A thinly rolled oatcake might take only three or four minutes on each side, for example, while a thick bannock may need 15 minutes on each side to cook through while only lightly browning its crust.

Even after being removed from the girdle, the thicker bannocks still required further baking. The undercooked edges might be rotated before the fire by laying the bannock on a pair of tongs bridging from the middle firebar to a stool, for example. Alternatively it could be finished by being popped on an easel-shaped 'cyek toaster' or 'bread sticks' before the fire to brown. The final drying out and storage took place on the cake-creel rack or the flakes, laths nailed to the underside of the kitchen ceiling joists, an ideal location, well away from rats, mice, cats, dogs and children. The following sections describe the different kinds of flatbreads made in the north-east.

OATCAKES

Oatcakes, sometimes called havercakes from the Norse *haver*, meaning oats, were known in the north-east, but did not form a major part of the regional diet. When they were made, they were crisp and rather similar to modern Scottish oatcakes, except for their shape.

Oatcakes
Mrs Marshall, Low Fell[10]

4oz/100g medium oatmeal	*pinch of salt*
½ tsp bicarbonate of soda	*1 tsp lard or dripping*

Mix the oatmeal, soda and salt, in a small bowl, add the lard, and pour in 2-3 tbs boiling water. Quickly stir together to form a dough, turn onto a board, sprinkled with sifted oatmeal (or flour) and form into a flat, round cake. Press the thumbs into the centre, until ⅛ins/3mm above the board, then use the thumbs to gradually extend this thin area, leaving a thick rim around the edge, meanwhile rotating it so that it does not stick to the board, until it has formed a 10ins/25cm circle. This takes a little practice, but is much better than using a rolling pin, which causes the cake to break up. Cut into four segments and bake each one on a medium-hot girdle until lightly browned on the underside and beginning to smell of scorching.

JANNOCK/RIDDLE-CAKE

Oatmeal contains very little gluten, the elastic substance which enables wheat bread to develop its fine spongy texture when fermented with yeast. This is why the oatcakes of Scotland, Wales and most of the northern counties are baked crisp and flat. In Northumberland, however, an unusual form of yeast-raised oatcakes was made which used yeast to give a lighter consistency. Since its delicate yeasted bubbles were easily burst if the uncooked dough was disturbed, it was left on a round, wood-rimmed riddle to rise, and then very carefully transferred to the girdle. Hence its name.[11]

Jannock/Riddle-cake

6oz/175g fine oatmeal   pinch of salt
½ tsp dried yeast   ¼pt tepid water

Mix the salt into the oatmeal, together with the dried yeast (unless the manufacturer's instructions state that it should be creamed) and mix in sufficient tepid water to form a mixture like sloppy porridge. Shake a thin layer of oatmeal through a sieve onto a piece of thin, stiff card, turn the oatmeal mixture onto it, and form into a flat-topped disc around 6ins/15cm in diameter [using the back of a fork]. Shake a little more oatmeal on top, cover with a light cloth, and stand in a warm place for about an hour to rise. Remove the cloth and slide the oatmeal 'jannock' on to the cool bakestone, leave to cook slowly for about 15 minutes on one side, then use the card again to turn it over, and cook the other side for about the same time. Continue turning if necessary until baked through and lightly browned on both sides.

The resulting jannock is crisp on the outside, and moist within. It eats well split in two, buttered, and eaten with either cheese or jams.

CRUPPY DOWS

In Northumberland, these jannocks/riddlecakes had fish added to their doughs. These were highly-esteemed, and a speciality of Spital-ford, as is described in this traditional verse recited by Mrs Aynsley of Embleton in 1891;

Dunstan-steads for loggerheads,
An' Craster for crowdies,
Spital-ford for cruppy-dows,
And Embleton for howdies.[12]

BARLEY BANNOCKS

Writing in 1805, John Bailey and George Culley recorded that in the northern parts of Northumberland;

Barley, or barley bread mixed with grey pease or beans is the common bread of the labouring people; previous to grinding, they are mixed in the proportions of two parts barley, and one of pease or beans; after being ground, the meal is sifted through a fine sieve, made of wood, to take out the rough husks and coarse bran; it is then kneaded with water, made into thin *unleavened cake*, and immediately baked on a girdle – In this district, barley or mixed meal is seldom, if ever, *leavened* and *baked in loaves*.[13]

This may have been the kind of barley cake which Thomas Bewick ate with cheese when walking up to Berwick, but other writers remembered the same mixture being baked as 'large thick loaves the size of the girdle'.[14] When the latter had been cooked on both sides, they were placed on an iron bracket and gradually turned to cook their edges. Most were made of coarsely-sieved barley flour but if coarse meal was used they became 'barley duggers'.

Barley Bannocks (thin)

for each cake take 3oz/75g barley flour, a pinch of salt and about 3 tbs cold water

Mix the ingredients together, kneading in the flour to form a firm dough. Shape as a round, flat cake on a floured board, press the thumbs down into the cake until almost touching the board, then thumb down the outer rim, expanding the central area and maintaining a thicker rim while rotating the cake, until it has been transformed into a large disc. Carefully roll out to 10ins/25cm diameter, slide onto a piece of thin, stiff card, and transfer to a moderately heated girdle. When the underside has slightly browned, turn over, using two pieces of card, and bake the other side.

Barley Bannocks (thick)

Since coarse barley meal is hardly ever stocked in shops, this version adds wheat bran to replace that removed from barley flour.

14oz/400g barley flour	*pinch of salt*
2oz/50g wheat bran	*½pt/300ml cold water*

Mix the ingredients and knead to form a soft dough. Turn on to a floured board and work with the hands to form a 10ins/25cm flat-topped circle. Use a piece of thin, stiff card to transfer to a cool girdle, and cook one side, and then the other, to a pale brown. To bake the edges, finish off at 200°C, 400°F, Gas mark 6 for 10 minutes.

THARF CAKE

Tharf cake was the common thin, crisp bread of the region. Elsewhere, to the south and west, oatcake supplied a similar alternative, but here oats were mainly used for making porridge and crowdy. The thin tharf cake combined barley flour and wholewheat flour with milk to produce a stiff dough which was then baked crisp.[15]

Tharf Cake

For each cake take:	*1oz/25g barley flour*
1oz/25g wholewheat flour	*pinch of salt*
2½ tbs milk	

Mix the milk into the dry ingredients, knead and work into a round, flat cake on a floured board, then roll out to 9ins/23cm diameter disc. Bake on a low/medium girdle for 3-4 minutes each side, then remove and cool on a flat surface.

Sometimes a thicker tharf cake was made of wheatmeal, pea-meal and dressed 'chissel' or bran. Whichever was available, it was considered to be quite poor food, since some groups of Northumbrians 'never gat owse better than thaaf-kyahyk'.

RYEBREAD

In the southern part of Northumberland rye, both locally grown and imported, was 'the most general bread of the labouring people. After being leavened until it gains a considerable degree of acidity, it is made into loaves and baked in a large brick oven, or made into cakes, one and a half, or two inches thick called 'sour-cakes' and baked on the girdle: the bread is very firm and solid, dark coloured, and retains its moisture or juiciness longer than any bread we know.'[16] This was the 'black, sour rye loaf' that Thomas Bewick ate as a child at Cherryburn, and the 'black rye bread' that fed the people of Teesdale.[17]

To make ryebread it is first necessary to make a 'sourdough starter';

Rye Loaves

20oz/550g rye flour   *½ tsp salt*

Mix a cup of flour with an equal amount of water, cover, leave overnight in a warm place, then mix in another cup of flour with enough water to make a thick paste, and keep covered in the warm for another two nights.

Knead the rest of the flour into an equal weight of the spongy, sour mixture, with the salt and enough tepid water to make a soft dough, then leave covered in the warm overnight.

Knead the dough again and either;

a) mould into round cakes 1ins/2·5cm thick, cover with a light cloth, leave to rise in the warm for 2 hours, then bake for 15 minutes each side on a cool girdle, or

b) put into a greased loaf tin, cover with a light cloth, leave to rise in the warm for 2 hours, then bake at 190°C, 375°F, Gas mark 5 for an hour, then reduce to 170°C, 325°F, Gas mark 3 for a further 30 minutes.

WHEAT FLATBREADS

White flour, 'bolted' by being shaken through a fine cloth was seen as a real luxury, and so was reserved for making the following enriched flatbreads for special occasions.

NED, NEDDY & NODDING CAKES

Because fats had to be kneaded into flour to make flatbreads, they became known collectively as 'knedding'. From this use, some breads became known as 'kned cakes', which later generations of housewives mistook for either the nick-name of all Edwards, or for nodding.[18] Earlier versions, made up to the mid-late Victorian period, were of white wheat flour, cream and fresh butter, but no sugar, to give a delicate white shortbread, sometimes called 'white loaf'.[19] Rolled out the size of a girdle and ½ins/12mm thick, it was baked on both sides on the girdle, cut in squares and piled up on plates especially for friend's visits or as a treat for youngsters.[20]

Neddycake[21]

8oz/225g plain flour	*¼ tsp salt*
3oz/75g butter	*6 tbs cream*

Rub the butter into the flour and salt, and mix in sufficient cream with a fork to form a light pastry. Pat out to some 8ins/20cm diameter, slide on to the cool girdle, and cook gently on both sides with little or no browning. Cut in squares and serve.

Later versions used lard instead of butter and cream, but also added baking powder to give a spongier texture.

Nodding Cake[22]

9oz/250g plain flour	*1 tsp baking powder*
4oz/100g lard	*3-4 tbs water*
¼ tsp salt	

Rub the lard into the flour, mix in the salt and baking powder, then the water, using a fork, to form a dough. Roll out 8ins/20cm in diameter, prick with a fork, and oven bake at 200°C, 400°F, Gas mark 6 for 12-15 minutes until risen and lightly browned.

The fatless version of nodding cakes were called Fancy Nancy, the use of baking powder enabling them to rise quickly on the girdle.

Fancy Nancy[23]

12oz/325g plain flour	*¾ tsp salt*
½pt/300ml buttermilk or soured milk	
1½ tsp baking powder	

Mix the dry ingredients, then stir in just sufficient liquid with a fork to form a soft dough. Roll out 10ins/25cm diameter and slide on to the girdle at a medium heat. Turn over when the underside is brown, using two pieces of thin, stiff card, then cook the other side, after which it will have doubled in thickness. Traditionally the under-baked edges were baked by the radiant heat of the coal-fired range. The long iron tongs formed a bridge between the middle firebar and a stool, so that the cake could be gradually rotated there until browned all round. Today the only practical alternative is to finish them by baking at 200°C, 400°F, Gas mark 6 for some 15 minutes.

When cold, they were cut into squares, split and buttered.

LOAVES

In order to bake loaves of bread it was essential to have access to an oven which provided an all-round heat. A cast-iron cauldron or 'yetling' hung over the fire might form a useful substitute, but nothing could replace a proper built-in oven. Castles, peel-towers, large houses and many farms had used them for centuries. They took the form of domed masonry chambers built into the thickness of a wall, a square opening at the front being provided for inserting the fuel and the loaves. In use, bundles of brushwood called faggots were speared by an iron fork, held over a fire until alight, and then thrust into the back of the oven. Here a steady current of fresh air was pulled in from the oven door, across the flat floor, to feed the flames that now licked the underside of the dome, to bring it up to a fierce heat. The smoke then escaped from the upper part of the oven door into either the main chimney, or into a specially-built smoke-hood with its own flue to the open air.

Once up to temperature, a hoe-like rake or fruggin was used to extract the embers, this being followed by a mailkin or malin, a few wet rags fastened to the end of a stick, which removed the finer ashes and also introduced a little steam into the oven, which helped to produce better loaves. If necessary the oven might also be 'brianed', or kept hot, by keeping some of the fire close to the mouth of the oven, either to illuminate its dark interior for arranging the bakery, or to maintain its heat. The bread was now inserted using a long-handled, flat-bladed oven-slice called a peel, the doorway closed and sealed in place with clay called ditten, and the contents left to bake.[24]

In the towns and larger villages those without an oven could take their oven-ready foods to the local baker, who would bake them in his

44. There was a long tradition of using communal open-air ovens in the North-east, one still remaining by the churchyard at Corbridge. Luke Clennell, one of Thomas Bewick's major pupils, painted this example on the quayside. The lady on the right has just now raked the burning embers out onto the ground, and is using her fruggin, an oven-mop just soaked in her bucket of water, to clean out the fire ashes before inserting her loaves

own oven for a small fee. This could be a risky business, however. One family on the Tweed sometimes found that the rabbit they had put into their pie had 'had an accident' at the bakers' and lost one of its legs, since the baker was adept at lifting up the crust and helping himself to part of the contents!²⁵

When new pit villages were being constructed in the early nineteenth century, few of the cottages were fitted with their own ovens. Instead, a communal oven was provided for each row, sometimes as part of a block of other conveniences, such as coal-places, privies and ash-holes. The 1841 report on child employment recorded that each row of pit cottages had such an oven. The Stella Colliery Company was still providing them in the 1850s-60s, one to serve about every five households, those built by Thomas March costing 55s (£2.75p) each. Every baking day the women took it in turn to clean the oven and bring it up to temperature with firewood she had gathered. On finishing her batch of loaves, which took about an hour, another brought hers, continuing in succession until all had finished.[26] Many continued in use after each cottage had been fitted with its own oven, even into the early twentieth century. However, the Ordnance Survey maps show that most of those built before 1856 had been demolished as they became obsolete, over the next forty years. As at Ryton in the 1840s, 'Baking day was religiously looked forward to by all the youngsters, who could be seen hanging round when the large brown loaves were being taken out. In the baking many of the loaves had developed a bump. This the good wife broke off and many hands were ready to catch the delicious morsel.[27]

YEASTS

The traditional yeasts used to convert solid dough into a spongy mass were usually either sourdoughs as used for ryebreads, or ale-yeasts derived from brewing ales. Other yeasts were home-made using blends of hops, sugar, flour and left-over yeasts, some housewives skilled in this craft making an additional income by selling their yeasts on to their neighbours.[28] These yeasts were slow to act, being mixed with flour and left overnight to form a sponge which could then be kneaded with extra flour and formed into loaves, but they produced good-flavoured bread which lasted quite a few days before going stale. The mid nineteenth century saw the first introduction of yeast in the form of a white, almost cheese-like solid called either dried, compressed, or German yeast. At first it was imported from Holland, but then began to be made by specialist producers in this country, and became our everyday yeast for all forms of bread. It had only to be brought from the grocers', 'creamed' with a little tepid water and sugar, and then kneaded with the flour to produce a reliable, comparatively speedy 'rise'.

45. After being kneaded and left to rise in a warm pank or bowl (left), the dough was formed into tin-loaves or stotty cakes. After baking, many families kept their bread in the large covered jars or bread-crocks made in the Sunderland and Newcastle potteries.

BREAD MUGS

The traditional brown-ware potteries of Tyneside, Sunderland, Preston Pans over the Scottish border, and a few more rural works, provided a ready source of glazed earthenware bowls for breadmaking.[29] The largest, up to 2ft/60cm diameter, were ideal for mixing and kneading dough, and for setting it on the fender by the fire for it to rise beneath a light cloth. They also made bread-pots, tall convex-sided jars with lids, handles near the rim, and frequently parallel encircling bands of white slip-trailed decoration. These were used to store the baked loaves, keeping them in good condition for up to a week.

BARLEY LOAVES

In 1942 the Rev. N.A. Wilson, the vicar of Alston, asked one of his oldest parishioners for the local recipes used for making barley loaves and barley cakes. Her mother had made sourdough rye loaves, but the method had already been forgotten. However, she was able to provide him with detailed information on barley loaves.

Barley Loaves[30]

1lb/450g barley meal	*1tbs salt*
8oz/225g plain flour	*½ tsp yeast*

'Put meal, flour, salt into bowl, mix well, make hole in centre and add water, then add yeast which has previously risen by the fire, in half a pint of water [and just under 1½pts tepid water]. Mix thoroughly to a nice soft dough, cover, keep warm, set to rise in a bowl ¾hour. Take up, form it into loaves in two large greased loaf tins, and set to rise ¾ of an hour. Then put into brick oven [or oven at 220°C, 425°F, Gas mark 7 for 15 minutes, then at 180°C, 350°F, Gas mark 4 for about 30-40 minutes]. Turn out of the tins and leave to cool.'

Barley Cake with Baking Powder

1lb/450g barley meal	*1¼ tsp baking powder*
about ½pt/300ml skim milk	*[pinch of salt]*

'Mix barley, salt, Baking powder and mix well with the milk. Divide into 2 cakes, form into balls, put out with the hand until the size of a cheese plate [6ins/15cm]. Put on a baking sheet and bake quickly [at 200°C, 400°F, Gas mark 6 for about 20 minutes].'

MASLIN BREAD

In 1810 John Bailey's *General View of the Agriculture of Durham* described the bread of 'the labouring classes' as being maslin, raised with yeast and baked as loaves known as brown bread. Maslin was a mixed crop of wheat and rye grown together then ground and baked to produce a well-flavoured and long-lasting bread. Its use was not restricted to this county, for it was made in Northumberland and Yorkshire too, but here it formed part of most meals, bread and milk appearing for breakfast, dinner and supper.

Maslin Brown Bread
Mrs Lucas, Low Fell[31]

Use the wholemeal loaf recipe below, but use 10oz/275g rye flour and 6oz/175g wholemeal flour, and mix well with 1½ tsp black treacle.

WHOLEMEAL BREAD

Wholemeal was the preferred working-class bread-flour wherever wheat was available. It might have the coarser husks removed, but many families used the meal just as it came from the mill.

Wholemeal Household Loaf

1lb/450g wholemeal flour	1 tsp dried yeast
½ tsp salt	11fl oz/325ml tepid water
1oz/25g lard	

Mix the flour and salt and rub in the lard. Mix in the dried yeast (or creamed with a little of the warm water and some sugar, according to the manufacturer's instructions). Stir in the water, then knead on a floured board for about 10 minutes, return to the bowl, cover with a light cloth, and leave to rise in a warm place for about an hour, until doubled in size. Turn the dough out onto a floured board, knead for a few minutes, into a smooth ball, and place in a greased 2lb/1kg loaf tin. Cover and return to the warm for about half an hour to rise again, then bake at 220°C, 425°F, Gas mark 7 for 15 minutes, then reduce to 180°C, 350°F, Gas mark 4 for a further 20-25 minutes.

If a finer loaf was needed, the wholemeal flour was sifted to remove the bran and mixed with sifted rye flour. The result was called booted or bolted bread. Some Newcastle bakers specialised in its production, an advertisement of 1828 reading; 'Hay and Maclean, Bolted bread

46. Ralph Hedley's 'Sounding the Bread' shows an elderly lady knocking the base of her loaf to hear the hollow sound which confirmed that it was done.

bakers, No. 14. Side, Newcastle.'[32] A modern version may be made by baking a mixture of half strong white bread flour and half rye flour, to the recipe above.

WHITE LOAVES

Some writers, such as William Cobbett, were already championing the continued use of wholewheat bread in the 1820s, claiming that 'The finest [white] flour is by no means the most wholesome; and, at any rate, there is more nutritious matter in a pound of [wholemeal] household bread, than in a pound of baker's [white] bread.'[33] Even so, bread made with finely sifted white flour was always seen as the very best by most working families, something especially good, particularly as it was the bread eaten by all the nobility, gentry, merchants and clergy. As a result, the use of white bread became widespread as conditions improved throughout the Victorian period.

White Loaf

Use the Wholemeal Loaf recipe above, but with strong white bread flour and 1/2pt/300ml warm water.

Most white loaves were baked in large rectangular tinplate loaf-tins, wider at the top than the bottom, and finished with a wired-edged rim for safety. Usually designed for two-pound loaves, they were in regular use in most large families where two or three might be eaten every day.[34] Other families might prefer to make cottage loaves, with a small round loaf baked on top of another.[35] Not only did this save space in the oven, but when torn apart, it provided two loaves which could be used separately. Any dough left over from either tin or cottage loaves was made up into small, round and flattish cakes called fadges, this being the local word for anything short, round and dumpy.

White bread dough was also used to make different kinds of loaves. At Catless Farm, North Tyne, Mrs M.A. Telfer used to roll out a piece of dough and then scatter it with some carefully sorted bran taken from the animals' feed bin.[36] When folded over and baked it made bran bread, delicious when spread with butter and jam. A pound of white dough could also be rolled out, sprinkled with 2oz/50g each or lard, sugar and raisins, folded over a few times and baked in a heavily greased tin to make a lardy cake. Delicious with its bands of toffee-like caramel and fruit, it was made by a number of north-eastern housewives, such as Mrs Elsie Ryan of Sherburn village, around 1914.[37] The unexpected appearance of this classic item of Hampshire, Wiltshire and Oxfordshire bakery in this region provides an interesting example of a recipe brought in by families moving from the rural south to the booming industries of the north.

FADGE

The traditional fadge of northern Northumberland was an oval bannock some two or three inches thick, made of pease-meal and some bean-meal, and baked hard on a girdle. By the mid nineteenth century 'Fadges' were also lighter and spongier rolls made from wheat flour, the *Keelmins Comic Annewel* of 1869 describing how 'She m'yeks hor fadjes o' breed.'[38] Some were made up of the dough left over after filling the loaf-tins, while others were made specially. The following recipe dates from around 1907 and was used by Margaret Robson of Thornburn Colliery. It uses some wholemeal flour, but many others were made from ordinary white bread dough.

Fadge[39]

3oz/75g wholemeal flour	*1oz/25g lard*
7oz/200g plain flour	*½ tsp salt*
2 tsp baking powder	

Mix the dry ingredients and rub into the lard, then make a well in the centre, pour in about ¼ pt/150ml cold water, work in from the sides and knead with a little more water if necessary to form a soft dough. Form into a round cake about 6ins/15cm across, place on a greased baking sheet and bake at 220°C, 425°F, Gas mark 7 for 30 minutes.

Within the next generation or two the fadge had disappeared from the local vocabulary. It was still being made in the same way, and had grown enormously in popularity, but was now known by a completely different name;

THE STOTTY

Every region has its 'national' dish, one that gives it a particular claim to fame, like Yorkshire's pudding and Cornwall's pasty. One of these, for the north-east, and Tyneside in particular, must surely be the stotty. It is a flattish, round breadcake made of spongy white dough, ideal for making sandwiches, being cut in half and spread with anything from dripping or butter to jam, or eaten alongside a meal. It is the regional version of the flat round white breadcakes once baked on both sides on a bakestone, like Yorkshire's oven-bottom cakes or Lancashire's barm cakes. As a fadge, it had a long history in the region, only becoming a stotty in the 1930s. The word itself has strong Scottish and Northumbrian roots and means 'to bounce'. A cork bound in worsted thread to make a bouncing ball, or later a rubber ball, was known here as a 'stotty-ball', for example.[40] The springy, spongy texture of the fadge/stotty appears to be the reason for the change of name. Interestingly enough, those asked to define the stotty in recent years all gave its previous titles;

'Oven-bottom cake is known as 'stotty cake'.
'My granny used to call stottie cakes 'oven bottom cakes'.'
'the stottie cake ... we used to call them fadges'[41]

Stotty Cakes

Roll out a lump of white bread dough (see the recipe on p.162) to about 8-9ins/20-23cm diameter and ½ ins/12mm thick, cover with a light cloth and leave in a warm place for 30-40 minutes until doubled in size. Bake at 220°C, 425°F, Gas mark 7 for about 30 minutes.

Enriched versions of the fadge/stotty were called;

WIGS & TEACAKES

Originating back in the fourteenth century, wigs were small yeast-raised bread-buns made of fine wheat flour. They were still popular throughout the Georgian period, those in Elizabeth Taylor's *Art of Cookery* being enriched with butter, sugar, eggs, milk, currants, candied peel and brandy.[42] By the mid nineteenth century their name had changed to the modern form 'teacake', a potential cause of real confusion, as one Newcastle lass discovered when working as a servant in London. Asking where she could buy wigs, she was directed to a barber's shop, where her request for half a dozen 'spice wigs' for tea quite astonished the proprietor. Mrs Rachel Pease of Darlington, who died in 1833, already preferred to call her spice wigs 'tea cakes' in her recipe book:

Tea Cakes

18oz of Flour, 4oz of Butter, 1 Gill of Milk, 1 Spoonful of Yeast, 2 Eggs & a little Sugar, Lemon & Currants.[43]

No method was given, since she already knew how to make tea cakes. However, very similar recipes were being used here a hundred years or more later:

Teacakes
Miss Hutchinson, Annfield Plain[44]

8oz/225g strong white flour	*½oz/12g candied peel*
½ tsp salt	*1oz/25g currants*
½oz/12g butter	*½ tsp dried yeast*
½ tsp sugar	*¼pt/150ml tepid milk*

Stir the salt into the flour, rub in the butter, mix in the sugar, peel and currants and add the yeast dry or creamed according to the manufacturer's instructions. Mix in the milk to form a dough, knead for 5 minutes and leave in a warm place until doubled in size. Knead lightly, make up as three round, flat cakes, set on a baking tray, cover lightly, and return to the warm until risen. Bake at 200°C, 400°F, Gas mark 6 for 10-15 minutes.

Other teacakes were made in the same way, perhaps mixed with buttermilk, sometimes enriched with sugar and eggs, and sometimes without any fruit, to be served as 'plain teacakes'. They were best served by being sliced in half, toasted on both sides before the fire, and spread with butter.[45]

MUFFINS

Today most people think that a muffin is a rich cup-cake, both of these words demonstrating the way in which American usage mangles the English language. A real, original muffin is quite different, being a light yeast-raised bread bun baked on a girdle or hotplate, its spongy crumb being designed to absorb lashings of butter when served piping hot.

Muffins

1oz/25g butter	*1lb/450g plain flour*
1 egg, beaten	*1 tsp salt*
½pt/300ml milk	*1 tsp dried yeast*

Warm the butter, beat in the egg and milk. Mix the flour with the salt, and the yeast either dried or creamed following the manufacturer's instructions, and the milk mixture, to form a soft dough. Knead for 5-10 minutes,

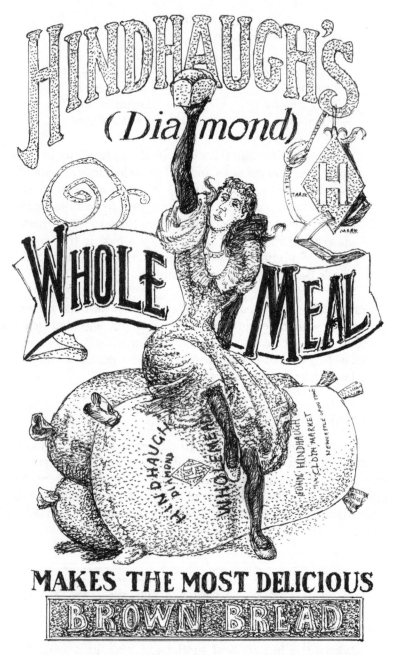

47. In the later Victorian period wholemeal bread began to be seen as a health food, rather than as the staple of an impoverished underclass. Hindhaughs, the great Newcastle millers, were leading promoters of wholemeal flour, using this design on its advertisements and flour bags.

then cover and leave in a warm place to rise for 1½ hours. Next, follow these instructions, given by Elizabeth Taylor of Berwick in 1769;

'then roll it with your hand, and pull it into pieces about the size of a large walnut; roll them in flour, and make them thin with your rolling-pin, cover them with flannel, and keep the dough also covered with flannel. When all your dough is done so, begin to bake what you made first. Lay them upon your iron [or girdle] and when one side is done, turn it. They must not be the least discoloured.

When you use them, they must be toasted crisp on both sides. Observe never to use a knife, but to cut them [around their sides] when they are going to table. Do not cut them [open], but pull them open with your fingers. They will look like a honeycomb if they are right made. Lay on as much butter as you choose, put it together again, and set it near the fire to melt the butter.[46]

As a degree of skill was required to make muffins, and as they couldn't be made in small batches, they became the province of the professional baker. Instead of a girdle, he or she used a hotplate, a thick iron sheet mounted on top of a rectangular brick base and coal-burning grate similar to those of a 'set-pot' washing boiler. Once baked, many were transferred to baskets, covered with a cloth and hawked around the streets for all to buy.

THE WHOLEMEAL REVIVAL

Fine white loaves had always been considered to be the best and healthiest for all breads. From the early nineteenth century a number of influential writers began to promote the use of wholemeal, partly because this was wheat 'as God had made it', partly for economic reasons, and, most importantly, because it aided good digestion and general health. As a result some millers responded by selling wholemeal flours, finding a growing market with better-off families.

The most important of these in the north were the Hindhaughs, John Hindhaugh (1794-1865) being the first of this family to take over the Gallowgate Mills in Newcastle. From around the 1890s their wholemeal flour for brown bread was being sold in 3½lb/1.6kg bags, each attractively printed with the company's name, diamond-H trademark, and this recipe;

Wholemeal Brown Bread

3½lb/1.6kg wholemeal flour
8oz/225g plain white flour
2 tsp salt
1oz/25g yeast

2 tsp black treacle
2oz/50g lard
1pt/600ml tepid milk

Mix the flours and salt. Mix the yeast, treacle and lard in another bowl, mix in the milk, and then work this into the flours, kneading for 5-10 minutes, then set to rise in a warm place for 45 minutes, until doubled in size. Knead lightly, divide into loaves, using large, greased loaf tins, then bake at 220°C, 425°F, Gas mark 7 for 15 minutes, then 180°C, 325°F, Gas mark 4 for a further 30 minutes.

As with almost all the bread recipes given above, this method still produces loaves just as good to eat today as they were over a century ago, when in widespread use in the northcountry.

CHAPTER FOURTEEN

OF CAKES

Delicious cakes, richly fruited and spiced, with plenty of butter and sugar, and raised with either yeast or eggs, were being made by the wives of the region's nobility and gentry from the mid-seventeenth century. They could afford all these expensive ingredients, and had the equipment, ovens and time required to make them. Professional and farming families also made cakes, but it was not until the mid-Victorian period that cakes began to be a regular part of working-class cookery, many women having developed their baking skills while in service at 'the big house'. Even so, cakes still continued to be considered as a treat, especially when made for a special celebration. The most important and earliest of all the region's working-class cakes was the singing hinny, a strong contender for being the north-easts 'national dish'.

THE SINGING HINNY

In 1825 John Brockett described the singing hinny as a 'kneaded spice cake on the girdle, indispensable in the pitman's family'. This description is admirably concise and accurate, though potentially misleading, since it uses everyday words which have a more particular meaning throughout the region. 'Kneaded' for example, means that they contained 'kneading' i.e. butter, dripping or lard, while 'spice' means currants, not imported spices. The other essential ingredient was plain white flour, Mrs. Gaskell's description of it in 1863 including 'fine wheat flour', along with cream for their 'kneading'.[1] Since it was made with rich ingredients still considered distinctly luxurious in most working-class homes in the north, it is not surprising that it was originally associated with pitmen, and their higher earnings. Thomas Wilson has 'singin' hinnies' served with 'rum-laced' tea in his *Pitman's Pay* of 1830, while William Howitt noted the pitman's 'great liking for kneaded cakes baked on a girdle, which with them are called singing-hinnies' in the 1840s.[2] In the early twentieth century Miss J. Barker of Hexham was still describing the singing hinny as 'the pitman's girdle-cake generally made very rich so that it "sings" on the girdle'.[3] The 'hinny' part of their name originated from the local pronunciation of honey, commonly used as a term of endearment in the north-eastern counties. 'Singing' meanwhile, came from the noise it made when baking on the hot girdle. In some households this was also called a fizz, J.P. Robson's *The Pitman's Happy Times* describing how 'Spice hinnies on the gurdle fizz'd.' As a result, singing hinnies were also known as spice fizzers.[4]

Anyone who has ever followed a singing hinny recipe will have found that it doesn't sing. It just lies there, perfectly dumb. The reason for this is that it has far too little fat. The true hinny used fat instead of raising agents to make it short, and had no sugar, since that would burn onto the girdle. It was, in fact, a rich currant pastry.

Singing Hinny/Spice Fizzer

8oz/225g plain flour	*4oz/100g currants*
5oz/125g butter	*2-3 tbs cream*
pinch of salt	

Mix the salt into the flour, rub in the butter, mix in the currants, stir in the cream using a fork, then turn out on to a floured board, dust with flour, and pat out to a 9ins/23cm diameter flat round cake. Place a girdle over a low heat (if using an electric cooker, place the girdle on the hob on a trivet and turn the oven on to its lowest setting to activate the fan, which will prevent damage to the internal wiring through overheating). The girdle should be just hot enough for a drop of water to boil away in 2-3 seconds.

Using a piece of thin, stiff card, slide the hinny onto the girdle, and leave to cook for 10-12 minutes on one side. Listen closely, and it will be heard to sing. Use two pieces of card again to turn the hinny over. This task was originally performed with a thin, broad wooden cake-turner, quite a skilful operation. After cooking the other side for a further 10 minutes, slide on to a board or flat plate, cut into squares, slice across horizontally, sprinkle with a little brown sugar, and serve immediately.

This, the true singing hinny, was always difficult to make well, and served as a real test of skill for any housewife. Its praise was celebrated in numerous verses, like these, published in the *Newcastle Chronicle* in 1885:

Sit doon, noo, man alive!
Te tell ye aa'll contrive
O' the finest thing the worl' hes iver gi'n ye, O.
It's not fine claes nor drink,
Nor owt 'at ye can think,
Can had [hold] a cannle up ti singin'-hinney, O.
Sing hi, the Puddin' Chare an' Elwick's lonnin', O!

Newcassels's fame [w]ill bide
Lang as its coaly tide;
But it winnet rest on what makes sic a shinney, O.
The pride o' a' the North
Is [be]'cas it forst ga borth [birth]
To the greatest charm o' life – a singin-hinney, O.
Sing hi, the Spital Tongues an' Javel Groupe, hi O!

Fre the day we forst draa breeth
To the day 'at brings wor deeth,
Fre the forst day ony on us kenned wor minnie, O,
We gan on step bi step,
An' each gaady day is kep,
Wiv a cheer 'ats elways crooned wi' singin hinney, O.
Sing hi, for Denton Chare an' the Bigg Markit, O! ...

An' se on, day bi day
As we trudge alang life's way,
We've troubles roond-like stoor – eneuf to blin' ye, O.
But whiles thor comes a stop,
An' wor tools we then can drop,
Te gan hyem [home], lads, an hev a singin' – hinney, O.
Sing hi, the Close, Waal -Knowl, an the Cat Bank, hi O!

An' when we can enjoy
Among wor hivvey 'ploy
A day 'at brings huz not a single whinney, O.
Let's elwis drop wor cares
An' set worsels [ourselves] for fairs,
Te celebrate it wiv a singin-hinney, O.
Sing hi, the Mushroom, Forth, an' Heed o' Side, hi O!

The status of the singing hinny was very clear in Betty Allen's home back in the 1780s. When two Methodist 'sisters' were entertained to tea 'a rich currant cake was placed on the girdle, which, in due time was cut into squares, piled upon a plate, and set before the ladies.' The menfolk of her family were only permitted to eat bread and butter until after the ladies had finished. Only then, with grudging permission, were they told that 'Ye may take a bit now, Wally and Charles.'[5]

As baking soda came into general use, the amount of butter began to be greatly reduced, and the singing hinnies become transformed into ordinary girdle scones. Since they no longer sing on the girdle, they should not be called singing hinnies, and so, in the following early twentieth-century versions, they are more appropriately called spiced hinnies or girdle scones.

Spiced Hinny
Miss Bell, Northumberland[6]

12oz/325g plain flour	2 tsp baking powder
2oz/50g ground rice	2oz/50g lard
2oz/50g sugar	3oz/75g currants
¼pt/150ml liquid, half milk, half cream	1 tsp salt

Mix the dry ingredients except the currants, rub in the lard, add the currants, mix to a soft dough and roll ¼in/6mm thick. Prick well all over with a fork and bake on the girdle until brown on both sides. It may be cut in half or quarters before baking to make it easier to turn.

Spiced Hinney
Miss Hutchinson, Annfield Plain[7]

8oz/225g plain flour	½ tsp cream of tartar
4oz/100g sugar	½oz/12g lard
¼ tsp salt	½oz/12g currants
½ tsp bicarbonate of soda	⅛pt/75ml milk

Make as in previous recipe, cutting into quarters before baking.

Spiced Hinny
Mrs Ferney, Chesters Farm, Middleton, Morpeth[8]

8oz/225g plain flour	*3oz/75g lard*
1 tsp baking powder	*2oz/50g currants*
1oz/25g sugar	*⅛pt/75ml milk*

Make as in previous recipe.

In rural Northumberland many of the hinnies were made without currants, sometimes being called 'white cakes' for this reason.

Plain Hinny or Northumberland Girdle Cake
Miss J. Barker, Hexham[9]

1lb/450g plain flour	*4oz/100g butter*
pinch of salt	*up to ¼pt/150ml cold milk*
2 tsp baking powder	

Mix the salt and baking powder into the flour and rub in the butter. Mix in just enough milk to form a firm dough, using a round-bladed knife. Turn out on to a floured board, roll out to the size of the girdle, slide on to a piece of stiff card to support it without cracking. Slide on to a girdle and bake on both sides. Finally remove from the girdle, cut into squares, split, spread with butter, and serve hot.

This, said Miss Barker, 'is the general cottage plan', but she preferred to cut them into small rounds like scones.

In an even greater departure from their original form, some hinnies gained fillings of fruit, transforming themselves into girdle-baked pasties.

Blackberry Hinny[10]

8oz/225g lard	*about 6-8 tbs cold milk*
1lb/450g plain flour	*2-4 tbs sugar*
4oz/100g fresh blackberries	*pinch of salt*
1½ tsp baking powder	
double cream as an accompaniment	

Rub the lard into the flour, mix in the baking powder and salt, and stir in the milk with a round-bladed knife to form a dough. Cut in two, and roll into two rounds about ¼ins/6mm thick, one a little larger than the other. Arrange the blackberries in an even layer on the larger round, brush the outer inch of pastry with a little milk, place the smaller round on top, turn the edges of the lower round over it, and pinch all round to seal them together. Slide onto the girdle and cook gently until the bottom is browned and cooked through, then turn over and cook the other side. Slide the hinny on to a plate, cut off the top and invert it on to another plate, cover it with half the blackberries from inside, then sprinkle both portions of blackberries with the sugar, mash them to a pulp with a fork, then cut into squares and serve with a jug of double cream.

Raisin Hinny[11]

1lb/450g plain flour	*6-8 tbs cold water*
pinch of salt	*1lb/450g raisins, chopped*
1½ tsp baking powder	*2 tbs caster sugar*
8oz/225g lard	*juice of 1 lemon*

Make the pastry and roll out as in the previous recipe, covering the larger round with a level mixture of the raisins, sugar and lemon juice, before sealing down. Brush the top with cold water, sprinkle with sugar, prick, slide on to a baking sheet, and bake at 190°C, 375°F, Gas mark 5 for about 15 minutes until crisp and brown. Serve hot or cold, cut into squares.

As the hinnies gradually went out of general use, the girdle was still used to make drop scones which were much lighter, and quicker and easier to make.

Dropped Scones
Mrs. Ridley, Hepscott W.I.[12]

5oz/125g flour	*1oz/25g sugar*
pinch of salt	*1 egg, beaten*
1 tsp cream of tartar	*¼pt/150ml milk*
½ tsp bicarbonate of soda	

Mix the dry ingredients, make a well in the centre and work in the egg and milk to form a thick batter. Drop large spoonfuls onto the greased girdle, leave to cook until the top is no longer glossy, then use a spatula to turn over, to cook the other side. They may be eaten cold, either plain, buttered, or with golden syrup.

CAKES

As the development of major industries drew families from the countryside into crowded urban centres, many women found it increasingly difficult to cope with the additional pressures of housekeeping. This was particularly evident in bakery, especially the home-baking of cakes and scones, for which the essential eggs were expensive, and yeast slow and, to the inexperienced, unreliable. To meet the growing need for a cheap and relatively fool-proof alternative, manufacturing chemists began to produce artificial raising agents in the form of bicarbonate of soda and baking powder. The latter was a blend of cream of tartar, bicarbonate of soda, and various alum, phosphate or ammonia powders which, when blended with flour and other ingredients, formed millions of tiny bubbles of gas during the baking process, aerating the mixture into a sponge. It was cheap, reliable and quick, its only major problem being bakery with a bitter 'chemical' taste and smell if used in excess, but this could be overcome by adding more sugar and flavourings.

One of the region's leading producers was Wilkinson and Simpson Ltd. of Low Friar Street in central Newcastle. One teaspoonful of their 'Castle' baking powder, plus a pinch of salt, would raise a pound (450g) of flour to produce moist cakes, scones and pastries. Another company, Joseph Lingford & Son, started in Bondgate, Bishop Auckland, in 1861, before moving on to Newgate Street. Here it dried, ground, mixed, sifted and packaged its 'Ideal' baking powder through into the twentieth century.

Among the numerous advantages claimed in its advertisements, were the absence of unhealthy alum, and even true 'domestic happiness'. The company's promotional booklet *Dainty Recipes* contained instructions for making 35 kinds of cakes, biscuits and puddings, but by the late Victorian period many north-eastern families had already developed their own favourite varieties.[13]

Some became particularly associated with towns in which they were made, these including;

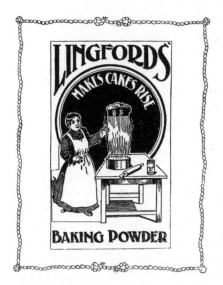
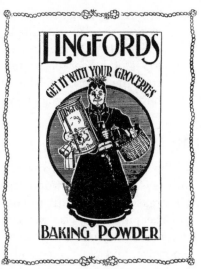

48. The introduction of baking powder revolutionised home baking in the later nineteenth century, lightening puddings and cakes, but not as much as this advert suggests!

Redcar Cake[14]

8oz/225g butter	*1½ tsp baking powder*
8oz/225g sugar	*8oz/225g currants*
4 eggs, beaten	*1oz/25g flaked almonds*
12oz/325g plain flour	

Cream the butter with the sugar, beat in the eggs little by little, then work in the flour sifted with the baking powder. Mix in the currants, turn into a greased and lined dripping tin, sprinkle with the almonds, and bake at 180°C, 350°F, Gas mark 4 for 2 hours.

Auckland Cake
Mrs Isabella Douglas, Sunderland[15]

8oz/225g butter	*few drops vanilla extract*
4oz/100g sugar	*5oz/125g plain flour*
3 eggs, separated	*3oz/75g ground rice*

Cream the butter with the sugar, fold in the yolks which have been beaten until light and creamy, and then the whites, beaten to a stiffness, with the vanilla, and finally the flour and ground rice. Butter a 7in/18cm diameter mould or tin, dust with a little mixed flour and caster sugar, and pour in the mixture. Bake at 180°C, 350°F, Gas mark 4 for 45 minutes.

Newcastle Cake [16]

1lb/450g plain flour	6oz/175g brown sugar
1 tsp bicarbonate of soda	½ tsp mixed spice
6oz/175g lard & butter	½ tsp ground nutmeg
8oz/225g sultanas	3 eggs, beaten
about ½pt/300ml warm milk	8oz/225g currants
3oz/75g chopped candied peel	

Sift the soda into the flour and rub in the fats. Mix in the dried fruits, sugar and spices, then the eggs beaten with half of the milk, and then sufficient milk to give a soft dropping consistency. Turn into a 8ins/20cm diameter greased and lined tin and bake at 180°C, 350°F, Gas mark 4 for 1½ –2 hours.

The other favourites were grannie cakes and vinegar cakes, both good everyday fruit cakes from which the family could 'cut and come again' as they wished.

Grannie Cake
Mrs Wake [17]

10oz/275g plain flour	1 tbs ground cinnamon
4oz/100g butter or lard	3 tbs treacle
7fl oz/200ml cream or milk	5oz/150g sugar
1lb/450g raisins or sultanas	1 tbs bicarbonate of soda

Rub the fat into the flour, mix in the sugar, dried fruit and cinnamon. Stir the treacle into the milk, stir in the soda, then mix into the flour and fruit. Turn into a greased and lined 7ins/18cm diameter tin and bake at 150°C, 300°F, Gas mark 4 for 1½ hours.

Vinegar cakes were popular in Northumberland from around the middle of the nineteenth century. They were fruited sponge cakes, raised with baking soda, sometimes including eggs, sometimes treacle, but always a small quantity of vinegar. This version is typical;

Vinegar Cake
Mrs M. Wilkinson, Morpeth area [18]

8oz/225g plain flour	*½ tsp bicarbonate of soda*
2oz/50g butter or lard	*¼pt/150ml milk*
4oz/100g sugar	*1½ tsp malt vinegar*
8oz/200g dried fruits	*[may add a little nutmeg]*

Rub the fat into the flour, mix in the sugar and fruit, then the soda mixed into the milk, and finally the vinegar. Turn into a greased and lined 2lb/900g loaf tin and bake at 180°C, 350°F, Gas mark 4 for 1½ hours.

The sharp taste of the vinegar is virtually undetectable in this rich, sweet cake, just as the taste of buttermilk disappeared when baking churn milk cakes. When making these, it is important to use the actual buttermilk left after churning the butter, rather than the yoghurt-like cultured buttermilk often sold in supermarkets.

Churn Milk Cake [19]

9oz/250g plain flour	*1 tsp bicarbonate of soda*
½ tsp ground allspice	*⅓pt/200ml buttermilk*
3oz/75g butter, lard or dripping	*3oz/75g sugar*
1oz/25g finely chopped candied lemon peel	

Mix the soda into the flour, rub in the fat, mix in the remaining dry ingredients, make a well in the centre, and stir in the buttermilk to make a soft mixture. Pour into a greased and lined 1lb/450g loaf tin, and bake at 180°C, 350°F, Gas mark 4 for 1 hour.

These cakes were most characteristic of the north-eastern counties, but of course there were many others, along with various buns, biscuits, pastries and scones. Their recipes were carefully collected by Peggy Hutchinson and published in her *North Country Cooking Secrets* of 1935. This has every variety of nut-and-date, walnut, seed, sultana, chocolate, rice, cherry, sponge, sweetheart and love cake, along with many more, an ideal selection for the home baker.

CHAPTER FIFTEEN

THE STORE CUPBOARD

Pickles and preserves were particularly useful for introducing a welcome relish to many everyday foods. Piquant sauces greatly increased the enjoyment of cooked meats, while jams made a delicious addition to bread and butter. Many were manufactured and sold on a commercial scale, the most important being mustard.

In 1720 'it occurred to an old woman of the name of Clements, resident at Durham, to grind seed in a mill and pass the seed through the various processes which are resorted to in making flour from wheat.' Taking it on packhorses from town to town, and collecting orders, she obtained the patronage of George I, and a national reputation.[1] The *London Journal* of 1723 advertised:

> TO ALL FAMILIES, etc. The Royal Flower of Mustard Seed is now used and esteemed by most of the Quality and Gentry. It will keep good in the Flower as long as in the seed, and one spoonful of the Mustard made of it will go as far as three of that sold at chandler's shops, and is much wholesomer.[2]

As a result, mustard became an important local crop, but it was already in decline by 1810. Its manufacture still continued in Durham, Newcastle and Gateshead, however, and its reputation remained undiminished. Victorian advertisements sometimes carried the initials 'D.S.F.', confident that the public knew that this meant 'Durham Super Fine' mustard. Usually just mixed with a little water or milk and served with roast beef, ham, sausages etc., it could also be transformed by 'some Epicures mixing it with Sherry or Madeira wine, or distilled or flavoured vinegar'.[3] Eliza Acton's recipe of 1845 preferred horseradish vinegar;

Strong Durham Mustard[4]

1oz/25g horseradish root   *mustard powder*
½pt/300ml vinegar

49. Bewick's depiction of a pantry in his *Fables of Aesop* of 1818 shows a ventilated and locked food safe to the left, and rows of pickle and preserve jars on the top shelf. Each has its mouth sealed with a chamoix leather cover, carefully tied down with twine.

> Scrape the root, cover it with the boiling vinegar, seal and leave for at least 4 days – but up to a few months. Strain off the vinegar and use it to make up the mustard to the required consistency.

Drying, grinding and sieving mustard seed was a long and troublesome process, and so most people found it most convenient to buy the prepared Durham mustard flour. Many other sauces were easily and cheaply made at home, their main ingredients being grown in gardens and allotments, or collected from the countryside, and made up as they came into season. They included the traditional varieties found in all other parts of the country, the selection given below recording typical local recipes. Anyone who wants to try the full range should read *Peggy Hutchinson's Preserving Secrets* and her *Old English Cookery*. Both are long out of print, but contain a wonderful range of very practical recipes collected by one of Britain's finest regional cookery writers.

For all the following recipes it is advisable to scald the jars with boiling water, empty these, and allow them to dry before filling with the ingredients and sealing down for storage.

Mint Sauce
Durham[5]

1oz/25g mint leaves, picked from the stalks
4 tbs vinegar   *1oz/25g sugar*

Finely chop the leaves (or blend, or use a food processor), add the sugar and grind in a pestle and mortar until they form a very smooth paste. Stir in the vinegar and seal down in a small jar. When required, dilute with a little more vinegar.

Mint Vinegar
Haydon Bridge[6]

1oz/25g mint leaves, picked from the stalks
1pt/600ml vinegar

Coarsely chop or bruise the leaves, pack into a jar, top up with vinegar, seal, and leave for at least 3 weeks. Pour off the vinegar into a clean bottle, seal, and keep for use.

Horseradish Sauce[7]

2 tbs freshly grated horseradish root   *3 tbs vinegar*
3 tbs cream or milk   *2 tbs ground mustard*
1oz/25g sugar

Mix all together, adding the vinegar last of all, and serve.

Gooseberry Sauce
Mrs Wren, Haydon Bridge[8]

1lb/450g gooseberries   *2 tbs chopped onion*
6oz/175g sultanas   *1pt/600ml vinegar*
1oz/25g currants   *5oz/125g sugar*
¼ tsp each ground chilli, allspice, ginger, mustard, nutmeg,
1oz/25g salt   *& turmeric*

Mix all but the sugar and spices in a pan, cover and simmer for 15 minutes. Blend smooth and pass through a sieve into a clean pan, add the sugar and spices. Return to the boil, stirring continuously, then bottle and seal for storage until required.

Plum Sauce
Mrs Dixon, Medomsley[9]

2lb/900g plums, halved	*1pt/600ml malt vinegar*
1lb/450g brown sugar	*½ tsp salt*

¼ tsp each, ground pepper & ground cloves
4oz/100g chopped preserved ginger or 1½ tsp ground ginger

Simmer all together in a covered pan until the plums are reduced to a soft pulp and will separate from their stones. Remove from the heat, rub through a sieve into a clean pan, stir thoroughly while re-heating to the boil, pour into bottles and seal down for storage until required.

Haw Sauce
Miss E. Rutherford, Tweedmouth[10]

1½lb/625g hawthorn haws	*½ tsp white pepper*
1½pt/900ml vinegar	*1oz/25g salt*
4oz/100g sugar	

Stew the haws in the vinegar in a covered pan for 30 minutes, then rub through a sieve into a clean pan. Add the remaining ingredients, stir and boil for 10 minutes, then pour into jars and seal down.

Rowan Jelly

Rowan/mountain ash berries, with twice their weight of crab	
apples	*sugar*

Put the berries and halved apples into a pan, cover with water and boil for 30 minutes, then strain through a thick muslin or jelly bag into a measuring jug. Transfer to a pan with 1lb/450g sugar to every 1pt/600ml juice, bring to a rapid boil and remove all scum. Continue testing until it forms a firm jelly when tested on a cold saucer, then pour into small jars and seal down for use.

This has a strong bitter-sweet flavour, and a rich colour, making it particularly suitable for accompanying all sorts of game and cold meats.

Haw Jelly [11]
Miss E. Rutherford, Tweedmouth

3lb/1.35kg hawthorn haws   fresh lemons
sugar

Stew the haws in 3pts/1.8l water in a covered pan for 1 hour, pour into a jelly bag and leave to drip through overnight. Measure the liquid, and add 1lb/450g sugar and the juice of 1 lemon for every pint/600ml. Boil rapidly, skimming off the rising scum, testing for a firm set by spooning a few drops onto a saucer and leaving in a cool place for a few minutes. Pour into small jars and seal down.

Pickled Leeks [12]

1lb/450g leeks   ½pt/300ml vinegar
1 tbs pickling spice (or a mix of allspice, celery seed, mustard seed, cloves, black peppercorns, ginger, chilli & garlic)

Boil the spices in the vinegar for 10 minutes and leave until cold. Cut the white parts of the leek into ½ins/12mm lengths (use the green parts in soups), pack into jars, cover with the strained vinegar, seal down and leave for at least a week before using with cold meats etc.

Pickled Red Cabbage [13]

about 3lb/1.4kg red cabbage   4 tbs salt
4pt/1.2l spiced vinegar, as in the previous recipe

Cut the cabbage into very fine slices and layer with the salt in a bowl, stir, and leave to soak for 24 hours. Pack the cabbage into jars, cover with the boiling vinegar, screw on the lids, and leave for at least a week before using. It can keep in good condition for a few weeks, but is best whilst still crisp.

A number of other pickles and sauces were made for almost immediate consumption, either cold or hot. The first of these is a close north-country version of the Yorkshire Ploughman's Salad, also eaten as a sharp, cool and fresh-tasting accompaniment to cold meats.

Lettuce Sauce [14]

1 crisp, firm-hearted lettuce	2 tbs sugar
6 sprigs fresh mint	4-6 tbs malt vinegar
1 tsp salt	

Pull the lettuce into separate leaves, rinse, shake dry and spread half the leaves on a chopping board. Add the mint on top, then the remaining leaves, and chop all together very finely. Layer with sprinklings of salt and sugar in a basin, stand for 10 minutes, then stir in the vinegar and eat immediately, while still crisp.

Onion Salad [15]

1 large mild onion	½ tsp salt
¼pt/150ml white wine vinegar	

Cut the onion in half vertically, then into ¼ins/7mm slices and layer with the salt in a bowl. Pour the vinegar over and leave overnight before using.

Another sauce, used continuously from the fifteenth century, used the tangy flavours of sorrel leaves or gooseberries to counteract the oiliness of some foods, or the fattiness of others. It was for this reason that sorrel was often known as goosegrass, and gooseberries became gooseberries.

Green Gooseberry Sauce
Darlington area[16]

8oz/225g gooseberries	*½oz/12g butter*
1pt/600ml sorrel leaves	*¼ tsp sugar*
salt & pepper	

Wash the sorrel leaves, cover them with boiling salted water and boil fast for 10 minutes, then drain and plunge into cold water. Drain again and rub through a sieve. Rub the raw gooseberries through a sieve, add to the sorrel with the remaining ingredients, stir over a gentle heat until hot, and serve with grilled oily fish such as mackerel, or with roast goose.

The final sauce to be described here can be used with cold meats, but is much more useful as an addition to stews and hashes. Easily made, it was the English housewife's version of the expensively-imported soy sauce, which it closely resembles.

Mushroom Ketchup

1lb/450g mushrooms	*2 blades mace*
piece of root ginger, bruised	*1½oz/35g salt*

Chop the mushrooms finely, layer with the salt in a bowl and leave for 3-4 days. Strain through a piece of muslin, squeezing out all the juice, and boil this with the spices until reduced by a half, then strain out the spices and bottle for use.

Moving on from the sour and salty contents of the store-cupboard to those that were rich and sweet, the northeast had a good regional tradition of bottling fruit and making jams. These skills developed slowly in most working-class homes, since sugar remained an expensive treat, and in many families an almost unknown luxury, until it became more affordable in the later Victorian period. From then on most housewives with sufficient time prided themselves on the jars of preserves lined up in their cupboards and larders. For jams, there was no need to write down any instructions, for the techniques were so well-known. Just prepare the fruit, simmer it until tender, strain out any unwanted seeds or skins, measure the volume of the remaining fruit, and boil it with a pound of sugar per pint until it set, then seal down in sterilised jars. If the fruit was unlikely to set, the addition of lemon juice introduced the required pectin, and all would be well. There are few local recipes which required any further information, these including;

Stanhope Black Jelly [17]

3½lb/1.6kg elderberries
1½lb/625g crab apples, halved
juice of 2 lemons

½oz/12g butter
sugar

Boil the elderberries in 1pt/600ml water for 10 minutes, meanwhile boiling the crab apples in a further 1pt/600ml water for 15 minutes. Mix together, boil for 5 minutes, then strain through a jelly bag. Measure the liquid, pour into a pan with the lemon juice and butter and bring to a rolling boil. Meanwhile heat 1lb/450g of sugar for each pint of liquid in a baking dish in the oven until very hot. Stir the sugar into the liquid and continue boiling and skimming until the jelly reaches setting point when tested on a cold saucer. Finally pour into sterilised jars and seal for storage.

Elderberry Syrup [18]

1pt/600ml ripe elderberries (with no stalks)
1 piece root ginger, bruised

sugar
3 cloves

Simmer the elderberries and spices in 1pt/600ml water for 30 minutes, then strain through a jelly bag into a measuring jug. Pour the juice into a pan with 8oz/225g sugar per 1pt/600ml of juice, boil for 10 minutes, and then seal in sterilised bottle for use.

Particular care was always taken when making lemon curd or lemon cheese, both being identical mixtures of expensive sugar, butter, eggs and lemons. When well made the result was an amazingly rich, glutinous, sweet and tangy jam. It was truly delicious when spread across good fresh white bread and well-flavoured butter, or baked as a lemon tart, the local type of cheesecake. Both these versions give good results, the first being even sweeter and richer than the second.

Lemon Cheese
Mrs Lewins, Morpeth area[19]

5 eggs, beaten and strained	*9oz/250g butter*
juice & grated zest of 3 lemons	*12oz/325g sugar*

Mix all the ingredients in a pan and cook over a gentle heat, stirring continuously until thickened, but not boiling, which would cause it to 'split'. Other local recipes recommend putting the ingredients into a large jar and standing this in a pan of simmering water, then stirring until it has thickened. This greatly reduces the chance of spoiling it by over-cooking. Finally, seal down in sterilised jars.

Lemon Curd
Mrs N. Potts, Medomsley[20]

3 eggs, beaten & strained	*8oz/225g butter*
juice & grated rind of 2 lemons	*1lb/450g sugar*

Cook as in the recipe above.

Jam or Lemon Curd Tarts

The usual way to make individual jam or lemon curd tarts was to line tart tins with shortcrust pastry, add the filling and bake, rather than blind-baking the pastry beforehand.

8oz/225g plain flour	*4oz/100g lard*
1 tsp baking powder	*pinch of salt*

Rub the lard into the flour until it forms very fine crumbs, add the baking powder and salt, stir in 3-4 tbs cold water, using a fork, form into a ball, cover, and leave in a cool place for 30 minutes. Roll the pastry out into a thin sheet on a floured board, cut into rounds a little larger than each tin, press gently into each greased tin, and trim the edges. Prick the base of each tart, using a fork, then three-quarters fill it with the jam or curd and bake at 200°C, 400°F, Gas mark 6 for about 20 minutes, then remove and allow to cool before removing from their tins.

CHAPTER SIXTEEN

DRINKS

The everyday drinks of most working people in the late eighteenth and early nineteenth centuries were very simple. Water from springs and clear-running streams was healthy enough, as was most of the water fed into the conduits or 'pants' erected for public use in towns such as Newcastle and Durham.[1] Other sources, particularly wells and pumps, could soon become dangerously polluted by industrial waste, leaking drains and sewerage, especially when towns and villages expanded without the construction of adequate toilets and sewers. The spread of cholera in the 1830s, this deadly disease first appearing in England in the port of Sunderland, was eventually discovered to be due to contaminated water supplies. As a result of this, the local authorities invested heavily in new reservoirs and water works to ensure that clean potable drinking water was available to all.

Wherever cows were kept, milk was the everyday drink of choice. Along with many others, Thomas Bewick drank it three times a day when in the country, and still enjoyed it in town. His Aunt Blackett, a freeman's widow in Newcastle's Pudding Chare, kept cows on the Town Moor, so that he was 'abundantly supplied with milk, which was the chief thing I lived upon.'[2] Milk was also the main beverage of the regions' farm labourers, so long as they had the use of their own house-cows.[3] As their wages began to be paid in cash rather than in kind, these cows disappeared, taking their copious milk supplies with them. By the 1890s, like the rest of the population, they had become tea drinkers.[4] This might be seen as an unhealthy alternative, but its boiling water and scalded milk killed off the bacteria which had caused so many digestive illnesses and fostered the spread of tuberculosis.

TEA & COFFEE

Tea had first been drunk in England in the 1650s, but the cost of transport, high taxation, and the silver and porcelain equipage associated with its use kept it within well-to-do polite society for several generations. The removal of its 100% import duty in 1784 encouraged others to try it, but it did not come into general use until the early years of the nineteenth century. By this time it had already become a very well-established part of the trade of grocers and the dealers in all the larger towns. In the late Victorian period even Allendale Town could boast of three tea-dealers' shops, but quantities were still being hawked around the countryside by pedlars. Isaac Holden served the Allendale area, for example, and John Smith, alias Tea Johnny, that around Wolsingham.[5] Those who first tried to make tea without the appropriate experience often got it all wrong. Every region has its own selection of such stories, the local version telling of an old woman of Cullercoats who once received a 1lb/450g package of tea from her sailor son. Declaring that she had never seen such odd-looking cabbage, she decided to try boiling it in her brass pan. Seeking advice from her neighbour, she also added pepper and salt to add to its flavour. Then;

> She boil'd it long, and she boil'd it strong
> And she tried it how it would eat;
> She slic'd some carrots and put them among
> To make it more of a treat.
> She boil'd it till it was twelve o'clock;
> She boil'd it away till four;
> She made up her mind to boil it well,
> So she boil'd it till she gave o'er.
>
> And then she call'd her neighbours all,
> To join in the feast and be
> Right merry withall, both great and small,
> On that wonderful pound of tea.
> She took out the leaves and butter'd them well,
> And the liquor away threw she;
> That's all at present I've got to tell
> Of the old woman's pound of tea.

Tea soon came into general use, however, for although often adulterated, it was quickly made, warming, satisfying, and helped to stave off feelings of hunger. In pitmen's homes it was carefully simmered, and, when the pay was good 'Mow tea had rum in't', but when the money had run out in baff week, it was drunk plain some three or four times a day, to save on food. In the 1850s it was taken with little or no milk, since the mines tended to be away from the best

50. Up to the early nineteenth century tea was imported from China rather than India, and formed part of the fashionable taste for Chinese porcelain, textiles, wallpapers and lacquer furniture. Following this trend, Mr Davidson chose the Chinese tea-drinking scene for his advertising woodcut.

dairy country, but those who remember the early 1900s could usually buy whole milk at a penny a pint, or skim milk at a penny for two pints, from local farmers.[6]

Coffee was never quite as popular as tea in working families, but the pitmen often drank it for breakfast, grinding the beans just before it was made. It was then well boiled, to give it a strong flavour.[7] In 1844 Richard Richardson, a hewer at Seaton Delaval Colliery was evicted from his cottage, and a complete list made of all his possessions. The amount of tea and coffee wares clearly shows how significant a part they played in his everyday life. They comprised;

1 tin caddie	5 teapots
1 coffee mill	18 cups & saucers
1 tea board	9 pint pots
2 tea trays	over 11 mugs.[8]

Some of these may have been kept for display on the dresser or cupboard, but this still left plenty for general use.

HOME-BREWING

Some traditional working-class communities, such as the weavers of West Yorkshire, maintained the practice of home-brewing their own beer throughout the nineteenth century. In the north-east, however, there is little evidence of it after around 1800.[9] The nobility, gentry and major farmers, just like their fellows elsewhere, continued to run their own brewhouses until it became cheaper and less troublesome to buy in their supplies from one of the major regional or national brewing companies. The only beers regularly brewed in the home appear to have been of the 'herbal' variety, quick and cheap to make, and excellent for quenching the thirst. They included;

Dandelion Beer[10]

3oz/75g fresh dandelion leaves   *3lb/1.35kg sugar*
½oz/12g root ginger, bruised   *2oz/50g hops*
½oz/12g liquorice   *½oz/12g yeast*

Put all but the sugar and yeast into a muslin bag and boil in 24pts/14.5l water for 30 minutes, then remove, and stir in the sugar until dissolved. Stir in the yeast when lukewarm, and leave overnight. Bottle, and leave for two days before drinking.

Nettle Beer
Morpeth area[11]

'Get the [4 handfuls of] nettles young, and put them into the pan, and boil them [in 12pts/7.2l water]; strain off into a vessel; put in the whole [1½oz] ginger, take a hammer, break the ginger, and bruise it, and put in a couple of lemons sliced; when it is cooled, put in a slice of toasted bread–crust with balm [yeast] spread on it; let it ferment three or four days [in the warm], put your hand in, and lift the bread up, and throw it away with all the scum on it; put one and a half pounds of brown sugar in it, strain it, let it cool and bottle it. And when you uncork it, take care it does not wash you!'

Treacle Beer [12]

1lb/450g Golden Syrup	*1 slice toast*
1 lemon, sliced	*½oz/12g fresh yeast*
¼oz/6g root ginger, bruised	

Boil the syrup, lemon and ginger in 16pts/9.6l water for 15 minutes. Leave to cool, floating the toast, spread with the yeast, on the liquid when lukewarm. Cover and leave to ferment for 2-3 days. Remove the toast and scum, then bottle and leave for a further 2-3 days before drinking.

Ginger Beer [13]

juice & zest of 3 lemons	*2oz/50g cream of tartar*
3lb/1.35kg sugar	*1oz/25g yeast*
2oz/50g root ginger, bruised	*1 slice toast*

Put the lemons, sugar, ginger and tartar into a large container, scald with 16pts/9.6l boiling water, and leave until lukewarm. Spread the yeast onto the toast, float on the liquid, and leave in a warm place to ferment for 24 hours, then remove the toast and scum, strain and bottle. It may be drunk after a couple of days.

N.B. for any of the above, it is best to use either lightly-corked glass bottles, or screw-top plastic bottles, since over-fermentation will shatter tightly-corked glass bottles.

WINES

The home production of wines tended to be more of a hobby than an everyday activity. Those in ordinary households who enjoyed the craft and developed the necessary skills usually preferred to make sweet rather than dry varieties, always making sure that they had plenty in stock for entertaining friends and family over Christmas and the New Year. Favourite varieties included ginger, rhubarb, elderberry and parsnip. The best selection of these and many other North-country wines was published in Peggy Hutchinson's Home-Made Wine Secrets in 1960.

SPIRITS

Beer brewed from malted barley and hops was readily available from every inn and ale-house, those working in mining and heavy industry consuming large quantities to provide both energy and a replacement for their arduous perspiration. Spirits were also drunk, but these were heavily taxed if legal, and were often of dubious quality. 'While rum an' brandy soak'd each chop [chin]' in heavy drinking sessions, there was also 'Jackey an' fine Ginger Pop.'[14] Jacky, an English gin also called Blue Dick in western Northumberland, could cause blindness, incontinence and unconsciousness, as at least one pitman discovered to his cost at Newcastle Fair in 1811.[15] There were well established means of smuggling brandy and rum into the area from overseas and whisky from Scotland over the remote hills of the largely unpatrolled border. All manner of ruses were employed to bring in the whisky. Some came in the newly-made pots carried into Northumberland by the potters of Preston Pans. At other times trains of thirty packhorses brought it in bulk over Carter Bar and down Redesdale. When one exciseman heard that the family of a recently-deceased Redesdale man had ordered his coffin from Jedburgh, he immediately galloped up to the border to intercept the hearse as it returned into England. His suspicions were well-founded, for both the coffin and the hearse were packed full of 'grey hens' (stoneware spirit bottles) full of whisky. As a result, he confiscated not only the whisky, but also the coffin, the hearse, and even the horses, a clear warning to all others who might try the same method.[16]

Smuggling over the border was always a risky business, but there were clear financial advantages so long as legitimately distilled spirits were taxed at a lower rate in Scotland than they were in England. The trade was even more profitable if no tax was paid, and so illicit stills flourished at both sides of the border. The remote hill country of the North Pennines and Cheviot Hills were ideal for this purpose, having ready access to the essential barley, peat and cold, pure and fast running streams. However, it was often more convenient to find a secluded spot much nearer to customers in the pit villages and towns. The woods and valleys a few miles to the west of Durham City maintained an active tradition of illicit distillers, these being known as 'smugglers' even though they never crossed any borders. In the 1830s–50s the glades of Lord Boyne's estate between Brandon and Waterhouses, and Lord Durham's Langley estate provided cover for Harry Carr's stills, for example. He had apparently learned his skills in Ireland, then passing them on to Norfolk-born John Cain or Kane, better known locally as 'Whisky Jack'. Another smuggler called 'Nat' operated about the nearby settlements of Greenland and Quebec a couple of miles to the north.

Their usual raw material was sour or stale ale obtained 'on the quiet' from local breweries. This was poured into a large boiler set up to its rim into the ground, and mixed with molasses or occasionally coarse sugar and a few stems of juniper. Having been boiled and cooled until lukewarm, yeast was added, and it was left to ferment. The resulting 'half-stuff' was then run off, probably strained, and then returned to the cleaned boiler for stilling, the alcoholic steam being directed into a tubular copper worm submerged in a fast-running stream of cold water. It was then stored in casks or stone jars. Having been released from Durham Gaol at the end of a two-year sentence for distilling, Nat went to a clump of thorns on the borders of the Rowley and Iveley estates, and began to dig. He expected to find eighteen gallons of his whisky, carefully hidden here to enable him to recommence his trade. However, someone must have known his secret, for not a trace of it remained to be distributed in his dried ox-bladders worn under his shirt.[17]

Local writers confidently state that all of these stills had been closed down by 1860 due to the increased vigilance of the police. By this time the same level of taxation on spirits was being charged throughout the United Kingdom, but, at eight shillings/40p a gallon, the illegal stills remained profitable. Even in the 1960s–70s the method of producing malt whisky was still well-known in the same area, starting with someone peeing on a sack of barley set behind a hedge to start the malting process.

HOT LIQUORS

The traditional drink of hot spirits used 'Thy stomach as well as thy fingers to warm' in cold Durham and Northumbrian winters was appropriately called a cheerer. It was made by scalding rum with about its own volume of boiling water.[18] The other regional speciality was stoory, made by sprinkling and stirring fine oatmeal and sugar into hot ale. About 3 tbs fine oatmeal and 3 tbs sugar to each pint of ale, mixed in cold and gently heated while being stirred until hot, is a surprisingly smooth, satisfying and warming drink for a winter evening.[19] A 'cocktail' meanwhile, was not a fashionable blend of spirits to be sipped elegantly, but a robust mix of rum, ginger and hot ale, ideal for reviving the frost-chilled traveller at the end of a long journey.[20]

CHAPTER SEVENTEEN

FEASTS, FAIRS & CELEBRATIONS

Whether living in a busy town, a port, a pit village, a farm, or an isolated cottage, everyone looked forward to those few days when work could stop, giving a rare opportunity for a carefree communal celebration. Ordinary market days provided a little of this atmosphere, but were as nothing when compared to the region's traditional feasts and fairs. Many of these had been founded by royal charters granted to lords of manors who wished to increase their incomes. Some were also survivals from the pre-reformation celebrations of the saint to whom the local parish church was dedicated, or who had some particular significance. St. Ninian's Fair at Ford, for example, was held every 27th September, his feast day (Old Style).[1] Like many other fairs, it was a great mart for the sale of sheep, cattle, horses, hardware, cooperage and earthenware. Perhaps the most important were those which took place every autumn for the sale of the vast herds of Scottish black cattle as they were driven down into England, there to provide salt-beef as a major winter food. When Robert Raine of Barford went to the great Brough Hill fairs in September/October 1827-9, he did a considerable volume of trade there:

> At Brough Hill Fair ... I bought 80 Kylo bullocks for Lord Harwood of Harwood House and Colonel Beaumont of Bretton Hall [both in West Yorkshire]. The price was £905. They were fat.
>
> At Brough Hill Fair. It was supposed that there were 50,000 Scots and Irish beasts shewn and more than 1000 Horses.[2]

The spring fairs were often more concerned with hiring, acting as a kind of labour-exchange for farm workers who had finished one contract, and were now looking for a new employer. Notices announcing 'A hiring for hinds' or 'A hiring for female servants will be held ...' were printed and circulated locally. Those seeking work then assembled, some carrying their 'lines' which certified that they were free from any previous contract: 'The bearer John Mather is at Liberty to hire with whom he please to Enter the 12ᵗʰ of May [1794] ... John Fenwick.' They also held a piece of straw in their mouth, this being taken out once they had been selected by a farmer and had received their 'godspenny', usually a shilling or more, to confirm the agreement.[3]

All the attractions of such events are fully described in the poem on Long Framlington fair, or tryst, published in 1812. Here were gathered:

> *Horn'd cattle, and horses, mules, asses and swine,*
> *And sheep of all sorts kept between Tweed and Tyne.*
> *A skilful collection of choice Cheviot rams,*
> *And also the best breed of black border lambs;*
> *Hard hogs from the Highlands, some long and some short,*
> *And some sightly samples of Leicestershire sort;*
> *Some South Downs, some Dishleys, some Dorsets and Harts,*
> *Some Bedfords and Bakewells, grace mayor Miller's marts ...*
> *Here potters with panniers of Stafford and Delph,*
> *And chests of choice china to shine on a shelf;*
> *Here's hampers of hardware-plate-polish'd and plain,*
> *With all tin utensils of varnish and stain ...*
> *From Morpeth, Newcastle and London likewise*
> *The puffers of paste here expose Penny pies!*
> *With cheese cakes and custards and other confects,*
> *Of rare aromatics, and summer selects,*
> *Scarce kickshaws more costly can be chewed with the chaps,*
> *Yet somewhat less sav'ry than Silas Swain's snaps ...*[4]
> *(He was the local confectioner).*

Food featured largely in the fun of the fair. At the 'Hoppings' around Newcastle boys would have their hands tied behind their backs before trying to eat treacle-dipped bread-rolls hanging from lines, their sticky faces and hair causing great amusement. Visitors would buy oranges from the stalls and toss them into the burn, or stream, so that men, women and children would scramble for them, while old women would run races for packets of tea. Those who went to Billy Fairplay's stall at Newcastle Fair in the 1850s could toss a marble into the hat of his wooden figure of a man, so that it ran down a spiral groove and, if it dropped down the appropriate hole at the bottom, win themselves a spice cake.[5] There might also be a greasy pole to climb, perhaps with a leg of mutton at the top for the winner, or blindfolded wheelbarrow races for sacks of potatoes.[6]

For eating on the day, there were always oranges, Barcelona nuts and pies. W. Nicholson could remember Wolsingham Fair in the 1830s when Old Joe Stephenson was shouting his, '"Hot pies! Hot pies!" - and what a voice he had; you might have heard him two miles off. His wife Gracey made the pies, real mutton pies, no mistake about that. Nothing could exceed one of Joe's nice savoury pies.'[7]

From their price, they were usually called penny pies.

Penny Pies
Ms. J. Douglas, Newcastle Road, Sunderland[8]

For 2 dozen;

1lb/450g roasted or boiled meat, together with its bones
1 onion, quartered *12oz/325g lard or dripping*
2lb/900g plain flour *1 egg, beaten*
1 tbs salt

Simmer the cooked meat and onion in a little water in a covered pan for an hour or so, until the meat falls from the bone. Strain off the stock, mix it with any good gravy, reduce it until thick, and season if necessary with a little salt and pepper. Coarsely chop the meat, and stir this into the stock.

Mix the flour and salt, make a well in the centre, pour in the lard which is boiling in 18fl oz/500ml water, mix quickly, and, when just cool enough, knead to form a smooth dough. Use three-quarters of this to raise 24 small pies (or mould in small pie tins), fill with the meat, moisten their rims, and top with lids made from the remaining pastry, carefully sealing them together. Cut a hole in the centre of each lid, brush the pastry with the beaten egg, and bake at 220°C, 425°F, Gas mark 7 for 30 minutes.

Such pies were also sold by Pennypie Jack around the Old Customs House on Newcastle's Sandhill in the 1820s, except for an eight-year period which he spent on Van Dieman's Land 'at His Majesty's Pleasure'.[9] Johnny the Pieman, dressed in silk top hat, dress suit, white bib and apron, and carrying a block-tin oven polished like silver, succeeded him in the 1850s. His cry was

'Hot pie, toss or buy, Mutton pie, have a try![10]

199

As described in 'The Mode of Wooing', it was not pies, but gingerbreads which were the most important of all the feast foods;

> *When e'er at market or at fair,*
> *Be sure that weel ye treat them there,*
> *With raisins, wine, or ginger-bread,*
> *A comb or ribbon for the head,*
> *When ye shall go a-wooing.*[11]

GINGERBREADS

Those who attended the Midsummer Fair at Corbridge found a long row of gingerbread and orange stalls lining the street, with dames crying 'bool up and buy away!' or 'London Spice [gingerbread] twopence a package!' or displaying twenty-four squares of gingerbread down the length of their arm – 'A shilling the lot!'[12] Further north, near Ford, one side of the field occupied by St Ninian's fair every 27th September (his feast day, Old Style), had a street of refreshment tents and stalls offering sweets, finery, and;

> gingerbreads made in moulds to represent the Royal Arms, men, horses and dogs; these being, par excellence, the 'fairing' that was always expected by the young and old people who, for any reason, could not be present.[13]

To the south, throughout County Durham, the best gingerbreads came from Barnard Castle. At Blanchland, for example;

> The stalls were filled with sweets and nuts
> With fruits all ripe and nice,
> Abounding most, in various cuts,
> Was "Barney Cassel" spice [gingerbread][14]

while at Wolsingham fair, 'we had splendid gingerbread from Barnard Castle, brandy snaps, oranges, and all kinds of sweets.'[15]

Considering the relatively bland and monotonous nature of most everyday foods of the past, it is not surprising that the rich, spicy, hot flavours of these moulded gingerbreads were greatly appreciated as a rare and luxurious treat. The following recipe was made by Mrs Ann Cook, sometimes landlady at the Queen's Head in Morpeth, in her *Professed Cookery* of 1760;

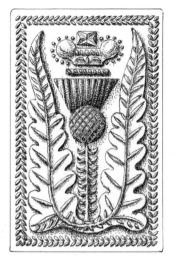

51. These moulded gingerbreads were sold as 'fairings' at St. Ninian's Fair. Since the moulds were carved in Scotland they show the thistle, and have the Scottish unicorn on the left side, the place occupied by the lion in England.

To make Gingerbread[16]

Take four Pounds of Treacle into a Pan, and set it on a clear Fire till it is scalding hot; then stir in half a Pound of Sweet-butter and a Jill of Brandy, and pour it into a Bowl; add to it two Ounces of best Ginger, the same Quantity of powdered Jamaica Pepper, an Ounce of Coriander Seeds, the same of Carraway Seeds, all well beat, and beat four pounds of Flour into it very well; when the Lumps are very well beat out, cut half a Pound of Lemon-peal into long Pieces, grease a large Cake-pan with Butter, and divide it into four Loaves, laying the fourth Part of the Lemon-peal on each Lair: It will take six Hours baking'

The resulting gingerbread is heavy, dense and intensely-flavoured compared to all modern gingerbreads, being intended to be eaten in small pieces, more like a sweet than a cake. The quantities, meanwhile, are those required by a confectioner, producing a block weighing over eight pounds/3.6kg, rather than just over a pound/450g, as in this reduced recipe;

Ann Cook's Block Gingerbread

8oz/225g black treacle	*1oz/25g butter*
12oz/450g plain flour	*1 tbs brandy*
1oz/25g candied lemon peel	
2 tsp each ground ginger & allspice	
1 tsp each ground coriander & caraway	

Place a small saucepan on the scales, weigh in the treacle and butter, and stir over a gentle heat until melted together. Remove from the heat, and stir in the brandy, spices and three-quarters of the flour to form a uniform dough. Turn this out on to the remainder of the flour, and knead until it has all been incorporated. Line the inside of a small loaf tin with greased paper, and enclose its base and sides with a few layers of paper to provide a degree of insulation. [Alternatively fold a sheet of thick cardboard to form an open-topped box some 4x6ins/10x15cm by 2ins/5cm high, and, line it with greased paper.] Form the dough into two slabs, drop one into the tin [or box], press it out until level, sprinkle with the peel, top with the remaining slab, level, and decorate either with wooden moulds, butter-prints or the back of a tablefork, before baking at 150°C, 330°F, Gas mark 2 for 1 hour.

When cold, it will be extremely hard, and so needs to be stored for a week or two in a cool, damp atmosphere until it can be sliced with a knife. It eats well on its own, or accompanied by a mild white cheese, in the northern tradition. I have made this for New Year's Eve parties in County Durham, the general verdict is 'The best gingerbread ever!', even if its digestive effects are quite noticeable if eaten to excess!

From at least the late eighteenth century the gingerbread made for the May and October fairs in Sunderland took the form of ginger-nuts, flat-bottomed balls about the size of a large walnut. Early in Queen Victoria's reign most were bought from John Young's chemist shop in the High Street. Here, as he recorded in his diary for Monday October 9th, 1843, he 'was kept constantly engaged in attending to the manufacture of Spice Nuts for the fair. Tuesday – I baked some nuts ourselves at night in the front warehouse ... in the shop very late wrapping up Spice Nuts.' Some were loaded into baskets and thrown into the crowds at the start of the fair, but 'many tons of these sweets were annually disposed of in pound and half-pound packages as presents to sweethearts and friends ... at 8d and 10d per pound' from his shop, its roof and windows being brilliantly illuminated with elaborate designs in flaring gas-lights. 'Mr Young had many rivals in the ginger nut trade and his popularity as the premier purveyor of them continued long after the abolition of the fair', the last one taking place in 1868. The recipe for such a popular product was always a closely-guarded secret, but this is the traditional local version;[17]

Sunderland Ginger Nuts [18]

11oz/300g plain flour	*4oz/100g sugar*
2oz/50g candied lemon peel	*4oz/100g butter*
1 tbs ground ginger	*9oz/250g black treacle*
1½ tsp each ground cinnamon & cardamom	

Mix the dry ingredients, rub in the butter, place the bowl on the scales, weigh in the warmed treacle, mix thoroughly, cover, and leave overnight. Next morning divide into walnut-sized balls, place on a greased baking tray, and bake at 150°C, 300°F, Gas mark 2 for 20 minutes.

The third form of gingerbread fairing was the ginger-snap. This probably originated from the crisp wafer-thin ginger biscuits of the late eighteenth century country-house tradition which continued through into the home bakery of Northumberland and Durham.[19] The following recipe was first published by Elizabeth Taylor of Berwick-upon-Tweed in 1769.[20]

Gingerbread
Mrs Raine, Darlington area [21]

4oz/100g black treacle	*1 tsp grated lemon zest*
1oz/25g butter	*8oz/225g plain flour*
3 tsp ground ginger	

Place a small saucepan on the scales, weigh in the treacle and butter, and stir over a gentle heat until melted. Pour in the remaining ingredients, mix and then knead to form a firm dough. Roll out very thin, cut into 2ins/5cm rounds, place on a greased baking sheet and bake at 150°C, 300°F, Gas mark 2 for 10-12 minutes.

With the introduction of baking soda in the mid nineteenth century, and Golden Syrup in the 1870s, the 'ginger snap' was transformed into the 'brandy-snap', or, to give it its local name, 'scarnchum'. This had so much sugar and raising agent that it spread into a molten, bubbling pool in the oven, enabling it to be rolled into a tubular shape before hardening to perfect crispness. It sold well at feasts and fairs – where the cry, 'nice brandy snaps, sixteen a penny' could be heard - the 'brandy' in its name hinting at an expensive ingredient that it rarely contained.

Brandy Snaps or Scranchum
Mrs F. Stephenson, Manor House Road, Newcastle.[22]

2oz/50g each, Golden-Syrup, butter, sugar & flour
½ tsp ground ginger

Weigh the syrup, butter and sugar into a saucepan, melt together while stirring, then remove from the heat and beat in the flour and ginger until smooth. Drop teaspoonfuls of the mixture some 4ins/10cm apart on a greased baking sheet and bake at 180°C, 350°F, Gas mark 4 for 7-10 minutes until bubbly and golden. Allow to cool for 1-2 minutes, then loosen with a palette knife, roll around the handle of a wooden spoon and leave until set. Use immediately or store in an airtight tin. They are delicious when piped full of whipped cream.

The use of baking soda similarly transformed the old black gingerbread into much lighter, softer and often moister forms of spongy cake. As a result, gingerbread became one of the most popular and regionally important specialities of northcountry housewives, many families developing their own social versions. Some contained orange, fig, walnut or coconut, and some were baked in cake, dripping or loaf tins, according to personal preference. A brief selection is given below, but anyone who wishes to explore their range more completely should read *Peggy Hutchinson's North Country Cooking Secrets*, which includes thirteen regional recipes.

Gingerbread,
from the Johnson family of Urpeth[23]

12oz/325g plain flour	*½ tsp bicarbonate of soda*
1 tbs ground ginger	*4oz/100g black treacle*
2oz/50g butter	*1 egg, beaten*
2oz/50g lard	*¼pt/150ml tepid milk*
6oz/175g sugar	

Sift the ginger into the flour, rub in the fats and mix in the remaining dry ingredients. Make a well in the flour, place the bowl on the scales, and weigh in the treacle. Add the egg and milk, and beat in to form a light mixture.

Pour the mixture into a greased and lined 2lb/900g loaf tin, half-filling it, and bake at 150°C, 300°F, Gas mark 2 for 1 ½ hours.

Wholemeal Gingerbread[24]

10oz/275g wholemeal flour	*½ tsp bicarbonate of soda*
2 tbs ground ginger	*2oz/50g lard*
2 tbs ground mixed spice	*¼pt/150ml milk*
2oz/50g sugar	*8oz/225g black treacle*

Mix the flour, spices and sugar, make a well in the centre and mix in the bicarbonate mixed with a little of the milk. Bring the remaining lard, milk and treacle to the boil, pour it into the dry ingredients, beat in, pour into a greased and lined 6ins/15cm square tin and bake at 170°C, 325°F, Gas mark 3 for about 2 hours.

Esh Winning Ginger Shortcake

12oz/325g plain flour	*3 tsp ground ginger*
6oz/175g butter	*1 tbs black treacle*
4oz/100g sugar	*1 egg, beaten*
2 tsp baking powder	

Rub the butter into the flour, mix in the dry ingredients, drop in the treacle and the egg, and work into a dough. Roll out ½in thick on a floured baking tray and bake at 170°C,

325°F, Gas mark 3 for 20-25 minutes. Dredge with sugar and leave to cool on its tray, before cutting up into square and triangles.

IN CHURCH AND CHAPEL

For anyone born after the 1950s and '60s, outside a church- or chapel-going family, it is difficult to appreciate the important role which these organisations played in the personal and social lives of their communities. Sundays, when all the shops were closed and there was little public transport, were spent at services and Sunday Schools in the morning, family dinners at mid-day, and, after tea, perhaps evening services, too. Choir practices, 'Bright Hours' and various parish meetings took place each week, and plans were made for special events, sometimes religious, sometimes purely social, and sometimes as a means of raising funds.

In the early days of Methodism in the 1730s, the former Christian practice of the Lovefeast was revived. Some were held in any conveniently large room. At Fell Grove, Blanchland, for example, Methodists welcomed from the surrounding area were first provided with refreshments.

> The folk that came from far away
> were asked to stay for tea,
> And welcomed to the choicest fare
> within a poor man's cot.
> As well to food more choice and rare
> with those of a happier lot

After tea, all entered a barn, where, above the cattle, they sang the Lovefeast hymn, perhaps Philip Doddridge's 'O Happy Day', the first of the Lovefeast hymns in the Methodist Hymn Book. After prayers;

> They rose with sweet and tuneful sound
> The grace for meat to sing;
> The biscuits then were handed round,
> With water from the spring[25]

These were happy, joyous and enthusiastic communal services, often drawing in large crowds. On hearing that Thomas Batty and Jeremiah Gilbert were to preach at one planned for 3rd August, 1823 at Colliery

52. A selection of the specially-made white earthenware Love Feast cups used in North-Eastern chapel congregations.

Dykes, Dipton, one enterprising publican arrived on the previous day, set up his beer tent, and began trading. At this period Methodists were rejecting their former use of alcohol, and enforcing teetotalism, so the preachers forcefully persuaded him to pack up and leave before the event took place.[26]

Lovefeasts held in large chapels presented no problems of this kind. In towns such as Sunderland they became a regular feature of chapel life. In his diary for April, 1842 John Young, a Methodist lay preacher, recorded that he had spent the afternoon at a Lovefeast at Philadelphia (a village towards Durham); next month he attended one at 8pm at Broughton Street Chapel and, a month later, another at South Durham Street.[27] On entering these, or any other Wesleyan or Methodist chapel for a Lovefeast, he would expect to find the congregation seated in their pews. A two handled vessel filled with cold water would then be passed around hand to hand, everyone taking a sip, this being followed by a plate of sliced bread and plain biscuits. Afterwards, any member who wished to speak, or provide a testimony of faith, then stood up and addressed the gathering.[28] As Peggy Hutchinson recalled in the 1930s, 'they got up one after another to give their religious experiences, finishing up with a sort of communion with a two-handled vessel filled with cold water, and everyone has a drink. They used to have a slice of currant bread, something like a granny loaf, but nowadays they eat a bath biscuit.'[29]

A number of Lovefeast cups are now in the collections of local museums. Made in white earthenware, they usually date from the Victorian period and take the form of either a footed bell-shaped goblet or a cylindrical mug with two handles, and the word LOVEFEAST painted or printed across them in black lettering. Others might be more decorative and specially made, one in the Beamish collection bearing floral sprays and the inscription 'Wesleyan Chapel, Witton Park. A.D. 1860'.[30]

Another great celebration in the nonconformist church was the Anniversary, originally commemorating the opening of an individual chapel. This attracted members of all the surrounding congregations to hear a popular preacher, and to enjoy the following tea. This might be of the potted meat sandwiches, rock cake, and tea stewed too long in the urn variety, or be an opportunity for the ladies to demonstrate the best of their home baking. At Burnhope near Lanchester, the ladies decided that a communal approach was best. Having purchased some 332lb/150kg of dry ingredients, they gathered together to mix them and knead them into dough. Meanwhile, little lads had been sent off to collect baking tins, which were now filled, returned to numerous homes for baking, and then returned to the chapel on the day of the tea. The following recipe is sufficient for a single large loaf.

Burnhope Chapel Spice Bread[31]

1lb/450g strong white flour	*½ nutmeg, grated*
1oz/25g each of brown sugar, butter, lard, currants, raisins and chopped candied lemon peel	
2 tsp ground cinnamon	*1 tbs dried yeast*

Follow the manufacturer's instructions for the dried yeast, either activating it with 1 tsp sugar in a little tepid water, whisking together and leaving in a warm place for about 20 minutes until frothy, and adding with the rest of the water, or adding the dried yeast with the spices.

53. Spice breads were often served at chapel teas. Many churches and chapels commissioned their own services of cups, saucers, plates, milk jugs, and sugar basins. If these were not available, each person would take their own cup etc., their ownership often marked by binding a coloured thread around the handle.

Mix the spices and sugar into the flour, rub in the butter and lard, make a well in the centre, and pour in a little over ¼pt/150ml water at blood heat, and mix to form a soft dough. Warm the dried fruit and peel, then work it into the dough. Cover, and leave in a warm place for 1½ hours.

Knead the dough for a few seconds, dust with flour, put in a greased and warmed 2lb loaf tin, and return to the warm for a further 30–45 minutes until fully risen. Bake at 220°C, 425°F, Gas mark 7 for 15 minutes, then reduce to 190°C, 375°F, Gas mark 5 for a further 15 minutes.

Both the Church of England and the various chapels held a series of social events which featured a meal of some kind. This was usually made by a combination of a carefully planned mass-production of sandwiches etc., by the ladies, and a 'faith tea', where everyone brought something to share. From time to time a local baker or confectioner might also be asked to provide the food, especially pie and peas. It would be impossible to describe all the different meals served in this way, but the following extracts taken from the *Wolsingham and Tow Law Parish Magazine* of 1889-90 are both typical and revealing.

Nov 26th Pie Supper at the Mechanics Institute, Tow Law. There was quite a rush of people, and the pies soon disappeared. Some of the waiters and others who had worked hard in connection with the affair having to go without. This was very hard ... However the supper was a great success.

Jan 15th Sunday School Tea & Entertainment

Jan 31st Day-Schools Magic Lantern Show. The children were given oranges and cake.

April Tea Many avoided paying for admission. Next year we propose to take the names of people who *attempt* to avoid the doorkeeper and publish them in the magazine for the benefit of the public, who may thus beware of swindlers.

May ? Band of Hope Annual Tea in the Mechanics Hall and evening service of song.

June 7th Choral Festival with a tea and 'Mrs. E. Robson's excellent beverage'.

Aug 12th Choral Festival. The Vicar provided the tea and edibles.

Aug 27th Choir trip to Durham, with a tea in the evening.

Sept 10th Sunday School Annual Tea & Fete for 200 children

Oct 9th Harvest Festival.

CORONATIONS

There were only three Coronations during the nineteenth century, those of George IV in 1821, William IV in 1831 and Victoria in 1838. Each was marked by major celebrations in every town, but perhaps the most lively of all took place in Newcastle in 1821. The town had strong republican leanings, and many had little respect for the monarchy. George IV's continuing liaisons with Mrs Fitzherbert and other mistresses were well known, as was his rejection of the popular Queen Charlotte, herself notorious for her relationship with one of her servants. However, in a show of loyalty, the Corporation decided to roast a couple of oxen to feed the crowds, and to pipe wine and beer into the pants, the public water-fountains. Having stuffed the oxen with potatoes;

They hung them both down [to roast] as it struck 12 at night;
But lang ere day-light was come in on the morning,

Both stuffing and 'tatoes were burnt in their kites (stomachs)
They turn'd them on spits till they've burnt like two cinders
And cut them both up about twelve of the day;
As they lay on the stages they smoak'd just like tinder,
And look'd like two muck heaps, the people did say ...

For this great celebration the horns of the oxen had been gilded and bedecked with ribbons. The populace was quick to relate these horns to those traditionally symbolising a cuckold, the husband of a faithless wife, and hence to the King;

Some come from afar, as did wise men of old,
To see our King's head branched thus with gold.
Success then, to horns, when they're gilded so clever;
May the King wear the horns, and wear them for ever.

In praise then of horns let all Newcastle sing;
For he who scorns horns, despises his King.
Let them boast of their garters, and boast of their stars,
But horns are far better than honours or scars.
Having detached the heads;
Then the carvers set to, with knives cutting and scraping,
And lumps of fat beef with such vengance were strew'd ...
The battle grew hot as they flung round the beef,
Disgusted they sought no Commander in chief,
The fires they demolish'd, while brickbats and beef
  Flew like rockets, in mad desperation
The butchers, now thinking their lives very sweet,
Soon threw down their gullies [knives] and beat a retreat;
Not wishing to die, just like dogs, in the street,
  On George the Fourth's Coronation.
Finally the oxen, now reduced to:
... mangled black carrion, was knock'd from the stage
And dragg'd round the town with republican rage
Till deposited safely i' th' Mansion-house yard, ...
It was sunk in the Tyne – to make broth for the fish.

The free ale and wine was similarly disregarded, some gulping it out of old hats and old shoes, while one naked keelman sprang in for a wash;

To see a keelman, from his huddock [cabin]
Within your wine trough wash his buttock,
Which ne'er before was drenched with wine,
But often plung'd in coaly Tyne.

The morning procession of the gentry to a service in St. Nicholas', the firing of the castle guns, and the £1000 spent in the preparation of the oxen, ale, wine, etc., had augured well, but the loyalty of the populace of Newcastle was not to be bought by beef and liquor. They deliberately made waste of everything provided by the Corporation and rampaged through the town. Although there were fights and struggles with the officers of the law, they finally dispersed without any clashes with the cavalry, who stood off nearby.[32] By the time of Queen Victoria's coronation in 1838, and her Golden and Diamond Jubilees in '87 and '97 the mood had changed completely, every town and village in the northcountry celebrating with true patriotic fervour.

A PIPEMAKER'S FEAST

Individual groups and societies often held communal feasts to celebrate a particularly significant event. The Gateshead guild of tobacco-pipe makers held radical views, and were delighted to hear of the release of John Wilkes from prison to which he had been committed following the publication of his seditious issue number 45 of the North Britain journal. Since an ox would be too large, they roasted a 45lb sheep, ate it with 45 large potatoes, 45 biscuits, and 45 quarts of beer. For smoking, Taylor Ansell made 45 clay pipes each 45 inches long, and stamped J.W.45. on the stem, an amazing feat of craftsmanship.[33]

CHAPTER EIGHTEEN

CALENDAR CUSTOMS

Today most of the surviving events which mark the passage of each year have been formalised into Bank Holidays by the government and commercialised by entrepreneurs. In addition, most people have moved away from the established and nonconformist churches which had formed the bedrock of northern communities for centuries. I have met north-easterners up to their thirties who have never read a page of the Bible, and so have little or no understanding of the great religious festivals which dominated the calendar in their grandparents' younger days.

By way of festive foods, we still have Christmas cakes, mince pies, hot cross buns and Easter eggs, most being shop-bought rather than home-made, but these are a poor substitute for the more numerous and interesting foods and ceremonies which were common in this region only a century into the past. One of the most surprising aspects of this group of foods is that, with the exception of eggs, virtually none of them have any meaningful connection with their related festivity. Whenever people arrange a special event, they usually try to make sure that it is done properly, as they and their community know it should be. As a result, elements which were once current features of everyday life become fossilised, only re-emerging on their particular day. This is why brides and grooms frequently adopt long, elaborate dresses, and morning coats and top hats respectively, and also tiered cakes covered in royal icing, just as if they were being married before 1918. In the same way, most festive foods are only the everyday dishes of past generations, maintained solely because they had always been served on their particular day.

The most remarkable survival of this kind is frummety, a dish of probable pre-historic origins which fell out of fashion in the sixteenth century. Because it had formerly been one of the everyday dishes served at Christmas Eve, as well as throughout the year, it was still made for every Christmas Eve long after it had gone out of general use. This tradition became so strong that it is still made every Christmas Eve by some families in Cleveland. Between the late sixteenth and late eighteenth centuries boiled suet puddings, enriched with dried fruits, were a standard dish on all polite dinner tables, being eaten with meat before their place was taken by potatoes. Because they too had once been an everyday dish, and as such served at the Christmas dinner, they were retained to become an indispensable part of the Christmas festivities. If invited to a Christmas dinner today, we still expect to see the whole family seated around the table with the host/hostess at its head, a tablecloth properly set with cutlery, a large roast ready to be carved, complete with all the trimmings, and afterwards a boiled pudding and perhaps mince pies. Every one of these features is a real anachronism, something once commonplace, but now totally abandoned throughout most modern homes – except for this single day.

Even though such foods were kept alive through this customary use, their recipes were frequently modified to meet changing tastes and expectations. The most significant of these was brought about by the effects of international trade in the late Victorian period. Up to that time sugar, spices and dried fruits had all been prohibitively expensive for most families, fruit cakes such as Yorkshire's 'Shouting Rodger' reputedly having so few currants that they had to shout to each other to discover if any others were present. Once availability had increased and prices fallen, more of these rich ingredients were added, to make their dishes especially good. In the twentieth century this practice got out of hand, resulting in modern Christmas puddings, mince pies etc. which are so heavily enriched with sugar, dried fruit, fats, spices and spirits that many people find them really unpleasant and indigestible.

This chapter describes the various food-related customs which have been practiced in Northumberland and County Durham, many of which have now disappeared, while some still continue. The recipes all come from local sources, and are well worth reviving today since they form a major part of the region's unique culinary heritage.

NEW YEAR'S DAY, JANUARY 1ST

The New Year is probably celebrated more in the north-east than in any other region of England. The most important visitor, the first to enter the house after midnight, is the first-footer, sometimes a fair-haired man, definitely without a squint, who must enter the house before anyone else leaves. He should bring a piece of coal, a piece of iron and a bottle of whisky with him, sometimes bread[1] and salt too, to ensure prosperity in the coming year. A glass of whisky was his usual reward, although some preferred a hot tea or coffee, along with welcoming food, such as bacon and egg breakfast.[2]

At Low Urpeth near Birtley, Peggy Hutchinson's family prepared for this ceremony by taking the pewter plates down from the dresser to hold a year-old fruit cake and cheese, and the best cut-glass decanter for the wine. As the pit-buzzer sounded midnight the door was flung open to let the luck in, and await the 'first foot' who here had to be a dark man, bearing his traditional gifts, and proclaiming 'Here's my sonse and here's my sele, and here's my happy New Year'. Sonse is Gaelic for abundance, and sele Germanic for happiness, an appropriate combination for a border region.[3]

COLLOP MONDAY

On the Monday before Shrove Tuesday collops, slices of bacon or ham, were eaten, this being a survival of the medieval practice of eating the last of the preserved meats before the start of Lent. They also produced fat for frying tomorrow's pancakes.[4] Around Belford gifts of rashers of bacon were carried to the houses of friends. Up to the early twentieth century ham and eggs were eaten for dinner, slices of 'home-fed' always being called 'collops' without adding the words 'ham' or 'bacon'.[5]

PANCAKE TUESDAY

Although this started as a normal working day, the ringing of the church bells around noon marked the start of a half-holiday, celebrated with sports and with pancakes to use up the last of the eggs and fat before Lent. In Newcastle, for example, the apprentices organised football competitions to occupy the afternoon. The main activity of the day, was, of course, the making and eating of pancakes.[6]

Pancakes

4oz/100g plain flour   *½pt/300ml milk*
½ tsp salt   *1 egg*
1-2oz/25-50g lard for frying

Sift the flour and salt, make a well in the centre, drop in the egg and half the milk, and beat regularly so as to slowly draw in the flour from the sides, without forming lumps. As it thickens, gradually add the remainder of the milk, then stand for an hour. Melt a little lard in a frying pan,

pour in just sufficient batter to cover the bottom, fry until
it has set, then toss and fry the other side.

Traditionally the pancakes were spread with treacle before being rolled
up, but this was later replaced by lemon juice and a sprinkling of
sugar.

The other traditional food eaten on this day was called a care-cake.
It was described as a small cake baked with eggs, using them up
before Lent, but no recipes appear to have survived.[7]

CARLING SUNDAY

If the origins of a custom have been long forgotten, its community
usually invents a plausible, but entirely mistaken, explanation.
Since everyone in the north-east ate dried peas on this day, it must
commemorate the arrival of a shipload of dried peas into Newcastle,
where the population were suffering the effects of a severe famine.
This popular story was, however, pure fiction.[8]

Passion Sunday, the fifth Sunday in Lent, marks the beginning
of Passiontide, the festival of Christ's last few weeks on earth,
terminating with the Crucifixion and Resurrection at Easter. The old
Germanic word for sorrow, mourning, or to be troubled, was *care*, a
word used in England as early as *Beowulf*. In Germany, Good Friday
was *kar-freitag* and Passion week *karwocke*, so in England Passion
Sunday was Care-Sunday.[9] It has been suggested that doles of dried
pulses had been distributed on this day before the Reformation, a
practical and timely form of poor-relief when winter food-stocks would
be running low. What is certain, is that Carling Sunday traditions were
already well-established here by the sixteenth century. In 1562 Turner's
Herbal described 'The perched burstled peasen which are called in
Northumberland Carlines.'[10]

The first detailed account of Northumberland carlings appeared in
the *Gentleman's Magazine* in 1788;

> 'Carlings ... are choice grey pease of the preceding
> autumn, steeped in spring water for 12 to 15 hours, till
> they are soaked or macerated, then laid on a sieve in the
> open air that they may be externally dry. Thus swelled,
> and enlarged to a considerable size, and on the verge of
> vegetating, they are put in an iron pot, or otherwise on a
> slow fire, and kept stirring. They will then parch, crack,

54. Dated to Carling Sunday, 1825, this Bewick wood-engraving shows mice enjoying a feast of the sprouted and fried carling peas. Behind, the ale jug bears the punning motto 'Pease & Plenty'.

and as we provincially call it, bristle; when they begin to burst they are ready to eat.

The genteeler sort [have them] after dinner to a glass of wine ... the honest peasant resorts to the best home-brewed, and there freely quaffs his Carling-groat in honour of the festival.'[11]

This process may seem strange to us today, but it replicates the methods used to convert barley into malt on a domestic scale, and would once have been familiar to many housewives.

By the 1820s, the grey, or dried field peas were being soaked overnight, half-boiled, and then fried in butter until crisp, and served with salt and pepper. In this way the 'lower orders' in Newcastle consumed 'immense quantities', as did many others throughout the north-east.[12] Within a few years the use of grey peas was being supplemented by a new imported variety called brandings, this name originating from their mottled appearance, being brown and yellow spots, but both remained in regular use.[13]

Carlings (1)

Carling, 'bristled, 'pigeon' or 'black' peas, with a brown and yellow brindled surface with fat [or oil] for frying and with salt

217

Soak the peas in water overnight, then drain and leave on a piece of wet cloth on a metal tray at room temperature for 3-4 days, until they have sent out a shoot about ¼–½ins/6–12mm long. Fry crisp in butter, until they start to pop, then pour into a bowl and stir in a little salt. They may be eaten either hot or cold, and taste rather like dry-roasted peanuts.

Before WWI, Mr. Moffett, the flour-dealer in Kirkwhelmington, used to bring in the necessary supplies beforehand, giving a quart of dried grey peas to each of his customers.[14]

Carlings (2)

Dried peas, butter for frying with sugar and rum

Soak the peas overnight in plenty of cold water, then drain and put into a saucepan with fresh water. Heat very slowly, and simmer for up to 2-3 hours until tender but not mushy. Drain the peas, fry them in butter, then sprinkle them with sugar and rum just before serving hot.

They were eaten in this way both in private houses, and in inns, both providing them free to anyone who called. It was a point of honour that every pea must be eaten, the person claiming the last one being believed to be the first to marry.[15]

If Newcastle men were in London on Carling Sunday, they would make their way to *The Hole in the Wall* at No. 60 Fleet Street, a tavern frequented by Thomas Bewick when he visited the capital. There they would enjoy their carlings specially prepared for them by the landlord. After moving into St Dunstan's Court nearby by 1826, this inn was demolished in 1860.[16]

GOOD FRIDAY

As in other parts of the country, hot-cross buns were sold on this day. Today they have largely lost their religious significance, and can be found in most supermarkets for at least the first half of the year.

Hot Cross Buns
A recipe from the Morpeth area[17]

1lb/450g strong white flour	*1 tsp salt*
2oz/50g currants or sultanas	*1½oz/35g sugar*
1 tsp ground mixed spice	*½pt/300ml tepid milk*
1oz/25g lard	*1 tsp dried yeast*
1oz/25g butter	

Sift the flour, salt and spice into a bowl, rub in the fats, and stir in the other ingredients, including the yeast, prepared according to the manufacturer's instructions. Knead to form a soft dough, until elastic and no longer sticky. Cover in a bowl, and leave in a warm place for 1½ hours until doubled in size. Turn out on to a floured board, knead lightly, cut into 12 pieces, and mould each into a round bun. Flatten, and mark each one deeply [with the back of a knife] to make a cross. Place on a greased baking tray, brush with a glaze of 1 tbs sugar dissolved in 1 tbs milk, and return to the warm to prove for a further 15 minutes.

Bake at 190°C, 375°F, Gas mark 5 for 15-20 minutes.

EASTER SUNDAY

Traditionally known as Pace-Egg Day (Pace deriving from pasch, meaning Easter), this was the day for giving and receiving decorated hen's eggs, symbols of the Resurrection, and formerly collected by the church as a tithe at this time of year.[18] As described in Northumberland in 1777:

'Eggs stained with various colours in boiling, and sometimes covered with leaf gold, are at Easter presented to children at Newcastle, and other places in the North – they ask for their Paste Eggs, as for a fairing, at this season. This custom, which had its beginning in childish superstition, seems to be ending in a way which, for whatever cause, had made eggs emblematic of the resurrection.'[19]

Meanwhile, here in 1788:

'Pas-eggs are still ... sent as presents for young folk in the Easter holidays. They are merely the eggs of our domestic fowl boiled and tinged of various hues, by adding to the water, when boiling, logwood, rose leaves [i.e. petals], the yellow blossoms of the whin, or furze, or other dyes, and are written on, figured, or ornamented, by an oiled pencil [i.e. fine brush], or any greasy matter, drawn lightly over the shell before they are boiled, according to the boyish taste of the artist. A pecuniary present at this season has the same name given to it.'[20]

'The Pitman's Courtship' of 1818 has the lines:

'And to please the pit laddies at Easter
A dishfull of gilty paste eggs.'

Gilding the eggs would only have been affordable by young pitmen without family commitments, most others relying on their own skill and ingenuity to produce the most decorative results.

The easiest way to decorate an egg using everyday materials was to boil it with the brown outer skins of onions, which would produce a rich chestnut colour. Much more interesting marbled effects were produced by binding a thick layer of onion skins around a freshly-rinsed egg, tacking a piece of cloth or tying a tape over them to keep them in position. A final polish with a little butter or bacon fat made their colours even deeper and more glossy. Alternatively the eggs could be dyed using commercial dyestuffs such as logwood for black, or analine dyes for brighter, vibrant colours.

Before plain-dyeing an egg, parts of it could be coated with wax. This ensured that the area covered would not take the dye, and so remain perfectly white. In the early twentieth century Mr. Herdman, part miner, part milk-delivery man at Acomb near Hexham, used this method to decorate an egg for each of his customers, each one having the recipients' name written across it in wax before being dyed. Two generations later every child at the local school was still receiving similarly inscribed pace eggs, these being written with a wax candle, before dipping into a dye made of coffee grounds. It is interesting to consider the source of this method, since melted wax was also used to write names or initials on eggs in Denmark.

While simple dyes were still used on fabrics or wallpaper their colours were often fugitive and ran when plunged into boiling water. Local egg decorators were quick to exploit this property, by tying pieces of the coloured materials or ribbon around their eggs, the

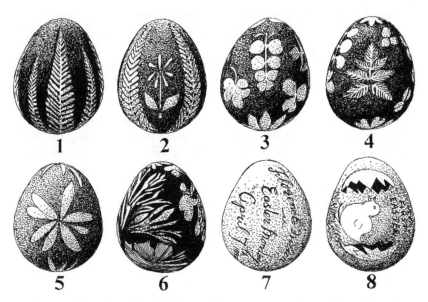

55. Fine examples of traditionally decorated pace-eggs. Numbers 1 & 2 were made in Newbrough near Haydon Bridge, 3 & 4 by Mrs Herdman of Acomb near Hexham, 5 by Mrs Thompson of Newbrough, and 6 by Mrs B. Alison of Halton Lea Gate. Number 7 was decorated with onion skins before being inscribed with a name and dated 1891, while 8 was painted in Durham around the 1950s.

shells absorbing the colours as they boiled. This could produce either overall mottled effects, or neat and vibrant designs, depending on the selection of cloths and colours. Peggy Hutchinson's mother used to sew parsley leaves on to plain calico, and wrap this around the egg, or even boil numerous eggs closely packed into a pan with parsley, to give dappled greeny-greys "rather like a peewit's egg without the brown spots."[21]

The finest Northumbrian pace eggs were made by combining both cloths and wild flowers. Near Hexham in the 1930s children collected petals and little flowers, which they pressed against the shell, after which coloured cloths chosen from the sewing basket were placed on top, with a final piece of linen to enclose everything tightly as it boiled for half an hour. It then emerged with finely outlined and coloured images of each flower set against their contrastingly tinted backgrounds. Since the Second World War egg decorating as a craft was promoted by the Womens' Institute, who held annual competitions. Mrs Herdman and her daughter from Acomb, Mrs Cyril Thompson of Newburgh and Mrs Beattie Allison of Halton-Lea-Gate were amongst the best known egg decorators in the region. Their patterns of neatly-arranged fronds of miniature ferns, leaves and flowers stand out in beautiful pale contrast to their rich purple, vivid blue, soft green, crimson and black backgrounds.[22]

Those without the time and skill to create such impressive effects still continued to decorate their eggs using simple penwork and paint. One set of three, made in County Durham in the 1950s and now at Beamish, show just how delightful these can be. Each bearing a newly-hatched yellow chicken and an egg, they are inscribed 'Did you lay it, Tommy Tucker', and 'My first Easter, Joyce', home-made mementoes of a significant family event.[23]

Returning to the nineteenth century, there were recognised penalties for refusing to accept the gift of a pace egg. If a woman refused one from a man, he felt free to seize her boots, while if a man refused one from a woman, she could snatch his cap.[24]

PACE EGG DAY

Easter Monday was dedicated to the destruction of pace eggs, only the finest, always intended for long-term display, surviving into evening. The first trial was booling - rolling them on the grass, preferably on a steep slope, to discover which ones broke first and could be eaten. Victorian participants in their sport could remember how;

> 'There was dancin', an footba's, an boolin pyest eggs.'
> 'The bells o' St Nicholas, when the Easter holidays myed thor appearance!
> Hoo leet was my yothful heart: ne stain was there to mar my happiness.
> Wi what pleshure aw booled maw peyste eggs on the Green!'
> 'Ne place to bool wor peyste eggs noo.'[25]

Next came jauping, when men and boys tried the strengths of their pace eggs. One held his egg securely in his palm, grasping it firmly so that only the pointed end protruded from his encircling thumb and forefinger. Grasping his egg in the same way, the 'jauper' then smashed it onto that of his opponent. Whichever broke was then forfeited to the victor, who then went off to challenge someone else. At the end of the day one jauper would emerge with a final, prize egg, along with sufficient hard-boiled eggs to guarantee severe indigestion if eaten that day.[26]

MAY DAY, 1ˢᵀ MAY

In the eighteenth century, as recorded in Hutchinson's *History of Northumberland*, syllabubs of wine, warm milk from the cow and sweet cake were made on Mayday, and a wedding ring dropped in. Each person then tried to dredge it out with a ladle, the successful participant expecting to be the first to get married.[27]

FLITTING DAY, 12ᵀᴴ MAY

On the larger farms, this was the day on which the hinds and their families packed up all their belongings and flitted, or removed, to the farm cottage provided by their new employer. Everyone was so busy, with so much to do, that there was little time to cook proper meals. For this reason, the wives prepared flitting dumplings, large boiled or steamed puddings which could be made beforehand, and hung from the ceiling in their cloths. Once inside the new cottage, they were easily and quickly re-heated to give a good, hot and satisfying meal when it was most needed.

ST JOHN'S DAY OR MIDSUMMER DAY, 24ᵀᴴ JUNE

On this day it was customary in Northumberland to cover the top of a stool with a layer of clay, onto which were stuck all kinds of flowers so closely and neatly arranged as to form a beautiful cushion. These were then displayed outside the houses in the villages, or at the ends of streets and at crossroads in the larger towns, with someone in attendance begging for money. That evening the proceeds were used to buy food and drink for a party.[28]

MICHAELMAS, 29ᵀᴴ SEPTEMBER

Throughout England well-to-do families celebrated this day with roast goose, these birds having been fattened by grazing on the stubble left after harvest. Some were probably paid as cottagers' rents since Michaelmas was a quarter-day. On 1ˢᵗ June, 1826, when Robert Raine was farming at Barford between Darlington and Barnard Castle, he invested in a flock of young geese, probably intending to fatten them up for sale at Michaelmas and Christmas. However, seventeen were stolen on 21ˢᵗ October, and so two days later he went to 'Barnard Castle and bid a reward of £10 -10 -0 to any person who could give information against the rogues who stole the geese.' This clearly demonstrates the local importance of Michaelmas geese.[29]

Elizabeth Taylor's *Art of Cookery* published in Berwick in 1769 recommended the cook to put shredded onions, a little sage, salt and pepper, all mixed in butter, into the goose just before it was put to roast. Later farmhouse cooks used a similar method, but without butter, since the goose provided ample fat.[30]

Roast Goose

9-11lb/4-5kg oven-ready goose	1 tbs chopped sage
3-4 large onions, parboiled	salt & pepper

Wash the goose, sew up the neck end, prick the breast with a fork, and rub with salt. Chop the onions, mix with the sage, season with salt and pepper, use to fill the inside of the goose, and skewer the vent together. Place on its breast in a roasting tin, and roast at 180°C, 350°F, Gas mark 4 for about 15 minutes per pound/450g, plus 15 minutes. When browned, turn the goose over onto its back [alternatively the goose may be cooked on a grid in the roasting tin] and baste frequently.

When ready, pour off the fat, add warm water, a little salt and gravy browning, and stir over a gentle heat for a few minutes to thicken before serving as gravy.

Apple Sauce for Roasting Goose

Peel, core and chop the apples and stew with a few tablespoons of water, stirring occasionally until tender. Pour off the liquid (if any) and stir in sugar to taste.

ALL HALLOWS' EVE, 31ST OCTOBER

The youngsters of Alnwick celebrated this night with apple-bobbing. In its simplest form every person threw an apple into a tub of water, and then took it in turn to bite one, and lift it out in the mouth without either sucking or using the side of the tub. To make the whole task more interesting a kind of beam was hung over the tub of water, and apple being stuck on one end, and a lit candle at the other, this being twirled so that they both spun round. Each person then had their hands tied behind their backs before trying to grip the apple with their teeth as it swung past, meanwhile having to dodge the advancing candle.[31]

Another activity involved the use of nuts to divine future happiness. Each couple threw a pair of nuts onto the fire: if these lay still and burned together, all would be well, but if they bounced or flew apart, their marriage would bring nothing but trouble. This custom led All Hallows' Eve to be popularly known as Nut-crack-night' in Northumberland.[32]

CHRISTMAS EVE

Preparations for the celebration of Christmas had started some weeks beforehand, with people gathering in all the various raw materials for the special seasonal dishes, and brewing the strong Christmas ale. Wherever possible, those foods which needed prolonged curing, boiling and baking had already been made, thus saving time and trouble over this busy period. All had to be ready for the evening of Christmas Eve, when the whole household gathered around their communal table to enjoy their first of their festive meals, a supper of frummety, yule cake and cheese.

FRUMMETY

Frummety is probably one of the oldest of all our cooked foods, being whole grains of corn simply prepared and stewed until soft. As soon as fires and cooking pots came into use, prehistoric people must have relished the transformation it brought to their everyday meals, their collected seeds or cultivated grains being rendered tender, succulent, hot and satisfying for the first time. Up to around the Tudor period, frummety made from wheat was a standard dish on the table of peasants and nobles alike, but then fell out of fashion, except for suppers on Christmas Eve. This tradition was followed throughout England, except in Northumberland and in the south-east, below a line extending from the Wash across to Dorset.

Frummety had remained an everyday food in Durham for centuries, being regularly served to the inmates of the Darlington workhouse from at least 1757 until 1834, when it was finally replaced by gruel.[33] Even in 1850 meals of 'posset an' honey an' bacon collops an' frummety' were being served on Tyneside, but from around that date it appears to have been regarded as a specifically Christmastime

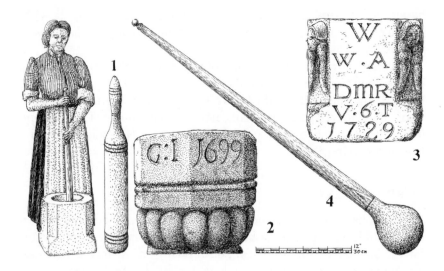

56. To prepare wheat or barley for making frummety, the ears of corn gleaned at the end of harvest were first threshed by being beaten with a wooden bittle, such as this example from Ford (1). The grain was then soaked in water, drained, placed in a stone knocking-trow (such as 2 & 3), and beaten with a knockin-mell (4, from Darlington) to remove the husks.

dish.[34] It was now being 'made of either wheat or barley. It is used by all classes on Christmas Eve, usually eaten … with plum loaf and cheese.'[35]

The traditional method of preparing frummety involved soaking the whole grains of wheat or barley in water, then beating them to remove the husk. This process took place in a large stone mortar called either a creeing trough or a knocking-trow, accompanied by its long wooden pestle or knocking-mell.[36] These used to be found in most farmhouses, but most have now been relegated to the garden to serve as sturdy flowerpots. They are usually of a hard gritstone, some 12–18ins/30–45cm square, and about the same height, and often bear their owners' initials and their date, mainly in the late seventeenth and eighteenth centuries. Some could be quite stylish, one owned by a Mr Davies of Hartlepool being octagonal, with a boldly gadrooned base and the inscription 'G:I 1699'.[37]

Knocking mells are much rarer, but one is preserved at Beamish, its bulbous head measuring some 6ins/15cm in diameter, fitted with a tapered shaft to make the whole mell just under 4ft/1.2m long.[38] Others were made of stone with a wooden handle, or even the shinbone of an ox, weighted with lead and sheathed in iron.[39] These creeing troughs were also used to prepare winter food for horses. At Cherryburn, Thomas Bewick used to set off early on dark winter mornings with his dyking mitten, apron and a broken sickle to gather the previous year's growth from the furze bushes. On returning from school, he would then strip off to energetically 'cree them with a Wooden Mell in a Stone trough, until these tops of Whinns were beaten to the consistency of soft, wet grass, & with this mess I fed the Horses before I went to bed, or in the morning.' As a result, they soon became very sleek.[40]

Once the soaked frummety corn had been beaten in the creeing trough, it was rinsed in water to float off the husks. The pearled grain was then placed in a pan or stoneware jar, covered with three times its volume of cold water, and kept hot for a day and a half to swell, soften and thicken into a glutinous mass. A quart of this was then mixed with two quarts of milk, three beaten eggs, four ounces of currants and a little grated nutmeg, before being re-boiled for about a quarter of an hour and served piping hot.[41]

Cooking frummety in this way was easy enough; it was the de-husking process which took most time and effort. From the later nineteenth century many families avoided this by using kibbled wheat which had the grains very coarsely milled or broken into pieces while still retaining their inner husk, and so not eating as smoothly as the earlier form. Mrs Symes' method was to simmer the kibbled wheat for twelve hours, then to stir in a knob of butter, a little mixed spice, sugar, cream, rum, and, if liked, some currants. She described it 'as near a liquid spice loaf as one can imagine, delightful and fragrant. One farmer I heard describe it as "Gruel with its best clothes on." '[42]

Since ready-pearled barley was readily available in most grocer's shops, it was found to be an effective substitute for pearled wheat. As early as 1849 the Christmas Eve frummety served in Teesdale was being made from either wheat or barley.[43] This practice continued throughout County Durham well into the twentieth century, some families introducing the term 'fluffin' to describe the barley version. Whichever its name, it was particularly popular around Coxhoe, Bishop Auckland, West Auckland and Stockton-on-Tees. The following recipe is based on the memories of Mrs Polly Gillham of Witton Park and Mrs O.B. Bannister of Bishop Auckland, who first stewed the barley in a large milk bowl in the oven before adding the other ingredients[44]

Frummety

8oz/225g pearl barley	*pinch of salt*
2oz/50g sugar	*½ tsp nutmeg*
1oz/25g butter	*1-2 tbs rum*
½pt/300ml milk or cream	
Optional additions: 1-2 tbs black treacle, 2oz/50g currants	

Put the barley in a casserole with 2pts/1.1l water, cover and bake at 170°C, 325°F, Gas mark 3 for 3 hours, adding a little more water towards the end of this time, if required. Remove from the oven, stir in the remaining ingredients, and stir over a gentle heat for 10 minutes before serving hot. (If it has become stiff, stir in a little more cream or milk).

On 23rd December, 1826, T.G. Wright, the Newcastle doctor, recorded that Mr Crawford had invited him 'to sup at Greenfield Place on Frumenty tomorrow evening.' There he would have been served a virtually identical seasonal dish.[45]

YULE CAKES

Unlike modern Christmas cakes, the Yule cakes of County Durham were fruited and spiced yeast-raised breads. Each measured about 10ins/25cm diameter by only an inch high, with rounded sides, since they were baked without a tin. Victorian recipes describe them as being decorated by marking the top 'in lines with the back of a fork', or 'Score it with a fork in the fashion of Christmas Cakes.'[46] Fortunately an example was once sketched by Lady Alice Gomme, this showing that the design comprised four diametric lines crossing in the centre, as with a Union Jack, and another line running around the perimeter, a short distance in from the outer edge.[47] These recipes produce the richer and the plainer yule cakes, as well as one which utilised a lump of dough left over from breadmaking on baking day.

Yule Cakes
Snow Hall, Jan 28th 1863[48]

14oz/400g strong white flour	*½ tsp dried yeast*
1 tsp mixed spice	*¼pt/150ml tepid milk*

57. Yule cakes made of fruited yeast-raised doughs were the original Christmas cakes, each part of the country having its own particular variety. The circular example incised with a fork was made at the historic Snow Hall, Gainford, while the other, designed to be broken into squares was made in Durham.

1½oz/35g sugar	*5oz/125g currants*
pinch of salt	*2oz/50g raisins*
1oz/25g chopped candied peel	*4oz/100g butter*

Sift the flour, spices, sugar and salt together, rub in the butter, add the yeast according to the manufacturer's instructions, and mix in sufficient milk to form a dough. Knead for a few minutes until smooth, then return to the bowl, cover, and leave in a warm place until doubled in size.

Knead in the remaining ingredients, and press with the heel of the hand to form a cake some 10-11ins/25-28cm diameter on a greased baking sheet. Use the back of a dinner fork to incise the decoration into the top (see fig 57), cover lightly with a cloth, return to the warm until risen again, then bake at 200°C, 400°F, Gas mark 6 for 20 minutes. After the first 10 minutes, briefly open the oven door and sprinkle the cake with a little sugar.

Stockton Yule Cake [49]
Mrs Webbs, Winston Rectory, near Staindrop

14oz/400g strong white flour	*½ tsp dried yeast*
1 tsp mixed spice	*¼pt/150ml tepid milk*
4oz/100g sugar	*3oz/75g currants*
3oz/75g butter	

Make up as in the previous recipe.

Durham Yule Cake [50]

14oz/400g strong white flour   *pinch of salt*
4oz/100g butter, creamed with 4oz/100g sugar
4oz/100g each currants, sultanas & citron
1 tsp allspice   *1 egg white, beaten*
½ tsp dried yeast
4oz/100g candied lemon peel, thinly sliced

Sift together the flour, salt and allspice, add 9fl oz/250ml tepid water and the yeast, prepared to the manufacturer's instructions. Mix together, then knead for 10 minutes to form a smooth dough. Return to the bowl, cover, and leave in a warm place until doubled in size. Mix the creamed butter and sugar, dried fruits and candied peels, knead into the dough, then roll out 1½in/4cm thick on a greased baking tray. Mark the top into squares with a greased knife, brush with egg white, and return to the warm to rise again.
Bake at 200°C, 400°F, Gas mark 6 for 20 minutes.

These yeast-raised yule cakes are delicious – especially the one from Durham, but in more prosperous homes rich egg-raised yule cakes were also being made in the late eighteenth century. The next recipe comes from a manuscript recipe book written in the Darlington area around 1789-1810.

Yule Cake
Mrs Jepson [51]

5oz/150g butter	*½ tsp ground nutmeg*
8oz/225g plain flour	*1 tbs brandy*

2 eggs, beaten	*5oz/125g currants*
3oz/75g chopped candied peel	*5oz/125g caster sugar*

Beat the butter until soft and creamy, then beat in half the flour. Beat the eggs with the sugar until very light and pale, fold in the remaining flour, add to the butter and flour mixture, and stir in with the nutmeg and brandy. Stir in the dried fruit, put into a greased and lined 6ins/15cm diameter cake tin, and bake at 150°C, 300°F, Gas mark 2 for about 2 hours.

Yule cakes and yule loaves, sometimes raised with yeast, sometimes with eggs, and sometimes with baking soda or baking powder, continued to be baked in many homes in County Durham throughout the nineteenth and twentieth centuries, despite the increasing popularity of the Christmas cake.

YULE DOOS

Before describing this most interesting yuletide cake, it should be explained that everyone appears to have their own definition of its correct spelling and pronunciation. It may appear as a hule-doo, he-yul-doo, hyull-doo, hull-doo, yull-doo, yule-babby or finally a yule-doo, the form adopted here. The earliest published definition was published in John Brand's *Popular Antiquities* of 1777; 'a kind of Baby or little Image of Paste, which our bakers used formerly to bake at this Season, to present to their customers'.[52] Despite giving the impression that it was already extinct, it was still thriving, and had at least another century and a half of regular use. In 1824 J.T. Brockett recorded that these little images of paste, studded with currants [are] baked for children at Christmas, probably intended for the virgin and child. About this time it was expected that every hewer, the pitman who picked the coal from the coalface, should give a yule-doo to his putter, the man or boy who pushed the loaded tubs away to the 'flat' ready for haulage to the shaft, and returned with a fresh supply of empty tubs. If the hewer failed to provide the yule-doo, he could expect to find that his clothes had disappeared mysteriously by the end of his shift.[53] Robson's *Pitman's Courtship* of 1849 described how the couple will sell 'hull-doos' from their shop, once they are married.

In 1891 Mrs Gomme received a letter from Mrs Jessie Barker of Hexham House, Hexham, telling her of the yule doos of Harbottle. In

58. Yule Doos (Yule Doughs) were made as Christmas gifts throughout the region. This one, sketched for Lady Gomme about a century ago, is a woman, as made for the girls. However, another cut in the dough would rapidly give it the separate legs to convert it into a man to be given to the boys.

this Coquetdale village on the fringe of the Cheviots, an old lady was still making them every year – a woman for the girls and a man for the boys. She simply cut them out with a knife. Fortunately Mrs Gomme's papers include a drawing of a yule doo, the only known representation of this most traditional north-eastern cake. It shows a piece of lightly-fruited dough which had been formed into a flat oval shape, then given a few knife-cuts to produce a head, body, and arms which touched in front. Currants provided the eyes, mouth, and probably buttons, while a triangle of candied peel served for the nose. Since the cake was solid below the waist, it must represent a woman, but another vertical cut would have given it separate legs to convert it into a man.[54]

Another contemporary description states that these cakes were between six and twelve inches/15-30cm long, with raisin eyes and nose, the arms crossed in front, and without feet. As to their recipe, it was a sweet, yeast-raised dough enriched with currants, sultanas and candied lemon peel. Combining all this information, they were probably made from ordinary bread dough, kneaded with sugar and dried fruits, just like the Durham yule cake (see p. 230), but with very little dried fruit.[55]

The yule doo was already in decline around 1900. In 1929 Mrs Thomas Hoyle of Cambo recollected that 'My mother always made Yule Dollies ... I don't make them now.'[56] About the same time Peggy Hutchinson remembered how at one time the young lads in the Chester-le-Street district used to call at all the surrounding farmhouses for their yule doos, but that in her day they were only given to children who regularly came to the farm to collect milk. These doos were not pieces cut from a yule cake, but had a different recipe. Some were still being made in northern Northumberland in the 1940s, but from that time they rapidly fell out of regular use, effectively ending a fine regional tradition.[57]

Whatever the kind of yule cake, it was always eaten with a piece of cheese. In Edwardian Bishop Auckland couples would often buy a whole or a half Cheshire cheese from the co-op. Here the manager took them into the storeroom to inspect 'his treasures, round and green and moulding and smelling. He inserts his knife and draws out the white pith. Father takes his piece and tastes, Mother takes her piece and tastes, the rest is put back in the cheese. They agree to have it sent home.'[58]

CHRISTMAS DAY

The chief meal of this day was, of course, the Christmas dinner, the best dinner of the entire year, with as many good things as the family could afford, always including its seasonal specialities. Up to the middle of the nineteenth century the housewife's first task was to make her Christmas pies, as recorded in the traditional Northumbrian rhyme sung to 'I saw Three Ships';

> 'Dames get up and make your pies
> And let your lazy maids lie,
> At Christmas Day in the morning.'[59]

CHRISTMAS PIES

The finest Christmas pies, those made in the region's major castles and halls, were truly magnificent, being designed to stand cold on the

sideboards of their great dining rooms, their rich ingredients ready to
be served whenever called for by the family members and their guests.
Those made by John Thacker, cook to the Dean and Chapter of Durham
Cathedral from 1739 to 1758, contained a whole goose and two ducks,
all boned, parboiled and seasoned before being baked in an elaborate
crust and filled with clarified butter. When it was served, the head and
feet of the goose garnished its lid, to readily identify the contents.[60]

Elizabeth Taylor of Berwick added a turkey or two hens to her goose
pie, while Ann Cook's version of 1760 was even richer;

'A Christmas Goose Pye'[61]

*Take a Stone of Flour, and boil up four Pounds of Butter in three
Quarts of Water, and mix the Flour with the Butter first; then take
as much of the Water as will mix the other Part of the Flour, work
it well together, and when it is cool raise an ovel crust, then take a
fat Goose and a Turkey, pick off all the Feathers, clean and cut up
their Backs, and take out all their Bones; take a Bullock's Tongue,
blanch and split it; season the Turkey and Goose with Nutmeg,
Jamaica and Black-pepper; Lay the Turkey on the Bottom of the
Pye, and upon it the split Tongue, cover it with the Goose; lay over
the Goose all the Seam, that is the Fat you took out of her; and
make a thick Lid, cover the Pye, and paper it well: It will take
six Hours baking; when you take it out of the Oven, pour into it a
Pound of melted Butter, and set it upon a cold Stone till it is cool'*

This pie, weighing some two stones, was certainly a major
achievement for any cook/housekeeper, adding considerably to her
reputation for fine food and hospitality, but it paled into insignificance
when compared with the following monster, described in the *Newcastle
Chronicle* for 6th January, 1770:

'Monday last was brought from Howick to Berwick, to
be shipp'd for London, for Sir Henry Grey, bart., a pie,
the contents wherof are as follows; viz. 2 bushels of flour,
20lb of butter, 4 geese, 2 turkies, 2 rabbits, 4 wild ducks,
2 woodcocks, 6 snipes, and 4 partridges; 2 neat's tongues,
2 curlews, 7 blackbirds; 6 pigeons; it is supposed to be
a great curiosity, was made by Mrs Dorothy Patterson,
housekeeper at Howick. It was nearly nine feet in
circumference at bottom, weighs about 12 stones, will take

59. Christmas goose pies were always an expensive upper-class delicacy. At Durham Cathedral in the 1750s the Dean and Chapter's goose pies were being made by John Thacker in the Great Kitchen. Just before serving each one was garnished with the bird's head and feet, to indicate its contents.

two men to present it at table; it is neatly fitted with a case, and four small wheels to facilitate its use to every guest that inclines to partake of its contents at table.'

Those without the resources and skills required to make their own Christmas goose pies could buy ready-made ones from town-centre confectioners.[62]

MINCE PIES

In the sixteenth century cooks added spices and dried fruits to their minced mutton pies, giving them a richer and more interesting flavour. Almost identical ingredients were still being used by their Georgian successors, the main difference being in their relative proportions, the fruit and spices now predominating. The meat content disappeared almost entirely during the Victorian period, only the beef suet remaining in general use, as in the following recipe of 1869 from Ryton Rectory, ten miles upriver from Newcastle.

Mincemeat
Mrs Webb[63]

1lb/450g peeled, cored & chopped apple   *8oz/225g suet*
8oz/225g flaked almonds   *½pt/300ml brandy*
½ tsp each ground cinnamon & nutmeg
[4oz/100g] chopped candied orange, lemon & citron peels
1lb/450g raisins   *12oz/325g currants*

This is a rich and expensive mixture, only to be found in the more prosperous households. For most working families rather plainer and more economical versions were used, as in this recipe of 1897;

Mincemeat
J. Dobson[64]

1lb/450g peeled, cored & chopped apples   *1 tsp mixed spice*
8oz/225g each, currants, raisins, sugar and suet

One of the disadvantages of including suet, was that it solidified when cold, so that eating a cold mince pie could leave an unpleasant fatty deposit in the mouth. To counteract this, the suet could be omitted, and more fresh fruit introduced, such as oranges, lemons, grapes, or plums.

Plum Mincemeat
Miss Williams, Durham Field Farm, Shotley Bridge[65]

2lb/900g plums, stoned & halved	*1 lemon*
2oz/50g candied peel	*2oz/50g chopped almonds*
4 large cooking apples	*1 tsp ground ginger*
2oz/50g currants	*1 tsp ground cloves*
2oz/50g sultanas	*8oz/225g sugar*

Stew the plums, lemon juice and ⅛pt/75ml water until tender. Rub through a sieve. Peel, core and finely chop the apples, and stir into the plum purée along with the other ingredients.

All these mincemeats benefit from being sealed down in jars and being left in a cool place for a few weeks to mature. They can then be used to fill shortcrust pie crusts and baked at 230°C, 450°F, Gas mark 8 for 20 minutes.

The next task was to prepare the haggis.

THE HAGGIS

The haggis is a fine old English dish, being made throughout this country from at least the fifteenth century and continuing into the nineteenth century. Its invented role as the national dish of Scotland owes far more to romantic patriotism than to historic reality. As made on both sides of the border, it was much sweeter, richer and spicier than the modern variety. In Northumberland the words haggish or haggish-meat referred to finely-minced tripe, formerly one of its principal ingredients.[66] Some haggises were quite plain, made 'only of oatmeal, suet and sugar, - stuffed into a sheep's maw and boiled'. But others of 1825 were:

'Made sometimes of fruit, suet and minced entrails ... it was till lately a common custom in many country places to have this fare to breakfast every Christmas Day, and some part of the family sat up all night to have it ready at an early hour. It is now used to dinner on the same day [and] sold in the Newcastle markets.'[67]

237

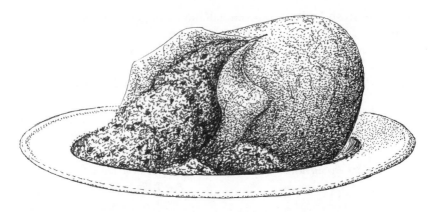

60. The modern haggis, always made to an almost uniform savoury recipe, is largely a creation of late Georgian Scotland's Romantic Nationalist revival. Haggises made both sweet and savoury had been made throughout England and Scotland from at least the fifteenth century, the fruited Northumbrian haggis still being sold in Newcastle market in the 1820s.

By combining these descriptions with those of Hannah Glasse of a Hexham family for an oatmeal pudding, and Charles Carter's for a Cumbrian hackin, it is possible to suggest a probable recipe for anyone wishing to recreate a Newcastle haggis.

Haggis

7oz/200g coarse oatmeal, soaked overnight in cold water
6oz/175g suet   *3oz/75g sugar*
8oz/225g currants   *pinch of salt*
4oz/100g minced tripe (or lamb)   *4oz/100g raisins*

Rinse, wring and lay flat a square of fine cloth or thick muslin, dust with flour, and shake off the surplus. Squeeze the oatmeal to remove the water, mix with the remaining ingredients, gather the cloth around them and tie tightly with string. Plunge into a large pan with sufficient boiling water to cover it, cover, and boil for 2½ hours. It may be kept for a week or two before needed, and then re-heated by re-boiling for an hour.

Years later one inhabitant of Belford, between Alnwick and Berwick, still remembered his mother making the haggis on the preceding night, to have it ready for Christmas morning.[68]

CHRISTMAS DINNER

The main dish for Christmas dinner was a roast, preferably of goose, if it could be afforded. Cooked just as at Michaelmas (p. 223), it was served with apple sauce, mashed potatoes, sprouts and gravy, as well as its stuffing of chopped sage and onion.[69] Before the introduction of battery houses, all types of poultry were too expensive for most families, unless home-bred, and many bought in a joint from the butchers. Ideally it would be a standing rib of beef, as described in Joe Wilson's poem on 'Christmas';

> *The beef on the tyeble looks temptin' an' lushus,*
> *An' tyests se much sweeter wi' bein' the prize,*
> *An' the holly seems noddin' as tho' it was laffin'*
> *At a' the glad fyeces an' bonny bright eyes.*
> *Mony a lump o' fine beef's tried, cut, and*
> *quartered; mony a fine prize beast gets a knock*
> *on the heed quite unexpected ...*

Other roasts were rather more economical. One Christmas dinner remembered from early twentieth-century Stakeford near Ashington comprised roast belly pork, sage and onion stuffing, and apple sauce, followed by a boiled sweet suet dumpling enriched with currants, raisins and spices, accompanied with cornflour sauce.[70] This cost far less than expensive poultry or beef, but well-cooked with crisp crackling, would be both delicious and satisfying. Sometimes in County Durham the Christmas dinner started with a separate course of Yorkshire Pudding, served with stuffing and lashes of gravy.[71]

As the Victorian period progressed, newspapers, popular magazines, and the works of writers such as Charles Dickens invented a nation-wide concept of the ideal Christmas. As a result, some of the old-established regional dishes began to be replaced by more standardised fare. The goose was now in competition with the turkey, for example, and the haggis with the Christmas pudding. The first generation of these puddings was much plainer, well-flavoured and digestible than those of today, and their recipes still give excellent results. It was customary for everyone in the house to stir the pudding mixture 'for luck', while some families always included a pinch of salt 'to avert the evil eye'.

61. Traditional Christmas puddings were much plainer, lighter and healthier than their over rich, over fruited, over spiced and indigestibly heavy commercially-made modern successors.

Christmas Pudding[72]

4oz/100g plain flour   *1 carrot, grated*
1 tsp bicarbonate of soda   *1 large apple, grated*
2 tsp cream of tartar   *1lb/450g mixed dried fruit*
1 tsp grated nutmeg   *2 eggs, beaten*
5oz/125g sugar   *⅓pt/200ml milk*
4oz/100g suet   *4 tbs sherry*
4oz/100g fresh white breadcrumbs

Sift together the flour, baking soda, tartar and nutmeg, stir in the dry ingredients, including the carrot and apple. Make a well in the centre, drop in the liquids, and mix all together very thoroughly. For a round pudding, rinse and wring out a piece of thin cloth or strong muslin, spread out flat, dredge with plain flour, and shake off the surplus. Lay this across a bowl, pack the mixture inside, gather the cloth over the top, twist it tight, and tie in place with string. Plunge into boiling water, cover, and boil gently for 6 hours, topping up with boiling water as necessary.

For a basin, grease the interior, pack the mixture inside, and cover with a piece of greaseproof paper, pleated down the centre, and across the middle, to allow for expansion. Traditionally this was topped with a square of cotton cloth or strong muslin, this being tied beneath the rim with strong string, and the corners brought together diagonally and knotted on top. This provided a 'handle' which enabled the hot pudding to be removed from the pot using a carving fork, or the handle of a wooden spoon. Placing a piece of cooking foil over the pudding and squeezing it tightly around the brim of the basin is much more convenient and just as effective as the muslin, but lacks the 'handle'. Place either in a steamer, or on a low trivet in a saucepan, with the boiling water half-way up the sides, cover, and steam for 6 hours.

Puddings such as these could be made weeks, even months, beforehand, being hung up against the ceiling to keep them safe and dry until required. Then they would be taken down and re-boiled or steamed for a couple of hours before being served with either custard or sweet white sauce laced with rum or brandy. A further dousing with more of the spirit enabled the puddings to appear dramatically swathed in blue flames, but this was never done in teetotal and strict Methodist households.

Today, when ingredients such as dried fruits and eggs are relatively inexpensive, it should be remembered that in the past they were still something of a luxury to many working families. Their recipes were appropriately plainer, as in these versions;

Economical Plum Pudding (1)
East Nubbock & Blossomhill Farms, Hexham[73]

8oz/225g each mashed potato, grated carrots, raisins & plain flour
6oz/175g brown sugar   *1 tbs ground mixed spice*
4oz/100g suet   *pinch of salt*

Mix together, leave overnight, and steam for 3-4 hours.

Economical Plum Pudding (2)
M. Gibson, Morpeth area[74]

4oz/100g each mashed boiled carrots, sultanas, raisins or
currants, suet, fresh white breadcrumbs and flour
2oz/50g each sugar & chopped dates
½ tsp each ground ginger, mixed spice & baking powder
1 tbs marmalade   milk for mixing

Mix together, and stir in sufficient milk to form a stiff mixture. Steam for 5 hours, and 2 hours when needed.

CHRISTMAS CAKES

The now universal Christmas cake comes from a completely different tradition to the yule cake. From before the 1590s huge fruit cakes had been made in great houses, these being occasionally cut to start the parties celebrating the end of the feast of Christmas on Twelfth Day and Twelfth Night, January 6th. During the eighteenth and nineteenth centuries these elaborately iced and decorated 'Twelfth Cakes' became a speciality for professional confectioners, giving ample scope for displaying their skills in bakery and sugarcraft.[75] On Twelfth Day 1827, Dr Thomas Wright of Newcastle received 'a present of a large twelfth cake &c from London', an extremely costly gift.[76] As the pressures of Victorian industrial and commercial life effectively killed off the Twelfth Night parties, use of these cakes retreated to Christmas Day, when they were cut at tea-time, and served to family and friends over the next few days. At the same time, they moved down the social scale, from the homes of the wealthy to those of the working class. Now more families could afford to buy the rich ingredients, especially as the booming Empire was importing the necessary spices and dried fruits at their lowest prices. Each family developed its own tried and tested recipe, typical examples being;

Plum Cake
Mrs Stafford, Brockley Hall, Alnwick[77]

8oz/225g each of butter, soft brown sugar, plain flour, currants
and chopped candied peel
3 eggs, beaten   1 tbs brandy

Cream the butter with the sugar, beat in the eggs and brandy little by little, and then the flour. Mix in the remaining ingredients, put in a greased and lined 6ins/15cm square or 7ins/18cm round tin, and bake at 150°C/300°F/gas mark 2 for 2½ hours.

Plum Cake
East Nubbock & Blossomhill Farms, Hexham[78]

5oz/125g butter	*1lb/450g currants*
8oz/225g caster sugar	*4 eggs, beaten*
4oz/100g chopped candied lemon peel	
4oz/100g flaked almonds	*2 tbs brandy*
2 tsp ground mixed spice	*12oz/325g plain flour*

a few lumps of sugar, rubbed on an orange peel to absorb the zest

Follow the instructions for the previous recipe.

The cakes were usually made in June or July, and never later than September, so that they would have sufficient time to mature or 'come again' in time for Christmas. Baking was a critical time, the temperature of the coal-fired ovens having to be carefully managed by stoking or adjusting the draught to ensure that the cake turned out well. It was then carefully wrapped and stored away until needed.

If to be served without icing, a sprig of holly was stuck in the centre. In Teesdale, the Christmas cakes were covered with almond paste and decorated with whole preserved fruits, while elsewhere the almond paste marzipan was finished with Royal icing, as most people still do today.[79]

NEW YEAR'S EVE /OLD YEAR'S DAY, 31ST DECEMBER

The north-east still celebrates the New Year much more than its southern neighbours. In Northumberland this day was traditionally known as hogmanay, just as in Scotland. For children, it was an opportunity to tour the usually better-off houses in their neighbourhood, chanting 'Hogmanay, hogmanay, Gis wor breed-an'-cheese, an' set's away' or else 'Please will you give us wor hogmanay.' This usually produced individual small cakes, the spice cake, cheese and liquor hospitality probably being reserved for adults.[80] A good range of food and plenty of drink was prepared for the evening's parties (as it still is in many homes), where everyone enjoyed themselves with traditional music and song. If there were teams in the area, the sword dancers might call in, or the mummers, appropriately dressed up and disguised as The Doctor, Nelson, Old Betty and the rest of the mumming play's characters. Having made their lively and boisterous contributions, they were rewarded with ginger-wine and cake before either going on to another party, or remaining to await the chimes of midnight, Auld Lang Syne, and the start of another year of traditional celebrations.[81]

CHAPTER NINETEEN

FROM CRADLE TO GRAVE

Threading of significant events in any person's life, birth, marriage and death, have always brought families and communities together to observe and share their mutual experiences. To those most closely involved, the parents or the bereaved, it was a matter of great pride that the assembled company should be received and provided with the foods and drinks expected for the particular event. For many working-class families this might involve considerable expense, leaving them in debt even after, in the case of funerals, there had been support from a friendly society or, later, an insurance policy. As with so many other aspects of social life, most of the centuries-old, homely local traditions gradually fell out of use in the Victorian period, as more fashionable, nation-wide replacements were gradually adopted, usually to the advantage of commercial suppliers.

GROANING

In Northumberland, as in many other parts of the country, confinement for childbirth was known as groaning. The room occupied by the sixteenth-century countesses of Northumberland at Wressle Castle near Selby was known as her 'Groaning Chamber', for example. Much lower down the social scale, preparations for the great event included the preparation of groaning malt in order to brew sufficient ale, the acquisition of a large groaning cheese, and the baking of a groaning loaf. These were to cater for the gathering of maids and women who came to visit the new mother, seated in her groaning chair, with her newborn child.[1] In some households, a medical man had to cut the cheese, while in others it was the father. As in the Borders, he probably cut 'a whang o' luck' for the lasses, from the edge of the cheese, dividing it into a portion for each one. If any went spare, it went to the spinsters of the family.[2] Sometimes more substantial food would be provided for this 'Upgetting', such as the 'goo speyce suet kyek, an' honey, an' bacon collops, an' frummety' served at one such celebration near Newcastle around 1850.[3]

Before setting out for the church for the christening a parcel was made up, its contents comprising a spice cake or loaf, a piece of cheese and a packet of salt. This was to be given to the first person the party met on leaving the house.[4] This custom is described in Wilson's poem, 'The Village Howdy' (i.e. midwife);

> *[Bella] deck'd us for church on the Christening day,*
> *Cut the bread-and-cheese meant to be stow'd*
> *In the first lucky pocket she met on her way*
> *To the church from their humble abode.*
> *Later, at the following reception:*
> *Her custom was always to cut up the cheese,*
> *To hand round the cake and the gin,*
> *Remarking afresh on the 'Stranger',*
> *To these, who afterwards kindly dropped in.*[5]

This cake baked for the christening was a spiced singing hinnie. Making one for this event, for a birthday or a wedding, was known as 'setting on a gordle'. Even though recipes for the modern kind of christening cakes had been published in up-market cookery books from the early nineteenth century, they only began to be generally made in this region around the 1890s–1900s. As a Belford lady informed Mrs Gomme, probably around 1931, 'The majority either buy the birth-cake, or make it some days before … Many make two, a currant and a seed one.'[6] By this time some families were already starting to keep one tier of their wedding cake to serve as the christening cake of their first child, a custom which still continues today.

The range and quality of the food provided for friends and relatives after the christening must have been very substantial before the Napoleonic wars, for as early as the 1820s Thomas Wilson was complaining that:

> *… christenin's now are suiner duin*
> *By far than what they us'd te be;*
> *Folks were not ax'd for efternuin*
> *Te get blawn out wi' blashey tea.*
>
> *For nowse but solids then wad please -*
> *Substantials that wad bide some cuttin' -*
> *A ham and veal, a round [of beef] and peas,*
> *Some turmits and a leg o' mutton.*
>
> *A dumplin like a sma' coal heap -*

A puil o' spice kyel i' the middle -
Wi' pies and puddins, wide and deep,
About myed up the savory siddell [schedule].

Here there was plenty gawin' and comin' -
Here we cou'd cut and come agyen -
And a' wesh'd down, by men and women,
Wi' bumpers frae the awd grey hen [stoneware bottle]

This was the kind o' belly timmin [belly-timber, i.e. food]
For myekin PITMEN strang and tuiff,
But now they run them up far slimmer
Wi' tea and other weshy stuff

Splash yan the spuins among the kyell [broth] -
De'il take the hindermost on they drive -
Through and through the bowl they wyell
For raisins how they stretch and strive

This ower, wi' sharp and shinin' geer
They now begin their narrow workin',
Whilst others, eager for the beer,
Are busy the grey hen uncorkin'.

Tho' still they're i' the hyel [hole] a' hewin',
Before they close the glorious day,
They jenkin a' the pillars [trim the pillars of coal] down,
And efter tyek the stooks [remains of the pillar] away. [7]

The pitmatic coal-cutting terms of the last two verses simply describe how the pitmen carved up every joint on the table, leaving nothing but bare plates and bones by the end of the meal.

THE ALMOUS

The Almous - also spelt aamus or omus in Northumberland, and the 'bairn's awmous' in County Durham, meant alms, or a present made to the new baby when it made its first visit to another house. It usually comprised a pinch of salt, a piece of bread and an egg to ward off all things evil and ensure good luck, but other items might include matches, a candle, or any small silver coin. [8]

BIRTHDAYS

In the north-east, Victorian birthdays were commemorated by the baking of a special spice hinnie. In addition to its usual currants, it had three extra, inedible ingredients, each one divining the future of those who found it in his or her portion. One was a threepenny piece, foretelling wealth, another a pearl button for bachelorhood, and the last a thimble indicating a single life or, if found by a girl, life as a thrifty housewife.[9] Around 1906-11 Mrs E.M. Birkett of Newbiggin, Hexhamshire, could remember having hot singing hinnies for birthdays, while Mrs Bet. Mills of Wylan remembered birthday hinnies containing pennies.[10] By the Edwardian period these were slowly going out of fashion as more people baked a modern birthday cake instead. This was sometimes a rich fruitcake, but sometimes a sponge or other lighter mixture.

Nellie's Birthday Cake[11]

8oz/225g plain flour	*2 eggs, beaten*
½ tsp baking powder	*1 tsp rum*
½ tsp grated nutmeg	*4oz/100g currants*
1oz/25g candied lemon peel	*4oz/100g butter*
4oz/100g caster sugar	

Sift the flour with the baking powder and nutmeg. Cream the butter with the sugar, beat in the eggs, little by little, then the flour, and finally the currants and peel. Put into a 6ins/15cm diameter greased and lined tin, and bake at 170°C, 325°F, Gas mark 3 for about 1¾ hours. When cold, spread the rum over the top and allow to soak in before cutting.

WEDDINGS

In true aristocratic style, the marriage of Earl Percy to the daughter of the Earl of Powis in 1817 was celebrated at Alnwick by the ringing of bells, the firing of guns, and the roasting of an ox in the market place. Impressive as this was, these celebrations probably lacked the boisterous joy which accompanied many working-class weddings.

The best account of a traditional northcountry wedding is a poem written by Edward Chicken (1698–1746). Entitled *The Collier's*

Wedding, it first describes the courtship of Tom, a young pitman, to Jenny from Benwell, and then their wedding day. As Tom rides to church, accompanied by Northumbrian pipers, streamers and a crowd of collier lads, his bride is led there by two groomsmen. After the service the colliers seize her garters, their customary prize, and all walk quickly back home, where the wedding feast should be ready. However;

> 'The greasy cook at once appears
> And thunders mischief in their ears ...
> Now runs to see her kettle boil,
> Meanwhile she lets her butter oil,
> Then boxes her who turns the spit
> And cries: "You jade, yoa'll burn the meat!"
> Fire, smoke and fury round her goes.
> She's burnt her apron, singed her clothes.
> "The dinner will be spoiled" she cries.
> "Good Lord, the baker's burnt the pies!"

Meanwhile, the guests;

> 'Impatient for the want of meat,
> They feak [twitch] and cannot keep their seat,
> Play with the plates, drum on the table,
> And fast as long as they are able ...
> Some eat the bread, some lick the salt,
> Some drink, and others find some fault ...
> They damn and sink and curse the cook,
> And give her many a frightful look.
> They call her bitch and jade and sour.
> She says she does what fire could do.'

However;

> 'At last the beef appears in sight,
> The groom moves slow the ponderous weight.
> Swift to the smoking beef they fly.
> Some cut their passage through a pie.
> Out streams the gravy on the cloth.
> Some burn their tongues with scalding broth.
> But rolling spices make them fain;
> They shake their heads and sup again.
> 'Cut up the goose!' cries one below,

'And send us down a leg or so.'
An honest neighbour tries the point,
Works hard, but cannot hit a joint.
The bride sat nigh. She rose in prim,
And cut and tore it limb from limb.
Now geese, cocks, hens, the fury feel,
Extended jaws devour the veal.'

The meal having ended, dancing follows, to the music of fiddles and pipes, and the vast consumption of ale and spirits.

'So now the drunken senseless crew
Break pipes, spill drink, piss, shit and spew ...
The labouring peasant, weary grown,
Embraces night and trudges home.'

At this late hour Jenny and her females enter her bridal chamber, clear out all others, and advise her how to sleep with Tommy. Then;

'The posset made, the bride is led
In great procession to her bed ...
[Nanny Forster] ran and catched the bowl
Where currant cakes in ale did roll,
Then with a smile said "Jenny lass
Come, here's thy health without a glass"
Her arm supports it to her head,
She drinks, and gobbles up the bread ...
And some prepare t' undress the bride,
While others tame the posset's pride."[12]

The women then leave, while Tommy is undressed, set in bed beside his new wife, and the couple finally left to themselves.

In contrast to the ample but badly cooked wedding dinner served to Tommy's and Jenny's guests, a far better one was promised to those attending Skipper and Moll's wedding, as described in;

The Invitation

Neighbores, I've come for to tell ye,
our Skipper and Moll's to be wed,
And if it be true what they're saying,

Published by John Sykes. Bookseller, Newcastle

62. Willy Purvis, violinist and singer, was better known as Blind Willy. One of the great characters of late Georgian Newcastle, he was celebrated in engravings, on pottery and in verse. The main attraction of 'Skipper and Moll's' wedding reception was that 'Blind Willy's to play on the fiddle'.

> 'Lang may wor Tyneside lads sae true
> In heart byeth blithe an' mellow,
> Bestow the praise that's fairly due
> To this bluff honest fellow.
>
> And when he's hamper'd in the dust
> Still I' wor memory springin'
> The times we've run till like to brust
> To hear Blind Willie singin?

egad we'll be all rarely fed;
They've brought home a shoulder of mutton,
besides two thumping fat geese,
And when at the fire they're roasting,
we're all to have sops in the grease
Blind Willy's [William Purvis] *to play on the fiddle.*

And there'll be pies and spice dumplings,
and there'll be bacon and pease;
Besides a great lump of beef boiled,
and they may get crowdies who please;
To eat such things as these are,
I'm sure ye've seldom had luck;
Besides, for to make us some pottage,
there'll be a sheep's head and a pluck.
Blind Willy's going to play on the fiddle.

Of sausages there'll be plenty,
blackpuddings, sheep fat and neat's tripes,
Besides, for to warm up your noses,
great store of tobacco and pipes.
A room, they say, there'll be provided,
for us all at 'The Old Jacob's Well'
The bridegroom he went there this morning,
and spoke for a barrel o' yell.
Blind Willy's to play on the fiddle ...

But neighbours, I'd almost forgot,
to tell ye exactly at one,
The dinner will be on the table,
and music will play till its done:
When you'll be all hearty welcome,
of this merry feast for to share,
But if you won't come at this bidding,
why then you must stay where you are.
Blind Willy's to play on the fiddle.[13]

These great dinners formed only part of the region's wedding customs. At a riding wedding, the male guests would set off from the church and gallop over the moors to the house where the dinner was to be served, the winner having the privilege of either kissing the bride, or receiving a dish of kail or broth that evening, this custom being called 'ride to kail' around Cambo. At Whitburn near Sunderland, as late as the 1870s, the departing bride and groom might find five or six women standing outside the left side of the church porch, each holding a large mug covered by a cloth. The mug was first presented to the groom, who handed it to his bride who, after taking a sip, returned it. The same ceremony was then repeated for each of the following couples as they emerged from church. One old lady could remember having seventy of these 'hot pots' at her wedding back around 1800. The contents of these pots, while certainly hot, alcoholic, and probably spiced, was not to everyone's taste, one drinker finding that 'The composition in these mugs was mostly, I am sorry to say, simply horrible; one or two were very fair, and one very good.'[14]

The journey to the new home might also include a horse-drawn cart called the bride's wain. This carried all the bride's goods and chattels, those at Wolsingham being topped by her spinning wheel decorated with ribbons.

On her arrival at the house where the dinner was to be held, the bride had to stand before the door and have a bride-cake, cut in pieces, and sometimes still on its plate, thrown over her head, to ensure good luck.[15] As described in Thomas Wilson's *The Pitman's Pay*:

> *'The bride-kyek neist, byeth sweet and short*
> *was toss'd in platefuls ower the bride;*
> *The lads and lasses scrammel'd for 't*
> *Wi' airms and mouths stritch'd far and wide.'*[16]

It must be stressed that this bride cake was not a rich, multi-tiered fruit cake covered in royal icing, but, as confirmed by the words 'sweet and short', it was nothing less than a spice singing hinnie.

The nobility and gentry had been making huge, heavily fruited and very expensive bride cakes from the late sixteenth century, the elaboration of their icing and growth into multiple tiers reaching a crescendo in the late Victorian and Edwardian period. They were completely beyond the skills and resources of the ordinary housewife, and were the province of the professional baker and confectioner, from whom they were usually purchased. Slowly, however, and driven by a combination of family pride, the reducing price of ingredients, and the need to be economical, good quality egg-raised bride cakes began to be home-made. This was rarely an easy task, however, the direction and strength of the wind being judged carefully to ensure that the coal-fired oven would 'behave', since an under-done or burned cake was a frustrating and expensive loss. This is a local family recipe from around the 1890s;

Mother's Bride Cake [17]

8oz/225g butter	*½ tsp bicarbonate of soda*
12oz/325g caster sugar	*½ tsp baking powder*
4 eggs, beaten	*½ tsp ground nutmeg*
3 tbs brandy	*1¼lb/550g currants*
3 tbs sherry	*8oz/225g candied peel*
1 tbs rosewater	*4oz/100g flaked almonds*
12oz/325g plain flour	

Cream the butter and sugar, and beat in the eggs and other liquids little by little. Sift the flour with the bicarbonate of soda, baking powder and nutmeg and beat it into the creamed butter, etc., until smooth. Mix in the remaining ingredients, put into a 8ins/20cm round or 7ins/18cm square greased and lined tin, and bake at 150°C, 300°F, Gas mark 2 for 3½ hours.

The final dish of the wedding day, the posset, was described in Richardson's *Borderer's Table Book* of 1842 as;

> 'a portion of white bread soaked in white milk instead of wine, into which the marriage ring was dropped; the bride and bridegroom tasted the contents first, then the bowl was assailed by the lasses and lads; and whoever 'fished' up the ring was accounted to have the best chance of being first married.' [18]

This sounds more like a flavourless milk sop intended for the sickroom and nursery, rather than a wedding night. It would certainly improve if served hot and sweetened, or if, as Edward Chicken tells us, it was made with (hot, spiced?) ale and currant cakes.

No original recipe for a wedding posset appears to have survived from the region, unless it is the following published in the 1890s as;

Durham Custard [19]

4 yolks, beaten	*4-5 tbs sugar*
¾pt/450ml mild/brown ale	*2pt/1.2l cream*
3-4 slices of white bread lightly toasted and cut in squares	

Beat the yolks with a little of the ale, and pour through a sieve into a large pan. Add the cream, remaining ale and sugar, and heat, stirring continuously, until hot, but not curdled (about 80°C), then pour over the toast arranged in a deep bowl, and serve hot.

A pinch of nutmeg, mace, cinnamon and ginger may also be cooked with the cream.

FUNERALS

As in other parts of the country, food formed an important part of any funeral, particularly as the mourners may have travelled a considerable distance. They needed some form of light refreshment on arriving at the home of the deceased, before following the cortège to the church, and something more substantial, and with more drink, on their return afterwards. The funeral accounts of gentry families give a good impression of what might be served. This example, dated 10th August, 1703, is for 'mad cosen Mary Haggerston's' funeral on Holy Island;

> ... and for cakes, bread, alle, brandy, sack, tobacco, pipes and wine, £6 " 11 " 0d [20]

and this of 16th January 1730 from the accounts of William Wilson of Walbottle;

of cheese 35 pound	8s	0d
of white bread 1/6	1	6
of sugar 2 pound		8
of tobacco 1 pound 1 half	1	0
of brandy 2 quarts	1	3
of pipes half a grose	2	6
of ale a firkin	15	0
a pound of candle		5
a bushel of wheat	4	0
£1	15	7d [21]

Excluding the ale, brandy, tobacco and pipes, it will be seen that the fare was relatively plain for a modest funeral, just white bread, cheese and cakes. This stands in contrast to the delicate sponge funeral biscuits, rich wines and the very best of foods served to the most important guests at the funerals of the great and wealthy. Our knowledge of the region's funeral cakes is entirely due to a survey undertaken by one of the pioneer scholars of English traditional cookery.

In 1931, when Lady Gomme was collecting information on this subject, an informant from Belford sent her the following details of the Northumbrian 'Dead Cake', as;

> She does not remember having seen one since she was a child of 7 & then it was only one here & there that made them ... they had to be *yellow*. They seem to have been made with yeast & flour, coloured with saffron or something she called "yellerin" [turmeric?]. They were flavoured with cinnamon & bit of orange peel ...
>
> As far as Old Peggy knows they were *never* eaten except at the time of a death, & the cake was placed, she says, on a table beside the bed in which the "Corpse" lay, or even on the bed itself, & all visitors had to cut a bit before looking at the "Corpse". She described them as "real yellow". [22]

One of the earliest local recipes for saffron cakes was published by Hannah Allgood (1708–1770), daughter of a Hexham clergyman. In her *Compleat Confectioner* published in 1760 under her married name of Hannah Glasse, she provided instructions for making a huge saffron cake, its dry ingredients alone weighing 6lb (2.7kg). [23] By combining elements of her recipe with the memories of 'Old Peggy' and practical experience, it is possible to recreate this traditional Northumbrian cake.

Northumbrian Dead Cake

1½lb/675g strong white flour	*1 tsp saffron*
6oz/175g candied orange peel	*¼ tsp turmeric*
2 tsp ground cinnamon	*6oz/175g sugar*
¾pt/450ml milk	*1½ tsp dried yeast*
8oz/225g butter	*2 eggs, beaten*

256

Simmer the saffron and turmeric in the milk for 2-3 minutes while stirring, remove from the heat, add the butter cut in pieces, and leave to melt.

Mix the remaining ingredients, except the eggs, into the flour in a large bowl, and leave in a warm place, but if the manufacturer's instructions require the dried yeast to be activated separately, do this and add it just before kneading. When the milk and butter have cooled to blood heat, stir in, knead for 5 minutes, then return to the bowl, cover, and leave in a warm place for about 2 hours.

When the dough has doubled in size, knead it lightly, dust with flour, place in a warmed and greased 9ins/23cm diameter cake tin, and return to the warm for at least 45 minutes until risen again. Bake at 200°C, 400°F, Gas mark 6 for 15 minutes, then reduce to 190°C, 375°F, Gas mark 5 for a further 20 minutes.

Like most of the other food described in this book, it is good to make at any time, without waiting for some particularly special event.

All of the recipes in this book have been developed by generations of Northumberland and Durham housewives over many centuries. They convert the north's fine produce into easily-made, economical, practical, nourishing and enjoyable family meals. They do not disguise natural flavours with curry, sweet-and-sour or other strong sauce, but subtly enhance them in the best tradition of fine English regional cookery. Here is the true taste of the northcountry.

BIBLIOGRAPHY

Acton, E., *Modern Cookery for Private Families* (1855).

Anon., *A Voice from the Coal Mines* (1825).

Anon., *Modern Cookery, Tested Recipes* (Barnard Castle 1932).

Anon., *Tyneside Songs* (Newcastle 1873).

Anon., *Teesdale Cookery Book* (Barnard Castle 1962?).

Armstrong, T., *Song Book ... of the late Thomas Armstrong* (Chester-le-Street 1930).

Atkinson, F., *Life & Tradition in Northumberland & Durham* (1977).

Bailey, J., & Cully, G., *General View of Agriculture of Northumberland*.

Bain, I. (ed.), *A Memoir of Thomas Bewick* (Oxford 1975).

Balfour, M. C. & Thomas, N.W., *County Folklore, Northumberland* (1904).

Balfour, M. C., & Thomas, N.W. (ed.), *County Folklore IV Northumberland* (1904).

Barker, 'Tea For the Cabin', *Whitby Lit. & Phil. Soc. Annual Report* (Whitby 2004) 36-41.

Barley, M., *The English Farmhouse & Cottage* (1961).

Bedford MS. Leeds University, Brotherton Library Special Collections MS 432.

Bell, G.H., manuscript memoirs Beamish Museum 9.1.1975.

Bell, J., *Rhymes of the Northern Bards* (Newcastle 1812).

Bell, J., *Collections Relevant to Colliers and Coal Trade in the Counties of Durham &
Northumberland* (1847).

Bewick, T., *The History of Quadrupeds* (1790) (1807 ed.).

Bishopwearmouth Parish Church Cookery Book (1949).

Bond, J., *Sea Cookery* (1917).

Bosanquet, R.E., *In Troublesome Times* (Newcastle 1929).

Brand, J., *Observations on Popular Antiquities* (1777) (1810 ed.).

Brears, P., *The English Country Pottery* (Newton Abbot 1971).

    Jellies and their Moulds (Totnes 2010).

Brook, M., *Herring Girls, and Hiring Fairs* (Newcastle 2005).

Bruce, J.C., & Stokoe, J., *Northumberland Minstrelsy* (Newcastle 1882).

Burnett, J., *Plenty & Want* (1966).

Byron, M., *Pot Luck* (1914) (1932 ed.).

Carr, G., *Bonnie Blanchland* (Crook n.d.).

Carr, G., *Pit Women* (2001)

Chadwick, E., *The Sanitary Conditions of the Labouring People of Great Britain* (1842).

Chambers, B. (ed.), *Friends of the Northern Lead Mines* (Kilhope 2002).

Cobbett, W., *Cottage Economy* (1823).

Collier, Coleman., *Gatherings from the Pit Heaps* (1868).

Colls, R., *The Pitmen of the Northern Coalfield* (Manchester 1987).

Colls, R., & Lancaster, B., *Newcastle upon Tyne, A Modern History* (Chichester 2001).

Cook, A., *Professed Cookery* (1760).

Cook, M., *Fishing in Hartlepool* (Stroud 2011).

Dallas, E.S., *Kettner's Book of the Table* (1877).

David, E., *English Bread & Yeast Cookery* (1977).

Davidson, C., *The World of Mary Ellen Best* (1985).

Day, M. (ed.), *Farmhouse Fare* (1940).

Defoe, D., *A Tour through England & Wales* (1948 ed.).

Dinsdale, F.T., *A Glossary of Provincial Words used in Teesdale* (1849).

Ditchfield, P.H., *Old English Customs* (1896).

Dixon, D.D., *Whittington Vale* (Newcastle 1895).

    Upper Coquetdale (Newcastle 1903).

Dixon, H., *The Allendale Miscellany* (Newcastle 1974).

Dougal, D., & Graham, F., *Northumberland & Durham, A Social Miscellany* (Newcastle 1969).

Durham County Hospital, *Cookery Book & Bazaar* (Durham 194?).

E.D.D., *The English Dialect Dictionary* (Oxford 1923).

Ellerington, M., *History & Guide of Corbridge* (Haltwhistle, n.d.).

Evelyn, M., *The Young Wife's Cookery Book* (Sheffield & London, 1928).

Fawcett, J.W., *The History of the Parish of Dipton* (Satley 1911).

Fiennes, C., *The Journals of Celia Fiennes* (1983 ed.).

Fleming Hospital New Cookery Book (Newcastle n.d.).

Fox, A., *Report upon the Poor Law Union of Glendale* (1893).

Fuller, J., *The History of Berwick upon Tweed* (Edinburgh 1799).

Garrett, T., *The Encyclopaedia of Practical Cookery* (1892-4).

Gilbert, C., *English Vernacular Furniture 1750-1900* (New Haven & London 1991).

Gilly, W.S., *The Peasantry of the Border* (Berwick upon Tweed 1842 ed.).

Gomme, Lady., Manuscripts, Private Collection.

Graham, J.J., *Weardale Past & Present* (Gateshead n.d.).

Grange Villa Primitive Methodist Church, Favourite Recipes and Housekeeping Hints
    (Chester-le-Street c. 1900-1910).

Grice, F., *The Bonnie Pit Laddie* (Oxford 1960).

Griffiths, B., *Stotty & Spice Cake* (Newcastle 2006).

    Fishing & Folk (Newcastle 2008).

Hair, P.E.H., *Coals on Rails* (Liverpool 1988).

Halliday, W., *Guide to Holy Island* (1907) (1934 ed.).

Hargreaves, B. (ed.), *Farmhouse Fare* (1984).

Harker, D., *Lands of Liddisdale*

Harker, D., *Songs & Verses of the North-Eastern Pitmen 1780-1844* Surtees Society CCIV (1999).

Harker, D.I., *Songs from the Manuscript Collection of John Bell* Surtees Society CXVI (1983-4).

Haydon Bridge Women's Institute Tried Recipe Book (1928).

Heath, R., *Golden Hours* (1871).

Henderson, W., *Notes on the Folk-lore of the Northern Counties of England and the Borders* (1879).

Henisch, B.A., *Cakes & Characters* (Totnes 1984).

Hepscott Women's Institute Cookery Book

Heslop, H., *The Earth Beneath* (1946).

Heslop, O., *Northumberland Words* (1892).

Higginbottom, P., *The Workhouse Cookery Book* (Stroud 2008).

Hindhaugh's Cookery Book (Newcastle n.d.).

Hone, W., *The Everyday Book* (1826).

Howey, P., *The Geordie Cook Book* (Morpeth 1988).

Howitt, W., *The Rural Life of England* (1840),
    Visits to Remarkable Places (1882 ed.).

Hutchinson, P., *Peggy Hutchinson's North Country Cooking Secrets* (1935).
    Peggy Hutchinson's Home-made Wine Secrets (1960).
    Old English Cookery (1973).
    Peggy Hutchinson's Preserving Secrets (n.d.).

Hutchinson, W., *A View of Northumberland* (1776).

Johnson, A., *The Diary of Thomas Giordani Wright, Newcastle Doctor 1826-1829* Surtees Society CCVI (2001).

Johnston, G., 'Our Visit to Holy Island in May 1854' *Berwick Naturalists' Club VII* (1873-5) 27.

King, R., *Old Tyneside Street Cries* (Tynemouth 1924).

Kitchiner, W., *The Cook's Oracle* (1822).

Lanagan, P., *Houghton Feast* (Houghton-le-Spring 2002).

Lingford, J. & Son, *Dainty Recipes* (Bishop Auckland n.d.).

Lloyd, A.L., *Come All ye Bold Miners* (1978).

Loudon, J.C., *Encyclopaedia of Cottage & Farm Architecture* (1846).

Low Fell Recipe Book (Gateshead 1910).

Mackenzie, E., *History of Newcastle upon Tyne* (Newcastle 182?).

MacRitchie, W., *Diary of a Tour through Great Britain in 1795* (1891).

Manders, F.W.D., *A History of Gateshead* (Gateshead 1973).

Mann, R. & Weir, R., *The Compleat Mustard* (1988).

Mason, L. & Brown, C., *Traditional Foods of Britain* (Totnes 1999).

McCracken, E., *The Geordie Cook Book* (Newcastle 1950).

Middlebrook, S., *Newcastle upon Tyne* (Newcastle 1950).

Medomsley Church Bazaar, *A Cookery Book of Tested Recipes* (1948).

Milburn, G.E. (ed.), *The Diary of John Young ... Surtees Society CXCV* (1982).

Milburn, T.A., *Life & Times in Weardale 1840-1910* (Ireshopeburn 1987).

Mowatt, A., Ratcheugh *Shorthorns & Border Leicesters* (Alnwick 1898).

Murrey, J., *The Handbook for Travellers in Durham & Northumberland* (1873).

Newall, V., *An Egg at Easter* (1971)

New Shildon, All Saints Church Modern Cookery (New Shildon n.d.).

Neville, H.M., *A Corner in the North* (Newcastle 1909).

Northern Counties Training School of Cookery *A Compilation of Household Cookery Recipes* (Newcastle n.d.).

Northern Counties Training School of Cookery & Domestic Science *A Compilation of Cottage Recipes* (Newcastle n.d.).

O.E.D., *The Oxford English Dictionary* (Oxford 1971).

Oliver, S., *Rambles in Northumberland & the Scottish Borders* (1853).

Parmeter, K. (ed.), *The Fleming Hospital New Cookery Book* (Newcastle n.d.).

Porteous, K. (ed.), *The Bonny Fisher Lad* (Seaham 2003).

P.S.A.N.T., *Proceedings of the Society of Antiquaries of Newcastle upon Tyne* (Newcastle).

Raistrick, A. & Jennings, B., *A History of Leadmining in the Pennines* (Newcastle & Littleborough 1989).

Redmayne, Sir R., *Men, Mines & Memories* (1942).

Reed, A., *Bruce's School* (London & Newcastle 1903).

Richardson, *The Borderer's Table Book* (1842).

Scott, R., *Over the Anvil* (Whitley Bay 1027).

Simond, L., *Journal of a Tour & Residence in Great Britain* (Edinburgh 1815).

Sinclair, L., *Easingden* (Oxford 1926).

Slack, M., *Northumbrian Fare* (Newcastle 1981).

Smith, I., 'Frummenty' *Durham County Local History Society Bulletin 7* (1967).

Smith, W.H., *Songs of Moor & Stream* (Durham 1910).

Souden, D. (ed.), *Byng's Tours: The Journal of the Hon. John Byng 1781-1792* (1991).

Summers, J.M., *The History & Antiquities of Sunderland* (1858).

Taylor, E., *The Art of Cookery* (Berwick upon Tweed 1769).

Teesdale Cookery Book (Barnard Castle 1912?)

Thacker, J., *The Art of Cookery* (Newcastle 1758).

Thompson, T. (et.al.), *A Collection of Songs ... in the Newcastle Dialect* (Newcastle 1827).

'a Traveller', *Our Coal and our Coal-Pits* (1853).

Tomlinson, W.W., *Life in Northumberland during the Sixteenth Century Historical Notices on Cullercoats, Whitley & Monksheaton* (reprinted Newcastle 1980).

Treherty, J., *Hard Times* (London, New York & Manchester 1987).

Turnbull, L., *Chopwalls's Story* (Gateshead c. 1979).

Uglow, J., *Nature's Engraver* (2007).

Warner, *A Tour through the Northern Counties of England* (1802).

Watson, A., *My Life* (1937).

Watson, R., *Poems & Songs of Teesdale* (Darlington 1930).

Wilkinson, A., *Barnard Castle Historic Market Town* (Otley 1998).

Wilson, T., *The Pitman's Pay* (1872 ed.).

Wolsingham & Tow Law Parish Magazine (Wolsingham 1890).

Wright, P., *The Penguin Book of Everyday Verse* (Harmondsworth 1983).

Wright, W.R., *Esh Leaves* (Durham 1914).

Wylam Women's Institute Practical Cookery Book (Hexham n.d.).

Young, A., *A Six Month's Tour ...* (1790).

NOTES

CHAPTER ONE

THE PITMEN

1. Harker, 103.
2. Johnson, 80-81.
3. Gilbert, 63.
4. Carr, 34.
5. Scott, 65.
6. Hone (1832) II, 653-5.
7. EDD., Baff.
8. Harker, 88, 307.
9. Armstrong, 3.
10. Burnett, 149.
11. Harker, 94; Howitt, 331.
12. 'A Traveller' 158.
13. Murray, 19; Heslop 'Bait'.
14. Morris, Beamish.
15. Howitt, 332.
16. Murray, 19.
17. Beamish Survey.
18. *ibid.*
19. 'A Traveller' 158.
20. *ibid.*, 200.
21. Hone (1832), 653-5.

CHAPTER TWO

FARMING FAMILIES

1. Barley, 267.
2. Bailey & Culley, 26.
3. Beamish Survey.
4. ibid., 28.
5. ibid., 23.

CHAPTER THREE

FARM WORKERS

1. Howitt (1840), 123.
2. *ibid.*, 136.
3. *ibid.*, 129.
4. Neville, 12-15.
5. Dixon (1895), 70; Loudon, 487, 492-5.
6. Howitt (1840), 134.
7. *ibid.*, 137.
8. Burnett, 122, 125-6.
9. Fox, 110.
10. Beamish Survey, 5.
11. *ibid.*
12. Information from Mr. J. Gill.
13. Beamish Survey.
14. Hutchinson (1973), 20; EDD., Crowdy; Neville, 132.
15. Neville, 14, 20, 21.
16. *ibid.*, 21; Fox, 110.
17. Neville, 21.
18. Atkinson, 148; EDD., 'Mell'; For the Corbridge version see Ellerington, 83.
19. EDD., 'Mell', 'Kirn'.
20. 11th February 1899.
21. Hutchinson (1973), 91.
22. Neville, 9, 67.
23. Howitt (1840), 121.
24. Heath, 765.
25. Beamish Survey, 7.

CHAPTER FOUR

THE LEAD MINERS

1. PSANT Series 3 Vol II (1905-6), 208.
2. Raistrick & Jennings, 290-94.
3. *Royal Commission for Inquiring into*

the *Employment of Children in Mines and Manufactures* (1842) includes all the subsequent quotations.

4. *Kinnaird Report on the Condition of Mines* (1862-4).
5. *Royal Commission* (1842) Appendix 2, 740-742.
6. Milburn, 13.
7. Raistrick & Jennings, 309.

28. Hair, 41.
29. Whitby Museum Library, 7332.
30. Barker, 40.
31. *ibid.*, 39, 41.
32. Hagar & Co., *Directory of Durham* (1851).
33. *Northern Counties*, 25.
34. Bond, 80.
35. *ibid.*, 86.
36. *ibid.*, 61.

CHAPTER FIVE

FISHERFOLK & SAILORS

1. For further details of the regional fishing industry see Griffiths (2008), Tomlinson (1980) & Cook 2011), & Brook (2005).
2. Tomlinson, 87-8.
3. *Sea Fisheries Report* (1879), 83.
4. Cook, 38.
5. Heslop, 'Creave'.
6. *ibid.*, 'Hully'
7. Porteous, 11.
8. Fuller, 421-3.
9. Heslop, 'Bab', 'Drift'.
10. Porteous, 81.
11. Brockett, 'Blaze', 'Click-hook'.
12. Fuller, 424.
13. Bailey & Culley, 21-2.
14. Beamish, Letters from Mr. Holmes of Berwick 16/5/1994 and Mrs K. Patterson 17/5/1994.
15. Porteous, 20, 108,110.
16. Tomlinson, 115.
17. Trehertz, 75-6.
18. Porteous, 11 & 14 above.
19. *ibid.*, 46.
20. *ibid.*, 114.
21. *ibid.*, 39; Griffiths (2008), 143.
22. OED., 'Slake'.
23. Heslop, 'Slauke'.
24. Porteous, 17.
25. Oliver, 23.
26. Johnston, 27.
27. 'A Traveller Underground' 73; Murray, 74

CHAPTER SIX

THE POOR

1. Middlebrook, 167, 170.
2. *ibid.*, 294; see also Watson (1937), 122; Chadwick, 95.
3. Hislop, 'Poverty Engine'.
4. Manders, 220.
5. *ibid.*, 234; Middlebrook, 290.
6. Higginbottom, 32; For the Berwick on Tweed dietary see Fuller, 340.
7. Mackenzie, 544; Slack, 14-15.
8. Royal Commission ... the Poor Laws (1834) (1905), 51-4.
9. Higginbottom, 82.

CHAPTER SEVEN

FUELS & FIREPLACES

1. Brockett, 'Flak', 'Flaw'.
2. EDD., 'Peat' (32).
3. *ibid.*, 'Cat' (14).
4. Fiennes, 238.
5. Heslop, 'Beans'.
6. Harker, 108.
7. Heslop, 'Rake'.
8. Sinclair, 3.
9. Heslop, 'Gethering – coal'.
10. Brockett, 'Hallen'.
11. *ibid.*, & Heslop, 'Galley-bauk'.
12. Brockett, 'End-irons'; Heslop, 'Clamps', 'Niggarts'.
13. Heslop, 'Hud'; Dinsdale, 'Hood-end'.

14. Beamish 2002.40.
15. Beamish 2008.125, 1999.3.13.
16. Grice, 6, 11.
17. Sinclair, 7.

CHAPTER EIGHT

OF MEAT

1. Bewick (1790) 36.
2. PSANT 3rd Series II (1905-6) 246-50.
3. Bewick (1790) 365.
4. Hutchinson (1973) 38.
5. *ibid.*
6. Wylan, 20.
7. Beamish 1961/52 a/q.
8. Beamish survey.
9. Haydon Bridge.
10. Beamish survey 9, Hepscott, 40, Anon (1932).
11. New Shildon 39.
12. Beamish 1961/52, 42.
13. Beamish 1978/256, 27.
14. Beamish 1993/251 & survey 18.
15. Low Fell.
16. Beamish 1993/251.
17. Low Fell 8.
18. Beamish Ms. Mrs E.M. Birkett, Newbiggin, Hexham.
19. *ibid.*
20. Haydon Bridge 9.
21. Bain 7.
22. Collingwood Bruce & Stokoe 109.
23. Beamish 1961/52.
24. Beamish survey.
25. Collier 44-5.
26. Haydon Bridge.
27. Taylor, 28.
28. Armstrong.
29. Beamish survey.
30. Beamish Ms E.M. Danby, Darlington area.
31. Bell (1812) 41.
32. King, 50, Brockett 'Black Pudding', Armstrong 42, Beamish Ms Mrs. O.B. Bannister, West Auckland.
33. Beamish Ms. Mrs O.B. Bannister.

34. Hutchinson (n.d) 102, Hargreaves, 250.
35. Northern Counties (n.d.) 21.
36. Medomsley, 77.
37. Hargreaves, 245.
38. Hutchinson (n.d.) 104.
39. Hutchinson (n.d.) 104.
40. Hutchinson (n.d.) 104.
41. Hutchinson (1937) 151
42. Beamish Ms Mrs Birkett, Newbiggin.
43. Beamish survey 17.
44. Taylor, 26, Alnwick Castle Library 121/85 p.102.
45. Dixon, 471.
46. Beamish Ms 441-5.
47. Haydon Bridge, 10.
48. Beamish survey.
49. Hutchinson (1973) 33.
50. Fleming, 41.
51. Armstrong, 10.
52. *ibid.* 9.
53. Watson, 79.

CHAPTER NINE

OF FISH

1. King, numerous refs; Tomlinson, 87-8.
2. Dobson, 42.
3. Reed, 143.
4. Defoe II, 251.
5. Beamish 1993.251.
6. Haydon Bridge, 7.
7. Day, 16.
8. Hepscott, 39.
9. Beamish 1993.251.
10. Wylam, 22; Teesdale, 53.
11. Northern Counties, 13.
12. Beamish 1993.251.
13. Hutchinson (1973), 109.
14. Fuller, 398.
15. Information from Mr George Muirhead.
16. Taylor, 121.
17. Cook (2011), 42.
18. Anon., *Tyneside Songs* 90.
19. Beamish 1995.251.

CHAPTER TEN

OF VEGETABLES

1. King.
2. Anon., (1873), 357.
3. Beamish Survey.
4. *ibid.,*
5. Hutchinson (1973), 37.
6. Evelyn, 131.
7. Hutchinson, 35.
8. Hargreaves, 57.
9. Haydon Bridge, 9.
10. Hutchinson, 35.
11. Hindhaugh, 11.
12. Heslop, 'Pea-mornin'.
13. Dinsdale & Brockett, 'Pee Scalding'.
14. Beamish 1961/52 a-q 47.
15. Northern Counties, 18.
16. Beamish 1978.256.7.
17. Beamish 1961/52 a-q 8.
18. Durham County Hospital.
19. Beamish Survey.
20. Hutchinson, 57.
21. EDD., 'Pan' 2 (2) 'Hag'; OED., 'Hag' sb.3.
22. Howey, 14.
23. Slack, 41.
24. Beamish 961/52 a-q p.8.

CHAPTER ELEVEN

OF PUDDINGS

1. Cother, 54.
2. Beamish Survey.
3. Beamish 1993 -251.
4. Hutchinson (1973), 43.
5. *ibid.,* 41.
6. Beamish 1961/52/a-q.
7. *ibid.*
8. Beamish 1978 – 256 -27.
9. Garrett II, 265.
10. *ibid.,* 158.
11. Hutchinson, 40.
12. *ibid.*
13. Tyne & Wear Museums R293, Brears (2010) 196-7.

14. Beamish 1978.526.27.
15. *ibid.*
16. Hepscott, 34.
17. Heslop, 'Sowers'.
18. *ibid.,* 'Lithies'.

CHAPTER TWELVE

THE DAIRY

1. Bell (1812), 151; Harker, 100.
2. Bailey & Cully, 154.
3. Fiennes, 240.
4. MacRitchie, 149.
5. Bewick (1807), 77-9.
6. Lloyd, 100.
7. Young, 42; Bewick (1807), 26-32.
8. All these terms are from Heslop.
9. PSANT 3rd Series II (1905-6) 209.
10. Bosanquet, 44.
11. Warner, 40.
12. Brockett, 'Yearning'.
13. Heslop, 'Whig'.
14. Souden, 145-6.
15. Mason & Brown, 122.
16. Mowatt.
17. Neville, 23.
18. Hutchinson (n.d.), 92-3; Hutchinson (1973), 114; Haydon Bridge, 30.
19. Medomsley, 79.
20. Haydon Bridge, 30.
21. Hepscott, 39.
22. Medomsley, 9.
23. Medomsley, 65.
24. Hepscott, 41.
25. Bishopwearmouth, 45.
26. Hutchinson, 54.
27. Collier, 88, 99.
28. Heslop, 'Cheese'.

CHAPTER THIRTEEN

OF BANNOCKS, LOAVES & STOTTYS

1. Colls, 105.
2. Neville, 133.

3. Heslop, 'Wite'.
4. Neville, 77; Heslop, 'Moulter'.
5. Bruce & Stokoe, 94.
6. Dixon (1903), 361.
7. PSANT 4th Series VI (1933-4) 105.
8. Heslop, 'Tense'.
9. *ibid.*, 'Bakestone'.
10. Low Fell, 72.
11. Heslop, 'Riddle'.
12. Heslop, 'Cruppy-dow'.
13. Bailey & Culley, 82; Young, 38, 100.
14. Uglow, 133; Neville, 24.
15. EDD. & Heslop, 'Tharf Cake'.
16. Bailey & Culley, 79.
17. Barnes, 7; Wilson (1930), 103.
18. Heslop, 'Kneading'.
19. Howitt, 177, 135.
20. *ibid.*; also Neville, 24.
21. Beamish Survey.
22. Hutchinson (1973), 71.
23. *ibid.*, 60.
24. Dinsdale, 'Dittin'.
25. Hutchinson (1973), 80.
26. Atkinson, 103.
27. *Hexham Courier* (1933).
28. Neville, 83.
29. Brears (1971), 197.
30. Bedford, 432/3.
31. Low Fell, 61.
32. Brockett, & Heslop, 'Booted Loaf'.
33. Cobbett (1974 ed.), 62.
34. Atkinson, Fig. 97.
35. Hutchinson (1973), 79.
36. Beamish Survey.
37. *ibid.*
38. p.14.
39. Beamish Survey.
40. EDD., 'Stott'.
41. Griffiths (2006), 116.
42. Taylor, 257.
43. *15 Books of Old Recipes*, 81.
44. Beamish 1979.1019.
45. Bishopwearmouth, 31. Low Fell.
46. Taylor, 256-7.

Chapter Fourteen

OF CAKES

1. OED., Singing hinnies.
2. Howett (1882), 32.
3. Gomme Manuscripts.
4. Heslop, 'Fizzer'.
5. Collier, 52.
6. Day (*Farmhouse Fare* 1940), 99.
7. Beamish Survey.
8. *ibid.*
9. *ibid.*
10. Hutchinson (1973), 63.
11. *ibid.*, 64.
12. Hepscott, 16.
13. Beamish Museum 1981/272.
14. *Teesdale Cookery Book*, 11.
15. Beamish Survey.
16. Rivers, 27.
17. Hepscott, 11.
18. *ibid.* 18; see also 11 & 24.
19. Beamish Museum 1978 – 5 26.27; see also Hepscott, 11.

Chapter Fifteen

THE STORE CUPBOARD

1. Dullas, 308.
2. Mann & Weir, 47.
3. Kitchener, 339.
4. Acton, 130, 153.
5. Durham County Hospital.
6. Haydon Bridge, 15.
7. Beamish 1961/57 a-q 105.
8. Haydon Bridge, 14.
9. Medomsley, 52.
10. Hargreaves, 144.
11. *ibid.*, 216.
12. Beamish 1978-526-27.
13. *ibid.*
14. Hutchinson (1973), 121.
15. *ibid.*, 35.
16. Beamish 1993 -251.
17. Hutchinson (n.d.), .40
18. *ibid.*, 95.

19. Hepscott, 47.
20. Medomsley, 54.

CHAPTER SIXTEEN

DRINKS

1. Fox, 110; Reed, 151.
2. Bain, 43, 50.
3. Howitt (1840), 130.
4. Neville, 14, 20, 21.
5. Dixon (1974), 74; Wolsingham CXV.
6. 'A Traveller' 199; Bell (1975).
7. Bell (1975).
8. Bell (1847), 221.
9. Bain, 60.
10. Hutchinson (n.d.), 95.
11. Bosanquet, 69.
12. *ibid.*
13. Hutchinson (1960), 117; Medomsley, 91.
14. EDD., 'Jacky' (4).
15. Bell (1812), 89.
16. Murray, 162.
17. Wright (1914), 63-9.
18. EDD., 'Cheerer'.
19. EDD., 'Stoory'.
20. Heslop, 'Cocktail'.

CHAPTER SEVENTEEN

FEASTS, FAIRS & CELEBRATIONS

1. Neville, 95-6.
2. PSANT 4th Series IX 115, 260.
3. EDD., 'Hire' & 'Godspenny'.
4. Bell, 245-7.
5. Reed, 181.
6. Ellerington, 80; Wolsingham XLII.
7. Beamish, *Survey.*
8. Hair, 71.
9. Reed, 143.
10. Collingwood Bruce & Stokoe, 105.
11. Ellerington, 88.
12. Neville, 96.
13. Carr, 18.
14. Wolsingham XLII.
15. Cook, 188.

16. Milburn (1982), 90, 150; *Sunderland Echo*, 21/10/1909.
17. Hutchinson (1935), 99.
18. OED. & EDD., 'Snap'.
19. Taylor, 255.
20. Beamish 1993.251.
21. Parmeter, 49.
22. Hutchinson (1935), 95.
23. Beamish 1978. 526. 27.
24. Carr, 17.
25. Fawcett, 9-10.
26. Milburn, 10, 14, 115.
27. PSANT 4th Series VI 19.
28. Beamish.
29. Milburn (1987), 50.
30. Thompson *et al*, 198-217.

CHAPTER EIGHTEEN

CALENDAR CUSTOMS

1. EDD., & Heslop, 'First-foot'.
2. Bosonaquet, 13-15.
3. Hutchinson (1973), 87.
4. Balfour & Thompson, 65.
5. Hutchinson (1973), 47-8.
6. Brockett & EDD., 'Pancake'; Bosanquet, 16.
7. Heslop, 'Care-cake'.
8. *ibid.*, 'Carlings'.
9. OED., 'Care' vb 2 & 'Care Sunday'.
10. *ibid.*, 'Carling'.
11. *Gents. Mag.* 1788 I 188-9.
12. Brockett & Dinsdale, 'Carlings'; Brand 1069, 378-9.
13. Heslop, 'Brandlings'.
14. Bosanquet, 16.
15. Balfour & Thomas, 69.
16. Bain, 75, 237.
17. Hepscott, 24.
18. EDD., 'Pace Egg'.
19. Brand (1777), 343.
20. *Gents. Mag.* 1788 I. 188-9.
21. Hutchinson (1973), 124.
22. Newall, 282-4 & plate XXII.
23. Brears (1989), 9.
24. Ditchfield, 80.

25. EDD., 'Bool' & 'Pace Egg'.
26. EDD., 'Jaup'; Bosanquet, 17.
27. Hutchinson (17) Appendix 14.
28. Hone (1826) I 849.
29. PSANT 4th Series IX 71, 115.
30. Taylor (1769), 37; Hutchinson (1973), 89.
31. Balfour & Thomas, 78.
32. Brockett, 'Nut-crack night'.
33. Smith (1967), 2-3.
34. EDD., 'Frummenty'.
35. *ibid.*
36. EDD., 'Cree', 'Knocking'.
37. PSANT 3rd Series IV (1909-10) 18.
38. Beamish 1975. 306. 5.
39. Smith (1967), 5.
40. Bain, 9.
41. NRO 2/DE/34/3/3 in Slack 58.
42. Day, 70.
43. Dinsdale, 'Frummety'.
44. Beamish Survey.
45. Johnson (2001), 138.
46. Beamish 1993.251.641.5.
47. Private Collection.
48. Beamish 1993. 251.641.5.
49. *ibid.*
50. Byron, 300.
51. Private Collection.
52. Brand, 163.
53. Brockett, 'Yule Doo'.
54. Private Collection.
55. *Notes & Queries* 7th Series XII, 429; & EDD., 'Yule'.
56. Bosanquet, 19.
57. Hutchinson (1973), 87.
58. Heslop, 112.
59. Bosanquet, 20.
60. Thacker, 292.
61. Taylor, 216; & Cook, 107.
62. Balfour & Thpmas, 79.
63. Beamish 1993.251.
64. Beamish 13/8/08.9. 641.5.
65. Fleming Hospital, 66; Hargreaves, 137.
66. Heslop, 'Haggish'.
67. Brockett, 'Haggish'.
68. Balfour & Thomas, 80.
69. Hutchinson (1973), 89.
70. Beamish Survey.
71. Hutchinson, 96.
72. *ibid.*, 90..
73. Beamish Survey.
74. Hepscott, 37.
75. Henisch, 26.
76. Johnson, 152.
77. Beamish Survey.
78. Heslop, 112.
79. Hutchinson, 86.
80. EDD., 'Hogmanay'.
81. Bosanquet, 23.

CHAPTER NINETEEN

FROM CRADLE TO GRAVE

1. EDD., OED., & Heslop, 'Groan'.
2. Henderson, 11; EDD., 'Groaning'.
3. Heslop, 'Upgetting'.
4. *ibid.*, 'Christening'.
5. Wilson (1872), 132-3.
6. Private Collection.
7. Wilson (1872), 132-3.
8. EDD., 'Almous'.
9. Hutchinson (1973), 62.
10. Beamish Survey.
11. Hutchinson (1934), 36.
12. Chicken in Wright (1983), 309-320.
13. Bruce & Stokoe, 302.
14. Henderson, 37; Bosanquet, 37; Heslop, 'Kail'.
15. Heslop, 'Thrain – the- Bride-Kyek'.
16. Wilson (1872), 49.
17. Beamish 1978 – 526-27.
18. Richardson, 344.
19. Garrett I, 510.
20. Surtees Soc. CLXXX (1969), 65.
21. PSANT Series 3 VIII (1917-18) 178.
22. Private Collection.
23. David, 445.

GENERAL INDEX

C

RECIPE INDEX

A

Apple
    & cheese savoury 142
    sauce   224
Auckland Cake   176

B

Bacon
    cake   99
    fritters   98
    & liver   94
    stovies   98
Bannocks, barley   151
Barley
    bannocks 151
    bread   151
    loaves   159
    tharf cake   152
Beef
    boiled   79
    Irish stew   81
    pressed   80
    roll   78
    savoury balls for   81
    sea pie   49
    shepherds pie 21
    tongue   83
Beer
    dandelion   193
    ginger   194
    nettle   193
    treacle   194
Birthday Cake   248
Biscuit Hash 49
Black
    jelly   187
    pudding 93

Bread
    barley bannocks 151
    barley cakes   159
    barley loaves   159
    brown   160,
    fadge   87, 162
    Fancy Nancy   154
    maslin   159–60
    muffins   165, 167
    rye   152–3
    spiced   208
    stotty cake   97
    tea cake   164
    white   162
    wholemeal   160, 168
Bride cake   253–4

C

Cake
    Auckland   176
    bacon   99
    barley   151, 159
    birthday   248
    bride   253–4
    Christmas   242–3
    churn milk   178
    dead   256
    gingerbread   200–5
    gingerbread (wholemeal)   205
    grannie   177
    ned   153
    neddy   153
    Newcastle   177
    nodding 154
    potato   124
    Redcar   176
    riddle   149–50
    spiced   172–3, 228